THE DAYS BEFORE

The Days Before

BY KATHERINE ANNE PORTER

❋ ❋
❋

Harcourt, Brace and Company

New York

FOR GAY PORTER HOLLAWAY

FOREWORD

It is my hope that the reader will find in this collection of papers written throughout my thirty years as published writer, the shape, direction, and connective tissue of a continuous, central interest and preoccupation of a lifetime.

They represent the exact opposite of my fiction, in that they were written nearly all by request, with limitations of space, a date fixed for finishing, on a chosen subject or theme, as well as with the certainty that they would be published. I wrote as well as I could at any given moment under a variety of pressures, and said what I meant as nearly as I could come to it: so as they stand, the pieces are really parts of a journal of my thinking and feeling. Then too, they served to get me a living, such as it was, so that I might be able to write my stories in their own time and way. My stories had to be accepted and published exactly as they were written: that rule has never once been broken. There was no one, whose advice I respected, whose help I would not have been glad to get, and many times did get, on almost any of these articles. I have written, re-written, and revised them. My stories, on the other hand, are written in one draft, and if short enough, at one sitting. In fact, this book would seem to represent the other half of a double life: but not in truth. It is all one thing. The two ways of working helped and supported each other: I needed both.

My thanks for permission to reprint previously published material are due to the editors of the following publications: *Books Abroad, Flair, Harper's Magazine, The Kenyon Review, The Nation, New Directions, The New Republic, The New York Times Book Review, The New York Herald Tribune Books,*

Mademoiselle, Partisan Review, Vogue, and *The Writer;* to Appleton-Century-Crofts, Inc., for material from *Century Magazine,* and to the Louisiana State University Press for an essay from *The Southern Review;* also to Doubleday and Company for permission to reprint the preface from their edition of Lizárdi's *The Itching Parrot.*

My thanks and best wishes go also to Mr. Paul Cadmus, whose portrait drawing of me is used on the jacket, for being such a good artist; and to Mr. Monroe Wheeler for being a good friend and letting us have the original drawing for reproduction.

Rue Jacob, Paris   K. A. P.
  25 July, 1952

CONTENTS

Critical

Personal and Particular

Mexican

CRITICAL

The Days Before

Really, universally, relations stop nowhere, and the exquisite problem of the artist is eternally but to draw, by a geometry of his own, the circle within which they shall happily *appear* to do so.—H.J.: Preface to *Roderick Hudson*.

❋

We have, it would seem, at last reluctantly decided to claim Henry James as our own, in spite of his having renounced, two years before his death, so serious an obligation as his citizenship, but with a disturbing tendency among his critics and admirers of certain schools to go a step further and claim him for the New England, or Puritan tradition.

This is merely the revival and extension of an old error first made by Carlyle in regard to Henry James the elder: "Mr. James, your New-England friend," wrote Carlyle in a letter; "I saw him several times and liked him." This baseless remark set up, years later, a train of reverberations in the mind of Mr. James's son Henry, who took pains to correct the "odd legend" that the James family were a New England product, mentioning that Carlyle's mistake was a common one among the English, who seemed to have no faintest care or notion about our regional differences. With his intense feeling for place and family relations and family history, Henry James the younger could not allow this important error to pass uncorrected. With his very special eyes, whose threads were tangled in every vital center of his being, he looked long through "a thin golden haze" into his past, and recreated for our charmed view an almost numberless family connection, all pure Scotch-Irish so far back as the records run, unaltered to the third generation in his branch of the family; and except for the

3

potent name-grandfather himself—a Presbyterian of rather the blue-nosed caste, who brought up his eleven or was it thirteen children of three happy marriages in the fear of a quite improbable God—almost nothing could be less Puritanic, less New England, than their careers, even if they were all of Protestant descent. The earliest branch came late to this country (1764) according to Virginia or New England standards, and they settled in the comparatively newly opened country of upstate New York—new for the English and Scotch-Irish, that is, for the Dutch and the French had been there a good while before, and they married like with like among the substantial families settled along the Hudson River. Thus the whole connection in its earlier days was spared the touch of the specifically New England spirit, which even then was spreading like a slow blight into every part of the country.

(But the young Henry James feared it from the first, distrusted it in his bones. Even though his introduction to New England was by way of "the proud episcopal heart of Newport," when he was about fifteen years old, and though he knew there at least one artist, and one young boy of European connection and experience, still, Boston was not far away, and he felt a tang of wintry privation in the air, a threat of "assault and death." By way of stores against the hovering famine and siege, he collected a whole closet full of the beloved *Revue des Deux Mondes*, in its reassuring salmon-pink cover.)

Henry James's grandfather, the first William James, arrived in America from Ireland, County Cavan, an emigrant boy of seventeen, and settled in Albany in 1789. He was of good solid middle-class stock, he possessed that active imagination and boundless energy of the practical sort so useful in ancestors; in about forty years of the most blameless, respected use of every opportunity to turn an honest penny, on a very handsome scale of operations, he accumulated a fortune of three million dollars, in a style that was to become the very pattern of American enterprise. The city of Albany was credited to him, it was the work of his hands, it prospered with him. His industries and projects kept hundreds of worthy folk gainfully employed the year round, in the grateful language of contemporary eulogy; in his time only John Jacob Astor gathered a larger fortune in New York state. We may as well note here an obvious irony, and dismiss it: James's grandfather's career was a perfect example of the sort of thing that was to become "typically American," and still is, it happens regularly even now; and Henry James the younger had great good of it, yet it did create the very atmosphere which later on he found so hard to breathe that he deserted it altogether for years, for life.

The three millions were divided at last among the widow and eleven surviving children, the first Henry James, then a young man, being one of them. These twelve heirs none of them inherited the Midas touch, and all had a taste for the higher things of life enjoyed in easy, ample surroundings. Henry the younger lived to wonder, with a touch of charming though acute dismay, just what had become of all that delightful money. Henry the elder, whose youth had been gilded to the ears, considered money a topic beneath civilized discussion, business a grimy affair they all agreed to know nothing about, and neglected completely to mention what he had done with his share. He fostered a legend among his children that he had been "wild" and appeared, according to his fascinating stories, to have been almost the only young man of his generation who had not come to a bad end. His son Henry almost in infancy had got the notion that the words "wild" and "dissipated" were synonymous with "tipsy." Be that as it may, Henry the first in his wild days had a serious if temporary falling out with his father, whom he described as the tenderest and most sympathetic of parents; but he also wrote in his fragment of autobiography, "I should think indeed that our domestic intercourse had been on the whole most innocent as well as happy, were it not for a certain lack of oxygen which is indeed incidental to the family atmosphere and which I may characterize as the lack of any ideal of action

except that of self-preservation." Indeed, yes. Seeking fresh
air, he fled into the foreign land of Massachusetts: Boston, precisely: until better days should come. "It was an age," wrote
his son Henry, "in which a flight from Albany to Boston . . .
counted as a far flight." It still does. The point of this episode
for our purposes was, that Henry the first mildewed in exile
for three long months, left Boston and did not again set foot
there until he was past thirty-five. His wife never went there
at all until her two elder sons were in Harvard, a seat of learning
chosen *faute de mieux*, for Europe, Europe was where they fain
all would be; except that a strange, uneasy, even artificially in-
duced nationalism, due to the gathering war between the states,
had laid cold doubts on their minds—just where did they belong,
where was their native land? The two young brothers, William
and Henry, especially then began, after their shuttlings to and
from Europe, to make unending efforts to "find America" and
to place themselves once for all either in it or out of it. But this
was later.

It is true that the elder Jameses settled in Boston, so far as a
James of that branch could ever be said to settle, for the good
reason that they wished to be near their sons; but they never
became, by any stretch of the word, New Englanders, any
more than did their son William, after all those years at Harvard; any more than did their son Henry become an Englishman, after all those years in England. He realized this himself,
even after he became a British subject in 1914; and the British
agree with him to this day. He was to the end an amiable, distinguished stranger living among them. Yet two generations
born in this country did not make them Americans, either, and
in the whole great branching family connection, with its "habits
of ease" founded on the diminishing backlog of the new fortune, the restless blood of the emigrant grandparents ran high.
Europe was not so far away as it is now, and though Albany
and "the small, warm dusky homogeneous New York world
of the mid-century" were dear to them, they could not deny,

indeed no one even thought of denying, that all things desirable in the arts, architecture, education, ways of living, history, the future, the very shape of the landscape and the color of the air, lay like an inheritance they had abandoned, in Europe.

"This question of Europe" which never ceased to agitate his parents from his earliest memory was paradoxically the only permanent element in the Jameses' family life. All their movements, plans, interests were based, you might say, on that perpetually unresolved problem. It was kept simmering by letters from friends and relatives traveling or living there; cousins living handsomely at Geneva, enjoying the widest possible range of desirable social amenities; other cousins living agreeably at Tours, or Trouville; the handsomest of the Albany aunts married advantageously and living all over Europe, urging the Henry Jameses to come with their young and do likewise for the greater good of all. There was an older cousin who even lived in China, came back to fill a flat in Gramercy Square with "dim Chinoiseries" and went on to old age in Surrey and her last days in Versailles. There was besides the constant delicious flurry of younger cousins and aunts with strange wonderful clothes and luggage who had always just been there, or who were just going there, "there" meaning always Europe, and oddly enough, specifically Paris, instead of London. The infant Henry, at the age of five, received his "positive initiation into History" when Uncle Gus returned bringing the news of the flight of Louis Philippe to England. To the child, *flight* had been a word with a certain meaning; *king* another. "Flight of kings," was a new, portentous, almost poetic image of strange disasters, it early gave to political questions across the sea a sense of magnificence they altogether lacked at home, where society outside the enthralling family circle and the shimmering corona of friends seemed altogether to consist of "the busy, the tipsy, and Daniel Webster."

Within that circle, however, nothing could exceed the freedom and ease with which artists of all sorts, some of them forgotten now, seemed to make the James fireside, wherever it happened to be, their own. The known and acclaimed were also household guests and dear friends.

Mr. Emerson, "the divinely pompous rose of the philosophical garden," as Henry James the elder described him, or, in other lights and views, the "man without a handle"—one simply couldn't get hold of him at all—had been taken upstairs in the fashionable Astor Hotel to admire the newly born William; and in later times, seated in the firelit dusk of the back parlor in the James house, had dazzled the young Henry, who knew he was great. General Winfield Scott in military splendor had borne down upon him and his father at a street corner for a greeting; and on a boat between Fort Hamilton and New York Mr. Washington Irving had apprised Mr. James of the shipwreck of Margaret Fuller, off Fire Island, only a day or so before. Edgar Allan Poe was one of the "acclaimed," the idolized, most read and recited of poets; his works were on every drawing room or library table that Henry James knew, and he never outgrew his wonder at the legend that Poe was neglected in his own time.

Still it was Dickens who ruled and pervaded the literary world from afar; the books in the house, except for a few French novels, were nearly all English; the favorite bookstore was English, where the James children went to browse, sniffing the pages for the strong smell of paper and printer's ink, which they called "the English smell." The rule of the admired, revered *Revue des Deux Mondes* was to set in shortly; France and French for Henry James, Germany and German for William James, were to have their great day, and stamp their images to such a degree that ever after the English of the one, and of the other, were to be "larded" and tagged and stuffed with French and German. In the days before, however, the general deliciousness and desirability of all things English was in the domestic air Henry James breathed; his mother and father talked about it so much at the breakfast table that, remembering, he asked himself if he had ever heard anything else talked about over the morning coffee cups. They could not re-live enough their happy summer in England with their two babies, and he traveled again and again with them, by way of "Windsor and Sudbrook and Ham Common"; an earthly Paradise, they believed, and he believed with them. A young aunt, his mother's sister, shared these memories and added her own: an incurable homesickness for England possessed her. Henry, asking for stories, listened and "took in" everything: taking in was to be his life's main occupation: as if, he said, his "infant divination proceeded by the light of nature," and he had learned already the importance of knowing in advance of any experience of his own, just what life in England might be like. A small yellow-covered English magazine called *Charm* also "shed on the question the softest lustre" and caused deep pangs of disappointment when it failed to show up regularly at the bookstore.

Henry James refers to all these early impressions as an "infection," as a sip of "poison," as a "twist"—perhaps of some psychological thumbscrew—but the twinges and pangs were all exciting, joyful, mysterious, thrilling, sensations he enjoyed and sought eagerly, half their force at least consisting of his imaginative projection of his own future in the most brilliant possible of great worlds. He saw his parents and his aunt perpetually homesick for something infinitely lovable and splendid they had known, and he longed to know it too. "Homesickness was a luxury I remember craving from the tenderest age," he confessed, because he had at once perhaps too many homes and therefore no home at all. If his parents did not feel at home anywhere, he could not possibly, either. He did not know what to be homesick for, unless it were England, which he had seen but could not remember.

This was, then, vicarious, a mere sharing at second-hand; he needed something of his own. When it came, it was rather dismaying; but it was an important episode and confirmed in him the deep feeling that England had something formidable in its desirability, something to be lived up to: in contrast to

France as he discovered later, where one "got life," as he expressed it; or Germany, where the very trees of the great solemn forests murmured in his charmed ear of their mystical "culture." What happened was this: the celebrated Mr. Thackeray, fresh from England, seated as an honored much-at-ease guest in the James library, committed an act which somehow explains everything that is wrong with his novels.

"Come here, little boy," he said to Henry, "and show me your extraordinary jacket." With privileged bad manners he placed his hand on the child's shoulder and asked him if his garments were the uniform of his "age and class," adding with brilliant humor that if he should wear it in England he would be addressed as "Buttons." No matter what Mr. Thackeray thought he was saying—very likely he was not thinking at all— he conveyed to the overwhelmed admirer of England that the English, as so authoritatively represented by Mr. Thackeray, thought Americans "queer." It was a disabling blow, recalled in every circumstance fifty years later, with a photograph, of all things, to illustrate and prove its immediate effect.

Henry was wearing that jacket, buttoned to the chin with a small white collar, on the hot dusty summer day when his companionable father, who never went anywhere without one or the other of his two elder sons, brought him up from Staten Island where the family were summering, to New York, and as a gay surprise for everybody, took him to Mr. Brady's for their photograph together. A heavy surprise indeed for Henry, who forever remembered the weather, the smells and sights of the wharf, the blowzy summer lassitude of the streets, and his own dismay that by his father's merry whim he was to be immortalized by Mr. Brady in his native costume which would appear so absurd in England. Mr. Brady that day made one of the most expressive child pictures I know. The small straight figure has a good deal of grace and dignity in its unworthy (as he feared) clothes; the long hands are holding with what composure they can to things they know: his father's shoulder, his large, and, according to the fashion plates of the day, stylish straw hat. All the life of the child is in the eyes, rueful, disturbed, contemplative, with enormous intelligence and perception, much older than the face, much deeper and graver than his father's. His father and mother bore a certain family resemblance to each other, such as closely interbred peoples of any nation are apt to develop; Henry resembled them both, but his father more nearly, and judging by later photographs, the resemblance became almost identical, except for the expression of the eyes—the unmistakable look of one who was to live intuitively and naturally a long life in "the air of the passions of the intelligence."

In Mr. Brady's daguerreotype, he is still a child, a stranger everywhere, and he is unutterably conscious of the bright untimeliness of the whole thing, the lack of proper ceremony, ignored as ever by the father; the slack, unflattering pose. His father is benevolent and cheerful and self-possessed and altogether pleased for them both. He had won his right to gaiety of heart in his love; after many a victorious engagement with the powers of darkness, he had Swedenborg and all his angels round about, bearing him up, which his son was never to have; and he had not been lately ridiculed by Mr. Thackeray, at least not to his face. Really it was not just the jacket that troubled him— that idle remark upon it was only one of the smallest of the innumerable flashes which lighted for him, blindingly, whole territories of mystery in which a long lifetime could not suffice to make him feel at home. "I lose myself in wonder," he wrote in his later years, "at the loose ways, the strange process of waste, through which nature and fortune may deal on occasion with those whose faculty for application is all and only in their imagination and sensibility."

By then he must have known that in his special case, nothing at all had been wasted. He was in fact a most glorious example in proof of his father's favorite theories of the uses and virtues of waste as education, and at the end felt he had "mastered the

particular history of just that waste." His father was not considered a good Swedenborgian by those followers of Swedenborg who had, against his expressed principles, organized themselves into a church. Mr. James could not be organized in the
faintest degree by anyone or anything. His daughter Alice wrote
of him years later: ". . . Father, the delicious infant, couldn't
submit even to the thralldom of his own whim." That smother-
ing air of his childhood family life had given him a permanent
longing for freedom and fresh air; the atmosphere he generated
crackled with oxygen; his children lived in such a state of mental and emotional stimulation that no society ever again could
overstimulate them. Life, as he saw it—was nobly resolved to
see it, and to teach his beloved young ones to see it—was so
much a matter of living happily and freely by spiritual, ethical,
and intellectual values, based soundly on sensuous richness, and
inexhaustible faith in the goodness of God; a firm belief in the
divinity in human nature, God's self in it; a boundlessly ener-
getic aspiration toward the higher life, the purest humanities,
the most spontaneous expression of feeling and thought.

Despair was for the elder James a word of contempt; he declared "that never for a moment had he known a skeptical state."
Yet, "having learned the nature of evil, and admitted its power,
he turned towards the sun of goodness." He believed that "true
worship is always spontaneous, the offspring of delight, not
duty." Thus his son Henry: "The case was really of his feeling
so vast a rightness close at hand or lurking immediately behind
actual arrangements that a single turn of the inward wheel, one
real response to the pressure of the spiritual spring, would
bridge the chasms, straighten the distortions, rectify the relations, and in a word redeem and vivify the whole mass." With
all his considerable powers of devotion translated into immediate
action, the father demonstrated his faith in the family circle;
the children responded to the love, but were mystified and re-
spectful before the theory: they perceived it was something
very subtle, as were most of "father's ideas." But they also knew

early that their father did not live in a fool's paradise. "It was of course the old story that we had only to *be* with more intelligence and faith—an immense deal more, certainly, in order to work off, in the happiest manner, the many-sided ugliness of life; which was a process that might go on, blessedly, in the quietest of all quiet ways. *That* wouldn't be blood and fire and tears, or would be none of these things stupidly precipitated; it would simply take place by *enjoyed* communication and contact, enjoyed concussion or convulsion even—since pangs and agitations, the very agitations of perception itself, are the highest privilege of the soul, and there is always, thank goodness, a saving sharpness of play or complexity of consequence in the intelligence completely alive."

Blood and fire and tears each in his own time and way each of them suffered, sooner or later. Alice, whose life was a mysterious long willful dying, tragic and ironic, once asked her father's permission to kill herself. He gave it, and she understood his love in it, and refrained: he wrote to Henry that he did not much fear any further thoughts of suicide on her part. William took the search for truth as hard as his father had, but by way of philosophy, not religion; the brave psychologist and philosopher was very sick in his soul for many years. Henry was maimed for life in an accident, as his father had been before him, but he of them all never broke, never gave way, sought for truth not in philosophy nor in religion, but in art, and found his own; showed just what the others had learned and taught, and spoke for them better than they could for themselves, thus very simply and grandly fulfilling his destiny as artist; for it was destiny and he knew it and never resisted a moment, but went with it as unskeptically as his father had gone with religion.

The James family, as we have seen, were materially in quite comfortable circumstances. True the fine fortune had misted away somewhat, but they had enough. If people are superior to begin with, as they were, the freedom of money is an added freedom of grace and the power of choice in many desirable ways. This accounts somewhat then for the extraordinary amiability, ease of manners, and artless, innocent unselfconsciousness of the whole family in which Henry James was brought up, which he has analyzed so acutely, though with such hovering tenderness. It was merely a fact that they could afford to be beyond material considerations because in that way they were well provided. Their personal virtues, no matter on what grounds, were real, their kindness and frankness were unfeigned. "The cousinship," he wrote, "all unalarmed and unsuspecting and unembarrassed, lived by pure serenity, sociability, and loquacity." Then with the edge of severity his own sense of truth drew finally upon any subject, he added: "The special shade of its identity was thus that it was not conscious—really not conscious of anything in the world; or was conscious of so few possibilities at least, and these so immediate, and so a matter of course, that it came to the same thing." There he summed up a whole society, limited in number but of acute importance in its place; and having summed up, he cannot help returning to the exceptions, those he loved and remembered best.

There were enough intellectual interests and consciousness of every kind in his father's house to furnish forth the whole connection, and it was the center. Education, all unregulated, to be drawn in with the breath, and absorbed like food, proceeded at top speed day and night. Though William, of all the children, seemed to be the only one who managed to acquire a real, formal university training of the kind recognized by academicians, Henry got his, in spite of the dozen schools in three countries, in his own time and his own way; in the streets, in theaters (how early grew in him that long, unrequited passion for the theater!), at picture galleries, at parties, on boats, in hotels, beaches, at family reunions; by listening, by gazing, dawdling, gaping, wondering, and soaking in impressions and sensations at every pore, through every hair. Though at moments he longed to be an

orphan when he saw the exciting life of change and improvisa-
tion led by his cheerful orphaned cousins, "so little sunk in the
short range," it is clear that his own life, from minute to minute,
was as much as he could endure; he had the only family he
could have done with at all, and the only education he was
capable of receiving. His intuitions were very keen and pure
from the beginning, and foreknowledge of his ineducability in
any practical sense caused him very rightly to kick and shriek
as they hauled him however fondly to his first day of school.
There he found, as he was to find in every situation for years
and years, elder brother William, the vivid, the hardy, the
quick-learning, the outlooking one, seated already: accustomed,
master of his environment, lord of his playfellows. For so Henry
saw him; William was a tremendous part of his education. William was beyond either envy or imitation: the younger brother
could only follow and adore at the right distance.

So was his mother his education. Her children so possessed
her they did not like her even to praise them or be proud of
them because that seemed to imply that she was separate from
them. After her death, the younger Henry wrote of her out of
depths hardly to be stirred again in him, "she was our life, she
was the house, she was the keystone of the arch"—suddenly his
language took on symbols of the oldest poetry. Her husband,
who found he could not live without her, wrote in effect to a
friend that very early in their marriage she had awakened his
torpid heart, and helped him to become a man.

The father desired many things for the children, but two
things first: spiritual decency, as Henry James says it, and "a
sensuous education." If Henry remembered his share in the
civilizing atmosphere of Mr. Jenks's school as "merely contemplative," totally detached from any fact of learning, at home
things were more positive. Their father taught them a horror
of priggishness, and of conscious virtue; guarded them, by precept and example, from that vulgarity he described as "flagrant
morality"; and quite preached, if his boundless and changing

conversation could be called that, against success in its tangible
popular meaning. "We were to convert and convert, success—
in the sense that was in the general air—or no success; and simply
everything that happened to us, every contact, every impression and every experience we should know, were to form our
soluble stuff; with only ourselves to thank should we remain
unaware, by the time our perceptions were decently developed,
of the substance finally projected and most desirable. That substance might be just consummately Virtue, as a social grace and
value . . . the moral of all of which was that we need never
fear not to be good enough if only we were social enough. . . ."

Again he told them that the truth—the one truth as distinguished from the multiple fact—"was never ugly and dreadful,
and (we) might therefore depend upon it for due abundance,
even of meat and drink and raiment, even of wisdom and wit
and honor."

No child ever "took in" his father's precepts more exactly
and more literally than did Henry James, nor worked them more
subtly and profoundly to his own needs. He was at last, looking
back, "struck . . . with the rare fashion after which, in any
small victim of life, the inward perversity may work. It works
by converting to its uses things vain and unintended, to the
great discomposure of their prepared opposites, which it by the
same stroke so often reduces to naught; with the result indeed
that one may most of all see it—so at least have I quite exclusively
seen it, the little life out for its chance—as proceeding by the
inveterate process of conversion."

The little life out for its chance was oh how deeply intent on
the chance it *chose* to take; and all this affected and helped to
form a most important phase of his interests: money, exactly,
and success, both of which he desired most deeply, but with the
saving justifying clause that he was able only to imagine working for and earning them honestly—and though money was only
just that, once earned, his notion of success was really his
father's, and on nothing less than the highest ground did it de-

serve that name. In the meantime, as children, they were never to be preoccupied with money. But how to live? "The effect of his attitude, so little thought out as shrewd or vulgarly providential, but . . . so socially and affectionately founded, could only be to make life interesting to us at worst, in default of making it extraordinarily paying." His father wanted all sorts of things for them without quite knowing what they needed, but Henry the younger began peering through, and around the corners of, the doctrine. "With subtle indirectness," the children, perhaps most of all Henry, got the idea that the inward and higher life, well rounded, *must* somehow be lived in good company, with good manners and surroundings fitting to virtue and sociability, good, you might say, attracting good on all planes: of course. But one of the goods, a main good, without which the others might wear a little thin, was material ease. Henry James understood and anatomized thoroughly and acutely the sinister role of money in society, the force of its corrosive powers on the individual; the main concern of nearly all his chief characters is that life shall be, one way or another, and by whatever means, a paying affair . . . and the theme is the consequences of their choice of means, and their notion of what shall pay them.

This worldly knowledge, then, was the end-product of that unworldly education which began with the inward life, the early inculcated love of virtue for its own sake, a belief in human affections and natural goodness, a childhood of extraordinary freedom and privilege, passed in a small warm world of fostering love. This world for him was never a landscape with figures, but a succession of rather small groups of persons intensely near to him, for whom the landscape was a setting, the houses they lived in the appropriate background. The whole scene of his childhood existed in his memory in terms of the lives lived in it, with his own growing mind working away at it, storing it, transmuting it, reclaiming it. Through his extreme sense of the

appearance of things, manners, dress, social customs, the light-
est gesture, he could convey mysterious but deep impressions
of individual character. In crises of personal events, he could
still note the look of tree-shaded streets, family gardens, the
flash of a grandmother's scissors cutting grapes or flowers; fan-
shaped lights, pink marble steps; the taste of peaches, baked
apples, custards, ice creams, melons, food indeed by the bushel
and the barrel; the colors and shapes of garments, the head-
dresses of ladies, their voices, the way they lifted their hands.
If these were all, they would have been next to nothing, but
the breathing lives are somewhere in them.

The many schools he attended, if that is the word, the children he knew there, are perfectly shown in terms of their looks
and habits. He was terrorized by the superior talents of those
boys who could learn arithmetic, apparently without effort, a
branch of learning forever closed to him, as by decree of nature.
A boy of his own age, who lived in Geneva, "opened vistas" to
him by pronouncing Ohio and Iowa in the French manner: an
act of courage as well as correctness which was impressive, surrounded as he was by tough little glaring New Yorkers with
stout boots and fists, who were not prepared to be patronized
in any such way. Was there anybody he ever thought stupid,
he asked himself, if only they displayed some trick of information, some worldly sleight of hand of which he had hitherto
been ignorant? On a sightseeing tour at Sing Sing he envied a
famous criminal his self-possession, inhabiting as he did a world
so perilous and so removed from daily experience. His sense of
social distinctions was early in the bud: he recognized a Dowager
on sight, at a very tender age. An elegant image of a "great
Greek Temple shining over blue waters"—which seems to have
been a hotel at New Brighton called the Pavilion—filled him
with joy when he was still in his nurse's arms. He had thought
it a finer thing than he discovered it to be, and this habit of
thought was to lead him far afield for a good number of years.

For his freedoms were so many, his instructions so splendid, and yet his father's admirable, even blessed teachings failed to cover so many daily crises of the visible world. The visible world was the one he would have, all his being strained and struggled outward to meet it, to absorb it, to understand it, to be a part of it. The other children asked him to what church he belonged, and he had no answer; for the even more important question, "What does your father *do?*" or "What business is he in?" no reply had been furnished him for the terrible occasion. His father was no help there, though he tried to be. How could a son explain to his father that it did no good to reply that one had the freedom of all religion, being God's child; or that one's father was an author of books and a truth-seeker ?

So his education went forward in all directions and on all surfaces and depths. He longed "to be somewhere—almost any-where would do—and somehow to receive an impression or an accession, feel a relation or a vibration"; while all the time a performance of *Uncle Tom's Cabin*, which gave him his first lesson in ironic appreciation of the dowdy and overwrought and underdone; or Mrs. Cannon's mystifyingly polite establishment full of scarfs, handkerchiefs, and colognes for gentlemen, with an impalpable something in the air which hinted at mysteries, and which turned out to be only that gentlemen, some of them cousins, from out of town took rooms there; or the gloomy show of Italian Primitives, all frauds, which was to give him a bad start with painting—such events were sinking into him as pure sensation to emerge from a thousand points in his memory as knowledge.

Knowledge—knowledge at the price of finally, utterly "seeing through" everything—even the fortunate, happy childhood; yet there remained to him, to the very end, a belief in that good which had been shown to him as good in his infancy, embodied in his father and mother. There was a great deal of physical beauty in his family, and it remained the kind that meant beauty to him: the memory of his cousin Minnie Temple, the face of his sister Alice in her last photograph, these were the living images of his best-loved heroines; the love he early understood as love never betrayed him and was love at the latest day; the extraordinarily sensitive, imaginative excitements of first admirations and friendships turned out to be not perhaps so much irreplaceable as incomparable. What I am trying to say is that so far as we are able to learn, nothing came to supplant or dislocate in any way those early affections and attachments and admirations.

This is not to say he never grew up with them, for they expanded with his growth, and as he grew his understanding gave fresh life to them; nor that he did not live to question them acutely, to inquire as to their nature and their meaning, for he did; but surely no one ever projected more lovingly and exactly the climate of youth, of budding imagination, the growth of the tender, perceptive mind, the particular freshness and keenness of feeling, the unconscious generosity and warmth of heart of the young brought up in the innocence which is their due, and the sweet illusion of safety, dangerous because it must be broken at great risk. He survived all, and made it his own, and used it with that fullness and boldness and tenderness and intent reverence which is the sum of his human qualities, indivisible from his sum as artist. For though no writer ever "grew up" more completely than Henry James, and "saw through" his own illusions with more sobriety and pure intelligence, still there lay in the depths of his being the memory of a lost paradise; it was in the long run the standard by which he measured the world he learned so thoroughly, accepted in certain ways—the ways of a civilized man with his own work to do—after such infinite pains: or pangs, as he would have called them, that delight in deep experience which at a certain point is excruciating, and by the uninstructed might be taken for pain itself. But the origin is different, it is not inflicted, not even invited, it comes under its own power and the end is different; and the pang is *not* suffering, it is delight.

Henry James knew about this, almost from the beginning. Here is his testimony: "I foresee moreover how little I shall be able to resist, throughout these notes, the force of persuasion expressed in the individual *vivid* image of the past wherever encountered, these images having always such terms of their own, such subtle secrets and insidious arts for keeping us in relation with them, for bribing us by the beauty, the authority, the wonder of their saved intensity. They have saved it, they seem to say to us, from such a welter of death and darkness and ruin that this alone makes a value and a light and a dignity for them. . . . Not to be denied also, over and above this, is the downright pleasure of the illusion yet again created, the *apparent* transfer from the past to the present of the particular combination of things that did at its hour ever so directly operate and that isn't after all then drained of virtue, wholly wasted and lost, for sensation, for participation in the act of life, in the attesting sights, sounds, smells, the illusion, as I say, of the recording senses."

Brother William remained Big Brother to the end, though Henry learned to stand up to him manfully when the philosopher invaded the artist's territory. But William could not help being impatient with all this reminiscence, and tried to discourage Henry when he began rummaging through his precious scrapbags of bright fragments, patching them into the patterns before his mind's eye. William James was fond of a phrase of his philosopher friend Benjamin Paul Blood: "There is no conclusion. What has concluded, that we might conclude in regard to it?"

That is all very well for philosophy, and it has within finite limits the sound of truth as well as simple fact—no man has ever seen any relations concluded. Maybe that is why art is so endlessly satisfactory: the artist can choose his relations, and "draw, by a geometry of his own, the circle within which they shall happily *appear* to do so." While accomplishing this, one has the illusion that destiny is not absolute, it can be arranged, temporized with, persuaded, a little here and there. And once the circle is truly drawn around its contents, it too becomes truth.

First version July 1943
Revised 27 February 1952

On a Criticism of Thomas Hardy

❊

The Bishop of Wakefield, after reading Thomas Hardy's latest (and as it proved, his last) novel, *Jude the Obscure*, threw it in the fire, or said he did. It was a warm midsummer, and Hardy suggested that the bishop may have been speaking figuratively, heresy and bonfires being traditionally associated in his mind, or that he may have gone to the kitchen stove. The bishop wrote to the papers that he had burned the book, in any case, and he wrote also to a local M.P. who caused the horrid work to be withdrawn from the public library, promising besides to examine any other novels of Mr. Hardy carefully before allowing them to circulate among the bishop's flock. It was a good day's work, added to the protests of the reviewers for the press, and twenty-five years of snubbing and nagging from the professional moralists of his time; Thomas Hardy resigned as novelist for good. As in the case of the criticism presently to be noted, the attack on his book included also an attack on his personal character, and the bishop's action wounded Thomas Hardy. He seems to have remarked in effect "that if the bishop could have known him as he was, he would have found a man whose personal conduct, views of morality, and of vital facts of religion, hardly differed from his own."

This is an indirect quotation by his second wife, devoted apologist and biographer, and it exposes almost to the point of pathos the basic, unteachable charity of Hardy's mind. Of all evil emotions generated in the snake-pit of human nature, theological hatred is perhaps the most savage, being based on intellectual concepts and disguised in the highest spiritual motives.

And what could rouse this hatred in a theologian like the sight of a moral, virtuous, well-conducted man who presumed to agree with him in the "vital facts of religion," at the same time refusing to sign the articles of faith? It was long ago agreed among the Inquisitors that these are the dangerous men.

The bishop threw the book in the fire in 1896. In 1928, Mrs. Hardy was happy to record that another "eminent clergyman of the church" had advised any priest preparing to become a village rector to make first a good retreat and then a careful study of Thomas Hardy's novels. "From Thomas Hardy," concluded this amiable man, "he would learn the essential dignity of country people and what deep and passionate interest belongs to every individual life. You cannot treat them in the mass: each single soul is to be the object of your special and peculiar prayer."

Aside from the marginal note on the social point of view which made it necessary thus to warn prospective rectors that country people were also human entities, each possessed of a soul important, however rural, to God, and the extraordinary fact that an agnostic novelist could teach them what the church and their own hearts could not, it is worth noting again that churchmen differ even as the laymen on questions of morality, and can preach opposing doctrine from the same text. The history of these differences, indeed, is largely the calamitous history of institutional religion. In 1934, a layman turned preacher almost like a character in a Hardy novel, runs true to his later form by siding with the bishop. Since his spectacular conversion to the theology and politics of the Church of England, Mr. T. S. Eliot's great gifts as a critic have been deflected into channels where they do not flow with their old splendor and depth. More and more his literary judgments have assumed the tone of lay sermons by a parochial visitor, and his newer style is perhaps at its most typical in his criticism of Thomas Hardy:

The work of the late Thomas Hardy represents an interesting example of a powerful personality uncurbed by any institutional attachment or by submission to any objective beliefs; unhampered by any ideas, or even by what sometimes acts as a partial restraint upon inferior writers, the desire to please a large public. He seems to me to have written as nearly for the sake of "self-expression" as a man well can, and the self which he had to express does not strike me as a particularly wholesome or edifying matter of communication. He was indifferent even to the prescripts of good writing: he wrote sometimes overpoweringly well, but always very carelessly; at times his style touches sublimity without ever having passed through the stage of being good. In consequence of his self-absorption, he makes a great deal of landscape; for landscape is a passive creature which lends itself to an author's mood. Landscape is fitted, too, for the purpose of an author who is interested not at all in men's minds, but only in their emotions, and perhaps only in men as vehicles for emotions.

After some useful general reflections on the moral undesirability of extreme emotionalism, meant as a rebuke to Hardy and to which we shall return briefly later, Mr. Eliot proceeds:

I was [in a previous lecture] . . . concerned with illustrating the limiting and crippling effect of a separation from tradition and orthodoxy upon certain writers whom I nevertheless hold up for admiration for what they have attempted against great obstacles. Here I am concerned with the intrusion of the *diabolic* into modern literature in consequence of the same lamentable state of affairs; . . . I am afraid that even if you can entertain the notion of a positive power for evil working through human agency, you may still have a very inaccurate notion of what Evil is, and will find it difficult to believe that it may operate through men of genius of the most excellent character. I doubt whether what I am saying can convey very much to anyone for whom the doctrine of Original Sin is not a very real and tremendous thing.

Granting the premises with extreme reservations, Thomas Hardy was a visible proof of the validity of this disturbing doctrine. He had received early religious training in the Established Church, and by precept and example in a household of the most sincere piety, and of the most aggressive respectability. He remarked once, that of all the names he had been called, such as agnostic (which tag he adopted later, ruefully), atheist, immoralist, pessimist, and so on, a properly fitting one had been overlooked altogether: "churchy." He had once meant to be a parson. His relations with the church of his childhood had been of the homely, intimate, almost filial sort. His grandfather, his father, his uncle, all apt in music, had been for forty years the mainstay of the village choir. He felt at home in the place, as to its customs, feasts, services. He had a great love for the ancient churches, and as a young architect his aesthetic sense was outraged by the fashionable and silly "restorations" amounting to systematic destruction which overtook some of the loveliest examples of medieval church architecture in England during the nineteenth century. His devotion to the past, and to the history and character of his native Wessex became at times a kind of antiquarian fustiness. His personal morals were irreproachable, he had an almost queasy sense of the awful and permanent effects of wrongdoing on the human soul and destiny. Most of his novels deal with these consequences; his most stupendous tragedies are the result of one false step on the part of his hero or heroine. Genius aside, he had all the makings of a good, honest, church-going country squire; but the worm of original sin was settled in his mind, of all fatal places; and his mind led him out of the tradition of orthodoxy into another tradition of equal antiquity, equal importance, equal seriousness, a body of opinion running parallel throughout history to the body of law in church and state: the great tradition of dissent. He went, perhaps not so much by choice as by compulsion of *belief*, with the Inquirers rather than the Believers. His mind, not the greatest, certainly not the most flexible, but a good, candid, strong mind, asked simply the oldest, most terrifying questions, and the traditional, orthodox answers of the church did not satisfy it. It is easy to see how this, from the churchly point of view, is diabolic. But the yawning abyss between question and answer remains the same, and until this abyss is closed, the dissent will remain, persistent, obdurate, a kind of church itself, with its leaders, teachers, saints, martyrs, heroes; a thorn in the flesh of orthodoxy, but I think not necessarily of the Devil on that account, unless the intellect and all its questions are really from the Devil, as the Eden myth states explicitly, as the church seems to teach, and Mr. Eliot tends to confirm.

There is a great deal to examine in the paragraphs quoted above, but two words in their context illustrate perfectly the unbridgeable abyss between Hardy's question and Mr. Eliot's answer. One is, of course, the word *diabolic*. The other is *edifying*. That struck and held my eye in a maze, for a moment. With no disrespect I hope to conventional piety, may I venture that in the regions of art, as of religion, edification is not the highest form of intellectual or spiritual experience. It is a happy truth that Hardy's novels are really not edifying. The mental and emotional states roused and maintained in the reader of *The Mayor of Casterbridge* or *The Return of the Native* are considerably richer, invoked out of deeper sources in the whole human consciousness, more substantially nourishing, than this lukewarm word can express. A novel by Thomas Hardy can be a chastening experience, an appalling one, there is great and sober pleasure to be got out of those novels, the mind can be disturbed and the heart made extremely uneasy, but the complacency of edification is absent, as it is apt to be from any true tragedy.

Mr. Eliot includes Lawrence and Joyce in his list of literary men of "diabolic" tendencies. Deploring Lawrence's "untrained" mind, he adds: "A trained mind like that of Mr. Joyce is always aware of what master it is serving . . ."

Untrained minds have always been a nuisance to the military police of orthodoxy. God-intoxicated mystics and untidy saints with only a white blaze of divine love where their minds should have been, are perpetually creating almost as much disorder within the law as outside it. To have a trained mind is no guarantee at all that the possessor is going to walk infallibly in the path of virtue, though he hardly fails in the letter of the law. St. Joan of Arc and St. Francis in their own ways have had something to say about that. The combination of a trained mind

and incorruptible virtue is ideal, and therefore rare: St. Thomas
More is the first name that occurs to me as example. Hardy's
mind, which had rejected the conclusions though not the ethical
discipline of organized religion (and he knew that its ethical
system in essentials is older than Christianity), was not altogether an untrained one, and like all true Dissenters, he knew
the master he was serving: his conscience. He had the mathematical certainties of music and architecture, and the daily,
hourly training of a serious artist laboring at his problems over
a period of more than half a century. That he was unhampered
by ideas is therefore highly improbable. He wrote a few fine
poems among a large number of poor ones. He wrote fifteen
novels, of which a round half-dozen are well the equal of any
novel in the English language; even if this is not to say he is
the equal of Flaubert or of Dostoievsky. His notebooks testify
to a constant preoccupation with ideas, not all of them his own,
naturally, for he inherited them from a very respectable race of
thinkers, sound in heterodoxy.

He had got out of the very air of the nineteenth century
something from Lucian, something from Leonardo, something
from Erasmus, from Montaigne, from Voltaire, from the Ency-
clopaedists, and there were some powerful nineteenth-century
Inquirers, too, of whom we need only mention Darwin, perhaps.
Scientific experiment leads first to skepticism; but we have seen
in our time, how, pursued to the verge of the infinite, it sometimes leads back again to a form of mysticism. There is at the
heart of the universe a riddle no man can solve, and in the end,
God may be the answer. But this is fetching up at a great distance still from orthodoxy, and still must be suspect in that
quarter. Grant that the idea of God is the most splendid single
act of the creative human imagination, and that all his multiple
faces and attributes correspond to some need and satisfy some
deep desire in mankind; still, for the Inquirers, it is impossible
not to conclude that this mystical concept has been harnessed
rudely to machinery of the most mundane sort, and has been

made to serve the ends of an organization which, ruling under divine guidance, has ruled very little better, and in some respects, worse, than certain rather mediocre but frankly man-made systems of government. And it has often lent its support to the worst evils in secular government, fighting consistently on the side of the heavy artillery. And it has seemed at times not to know the difference between Good and Evil, but to get them hopelessly confused with legalistic right and wrong; justifying the most cynical expedients of worldly government by a high morality; and committing the most savage crimes against human life for the love of God. When you consider the political career of the church in the light of its professed origins and purposes, perhaps Original Sin *is* the answer. But Hardy preferred to remove the argument simply to another ground. As to himself, in his personal life, he had a Franciscan tenderness in regard to children, animals, laborers, the poor, the mad, the insulted and injured. He suffered horror and indignation at human injustice, more especially at the kind committed by entrenched authority and power upon the helpless. In middle age he remembered and recorded an early shock he received on hearing that, in his neighborhood, a young boy, a farm laborer, was found dead of sheer starvation in the fruitful field he had worked to cultivate. When he was planning *The Dynasts*, he wrote in his notebook: "The human race is to be shown as one great net-work or tissue which quivers in every part when one point is shaken, like a spider's web if touched." For Hardy, the death of that boy was a blow that set the whole great web trembling; and all mankind received a lasting wound. Here was a human fate for which human acts were responsible, and it would not serve Hardy at all to put the blame on Original Sin, or the inscrutable decrees of Divine Providence, or any other of the manifold devices for not letting oneself be too uncomfortable at the spectacle of merely human suffering. He was painfully uncomfortable all his life, and his discomfort was not for himself—he was an extraordinarily selfless sort of man—but the pervasiveness of what he considered senseless and unnecessary human misery. Out of the strange simplicity of his own unworldliness he could write at the age of 78: "As to pessimism. My motto is, first correctly diagnose the complaint—in this case human ills—and ascertain the cause: then set about finding a remedy if one exists. The motto or practise of the optimists is: Blind the eyes to the real malady, and use empirical panaceas to suppress the symptoms." Reasonableness: the use of the human intelligence directed toward the best human solution of human ills; such, if you please, was the unedifying proposal of this diabolic soul.

He himself in his few remarks on public and practical affairs, had always been very reasonable. War, he believed, was an abomination, but it recurred again and again, apparently an incurable ill. He had no theories to advance, but wished merely that those who made wars would admit the real motives; aside from the waste and destruction, which he viewed with purely humane feelings, he objected to the immoralities of statecraft and religion in the matter. He was opposed to capital punishment on the simple grounds that no man has the right to take away the life of another. But he believed it acted as a material deterrent to crime, and if the judges would admit that it was social expediency, with no foundation in true morality, that was another matter. On the Irish question he was acute and explicit in expressing his view in this direction. "Though he did not enter it here [in his notebook] Hardy . . . said of Home Rule that it was a staring dilemma, of which good policy and good philanthropy were the huge horns. Policy for England required that it should not be granted; humanity to Ireland that it should. Neither Liberals nor Conservatives would honestly own up to this opposition between two moralities, but speciously insisted that humanity and policy were both on one side—of course their own." At another time he complained that most of the philosophers began on the theory that the earth had been designed as a comfortable place for man. He could no more accept this theory than he could the theological notion that the world was a testing ground for the soul of man in preparation for eternity, and that his sufferings were part of a "divine" plan, or indeed, so far as the personal fate of mankind was concerned, of any plan at all. He did believe with a great deal of common sense that man could make the earth a more endurable place for himself if he would, but he also realized that human nature is not grounded in common sense, that there is a deep place in it where the mind does not go, where the blind monsters sleep and wake, war among themselves, and feed upon death.

He did believe that there is "a power that rules the world" though he did not name it, nor could he accept the names that had been given it, or any explanation of its motives. He could only watch its operations, and to me it seems he concluded that both malevolence and benevolence originated in the mind of man, and the warring forces were within him alone; such plan as existed in regard to him he had created for himself, his Good and his Evil were alike the mysterious inventions of his own mind; and why this was so, Hardy could not pretend to say. He knew there was an element in human nature not subject to mathematical equation or the water-tight theories of dogma, and this intransigent, measureless force, divided against itself, in con- flict alike with its own system of laws and the unknown laws of the universe, was the real theme of Hardy's novels; a genu- inely tragic theme in the grand manner, of sufficient weight and shapelessness to try the powers of any artist. Generally so reluctant to admit any influence, Hardy admits to a study of the Greek dramatists, and with his curious sense of proportion, he decided that the Wessex countryside was also the dwelling place of the spirit of tragedy; that the histories of certain ob- scure persons in that limited locality bore a strong family re- semblance to those of the great, the ancient, and the legendary. Mr. Eliot finds Hardy's beloved Wessex a "stage setting," such as the Anglo-Saxon heart loves; and Hardy's Wessex farmers "period peasants pleasing to the metropolitan imagination."

Hardy was Anglo-Saxon and Norman; that landscape was in his blood. Those period peasants were people he had known all his life, and I think that in this passage Mr. Eliot simply speaks as a man of the town, like those young rectors who need to be reminded of the individual dignity and importance of the country people. Further, taking all the Hardy characters in a lump, he finds in them only blind animal emotionalism, and remarks: ". . . strong passion is only interesting or significant in strong men; those who abandon themselves without resistance to excitements which tend to deprive them of reason become merely instruments of feeling and lose their humanity; and unless there is moral resistance and conflict there is no meaning." True in part: and to disagree in detail would lead to an endless discussion of *what* exactly constitutes interest in the work of a writer; *what* gives importance to his characters, their intrinsic value as human beings, or the value their creator is able to give them by his own imaginative view of them.

Hardy seems almost to agree with Mr. Eliot for once: "The best tragedy—highest tragedy in short—is that of the WORTHY encompassed by the INEVITABLE. The tragedies of immoral and worthless people are not of the best." My own judgment is that Hardy's characters are in every way superior to those of Mr. Eliot, and for precisely the reason the two writers are agreed upon. Hardy's people suffer the tragedy of being, Mr. Eliot's of not-being. The strange creatures inhabiting the wasteland of Mr. Eliot's particular scene are for the most part immoral and worthless, the apeneck Sweeneys, the Grishkins, and all. . . . They have for us precisely the fascination the poet has endowed them with, and they also have great significance: they are the sinister chorus of the poet's own tragedy, they represent the sum of the poet's vision of human beings without God and without faith, a world of horror surrounding this soul thirsting for faith in God. E. M. Forster has remarked that *The Waste Land* is a poem of real horror, the tragedy of the rains that came too late—or perhaps, never came at all. For how else can one explain the self-absorbed despair of Eliot's point of view, even in religion? That uncontrolled emotion of loathing for his fellow pilgrims in this mortal life? Was there not one soul worth tender treatment, not one good man interesting enough to the poet to inhabit his tragic scene? It is a curious paradox. Hardy feels no contempt for his characters at all; he writes of them as objectively as if they existed by themselves, they are never the background, the chorus, for the drama of his own experience. Beside Eliot's wasteland, with its inhuman beings, Hardy's Wessex seems an airy, familiar place, his characters at least have living blood in them, and though Mr. Eliot complains that Hardy was not interested in the minds of men, still their headpieces are not deliberately stuffed with straw by their creator.

Hardy's characters are full of moral conflicts and of decisions arrived at by mental processes, certainly. Jude, Gabriel Oak, Clym Yeobright, above all, Henchard, are men who have decisions to make, and if they do not make them entirely on the plane of reason, it is because Hardy was interested most in that hairline dividing the rational from the instinctive, the opposition, we might call it, between nature, and second nature; that is, between instinct and the habits of thought fixed upon the individual by his education and his environment. Such characters of his as are led by their emotions come to tragedy; he seems to say that following the emotions blindly leads to disaster. Romantic miscalculation of the possibilities of life, of love, of the situation; of refusing to reason their way out of their predicament; these are the causes of disaster in Hardy's novels. Angel Clare is a man of the highest principles, trained in belief, religion, observance of moral law. His failure to understand the real nature of Christianity makes a monster of him at the great crisis of his life. The Mayor of Casterbridge spends the balance of his life in atonement and reparation for a brutal wrong committed in drunkenness and anger; his past overtakes and destroys him. Hardy had an observing eye, a remembering mind; he did not need the Greeks to teach him that the Furies

do arrive punctually, and that neither act, nor will, nor intention will serve to deflect a man's destiny from him, once he has
taken the step which decides it.

A word about that style which Mr. Eliot condemns as touching
"sublimity without ever having passed through the stage of
being good." Hardy has often been called by critics who love
him, the good simple man of no ideas, the careless workman
of genius who never learned to write, who cared nothing for
the way of saying a thing.

His own testimony is that he cared a great deal for *what* he
said: "My art is to intensify the expression of things, as is done
by Crivelli, Bellini, etc., so that the heart and inner meaning is
made vividly visible." Again: "The Realities to be the true
realities of life, hitherto called abstractions. The old material
realities to be placed behind the former, as shadowy accessories."
His notebooks are dry, reluctant, unmethodical; he seems to
have spent his time and energies in actual labor at his task rather
than theorizing about it, but he remarks once: "Looking around
on a well-selected shelf of fiction, how few stories of any length
does one recognize as well told from beginning to end! The first
half of this story, the last half of that, the middle of another . . .
the modern art of narration is yet in its infancy." He made few
notes on technical procedure, but one or two are valuable as
a clue to his directions: "A story must be exceptional enough
to justify its telling. We tale tellers are all Ancient Mariners,
and none of us is warranted in stopping Wedding Guests . . .
unless he has something more unusual to relate than the ordinary
experiences of every average man and woman." Again: "The
whole secret of fiction and drama—in the constructional part—
lies in the adjustment of things unusual to things eternal and
universal. The writer who knows exactly how exceptional, and
how non-exceptional, his events should be made, possesses the
key to the art."

So much for theory. Not much about the importance of style,

the care for the word, the just and perfect construction of a paragraph. But Hardy was not a careless writer. The difference between his first and last editions proves this, in matters of style aside from his painful reconstruction of his manuscripts mutilated for serial publication. He wrote and wrote again, and he never found it easy. He lacked elegance, he never learned the trick of the whip-lash phrase, the complicated lariat twirling of the professed stylists. His prose lumbers along, it jogs, it creaks, it hesitates, it is as dull as certain long passages in the Tolstoy of *War and Peace*, for example. That celebrated first scene on Egdon Heath, in *The Return of the Native*. Who does not remember it? And in actual re-reading, what could be duller? What could be more labored than his introduction of the widow Yeobright at the heath fire among the dancers, or more unconvincing than the fears of the timid boy that the assembly are literally raising the Devil? Except for this; in my memory of that episode, as in dozens of others in many of Hardy's novels, I have seen it, I was there. When I read it, it almost disappears from view, and afterward comes back, phraseless, living in its somber clearness, as Hardy meant it to do, I feel certain. This to my view is the chief quality of good prose as distinguished from poetry. By his own testimony, he limited his territory by choice, set boundaries to his material, focused his point of view like a burning glass down on a definite aspect of things. He practiced a stringent discipline, severely excised and eliminated all that seemed to him not useful or appropriate to his plan. In the end his work was the sum of his experience, he arrived at his particular true testimony; along the way, sometimes, many times, he wrote sublimely.

1940

Gertrude Stein: Three Views

❊

"EVERYBODY IS A REAL ONE" (1927)

All I know about Gertrude Stein is what I find in her first two
books, *Three Lives* and *The Making of Americans*. Many persons
know her, they tell amusing stories about her and festoon her with
legends. Next to James Joyce she is the great influence on the
younger literary generation, who see in her the combination of
tribal wise woman and arch-priestess of aesthetic.

This is all very well; but I can go only by what I find in these
pages. They form not so much a history of Americans as a full
description and analysis of many human beings, including Gertrude Stein and the reader and all the reader's friends; they make
a psychological source book and the diary of an aesthetic problem
worked out momently under your eyes.

One of the many interesting things about *The Making of
Americans* is its date. It was written twenty years ago (1906-1908),
when Gertrude Stein was young. It precedes the war and cubism;
it precedes *Ulysses* and *Remembrance of Things Past*. I doubt if
all the people who should read it will read it for a great while yet,
for it is in such a limited edition, and reading it is anyhow a sort
of permanent occupation. Yet to shorten it would be to mutilate
its vitals, and it is a very necessary book. In spite of all there is in
it Gertrude Stein promises all the way through it to write another
even longer and put in it all the things she left unfinished in this.
She has not done it yet; at least it has not been published.

Twenty years ago, when she had been living in Paris only a
few years, Gertrude Stein's memory of her American life was
fresh, and I think both painful and happy in her. "The old people

36

in a new world, the new people made out of the old, that is the story that I mean to tell, for that is what really is and what I really know." This is a deeply American book, and without "movies" or automobiles or radio or prohibition or any of the mechanical properties for making local color, it is a very up-to-date book. We feel in it the vitality and hope of the first generation, the hearty materialism of the second, the vagueness of the third. It is all realized and projected in these hundreds of portraits, the death-like monotony in action, the blind diffusion of effort, "the spare American emotion," "the feeling of rich American living"—rich meaning money, of course—the billion times repeated effort of being born and breathing and eating and sleeping and working and feeling and dying to no particular end that makes American middle-class life. We have almost no other class as yet. "I say vital singularity is as yet an unknown product with us." So she observes the lack of it and concerns herself with the endless repetition of pattern in us only a little changed each time, but changed enough to make an endless mystery of each individual man and woman.

In beginning this book you walk into what seems to be a great spiral, a slow, ever-widening, unmeasured spiral unrolling itself horizontally. The people in this world appear to be motionless at every stage of their progress, each one is simultaneously being born, arriving at all ages and dying. You perceive that it is a world without mobility, everything takes place, has taken place, will take place; therefore nothing takes place, all at once. Yet the illusion of movement persists, the spiral unrolls, you follow; a closed spinning circle is even more hopeless than a universe that will not move. Then you discover it is not a circle, not machine-like repetition, the spiral does open and widen, it is repetition only in the sense that one wave follows upon another. The emotion progresses with the effort of a giant parturition. Gertrude Stein describes her function in terms of digestion, of childbirth: all these people, these fragments of digested knowledge, are in her, they must come out.

The progress of her family, then, this making of Americans, she has labored to record in a catalogue of human attributes, acts and emotions. Episodes are nothing, narrative is by the way, her interest lies in what she calls the bottom natures of men and women, all men, all women. "It is important to me, very important indeed to me, that I sometimes understand every one." . . . "I am hoping some time to be right about every one, about everything."

In this intensity of preoccupation there is the microscopic observation of the near-sighted who must get so close to their object they depend not alone on vision but on touch and smell and the very warmth of bodies to give them the knowledge they seek. This nearness, this immediacy, she communicates also, there is no escaping into the future nor into the past. All time is in the present, these people are "being living," she makes you no gift of comfortable ripened events past and gone. "I am writing everything as I am learning everything," and so we have lists of qualities and defects, portraits of persons in scraps, with bits and pieces added again and again in every round of the spiral: they repeat and repeat themselves to you endlessly as living persons do, and always you feel you know them, and always they present a new bit of themselves.

Gertrude Stein reminds me of Jacob Boehme in the way she sees essentials in human beings. He knew them as salt, as mercury; as moist, as dry, as burning; as bitter, sweet or sour. She perceives them as attacking, as resisting, as dependent independent, as having a core of wood, of mud, as murky, engulfing; Boehme's chemical formulas are too abstract, she knows the substances of man are mixed with clay. Materials interest her, the moral content of man can often be nicely compared to homely workable stuff. Sometimes her examination is almost housewifely, she rolls a fabric under her fingers, tests it. It is thus and so. I find this very good, very interesting. "It will repay good using."

"In writing a word must be for me really an existing thing." Her efforts to get at the roots of existing life, to create fresh life from them, give her words a dark liquid flowingness, like the murmur of the blood. She does not strain words or invent them. Many words have retained their original meaning for her, she uses them simply. Good means good and bad means bad—next to the Jews the Americans are the most moralistic people, and Gertrude Stein is American Jew, a combination which by no means lessens the like quality in both. Good and bad are attributes to her, strength and weakness are real things that live inside people, she looks for these things, notes them in their likenesses and differences. She loves the difficult virtues, she is tender toward good people, she has faith in them.

An odd thing happens somewhere in the middle of this book. You will come upon it suddenly and it will surprise you. All along you have had a feeling of submergence in the hidden lives of a great many people, and unaccountably you will find your-self rolling up to the surface, on the outer edge of the curve. A disconcerting break into narrative full of phrases that might have come out of any careless sentimental novel, alternates with scraps of the natural style. It is astounding, you read on out of chagrin. Again without warning you submerge, and later Miss Stein explains she was copying an old piece of writing of which she is now ashamed, the words mean nothing: "I commence again with words that have meaning," she says, and we leave this limp, dead spot in the middle of the book.

Gertrude Stein wrote once of Juan Gris that he was, somehow, saved. She is saved, too; she is free of pride and humility, she confesses to superhuman aspirations simply, she was badly fright-ened once and has recovered, she is honest in her uncertainties. There are only a few bits of absolute knowledge in the world, people can learn only one or two fundamental facts about each other, the rest is decoration and prejudice. She is very free from decoration and prejudice.

❋

SECOND WIND (1928)

Spirals and corkscrews are whirlwinds if we spin a big top and not stop. Not stop nor drag a herring. She confused them all, yet called every day offering new feather pillows. If you wish to amuse yourself you may have your palm read, or do you drink gin? There is also the flea circus, and there is a Congressman. Romance is useful knowledge; America is romance, but you must first live in Paris. Theaters and ticker tape and the states to escape. Ticker tape and ticker tacker, tick tack toe.

Now you know.
This is so.
This sounds silly.
As you please.
Now I will explain.

She mentioned a little of everything reasonable in order not to tell the secret. When the photographs came she said there had been a mistake. Dead things when they go dead go dead and do not come alive. They go dead. They said yes it is pretty but we miss the color. This was ended then.

This was not all. This was another one a younger one a sadder one a wiser one a smaller one a darker one with gray skin being reading the Making of Americans three times all summer. It was ended then. But you say she is wiser then why is she sadder then it is not sadder to be wiser then. Oh, yes, but when things go dead it is different.

You don't understand. Let me tell you then.

We were saying it is different now it was different then it is finished now it was finished then you may go up close and look if you like. This is an American habit with romance.

In *Useful Knowledge* you will look for sex to vex. There is no sex to vex. Look visibly. Stimulation is one and irritation is an-

other. Another to smother Americans, who wear glasses and read
if a hat is dropped suddenly. They send white wedding cake too
in painted boxes. We are told this is being American, but it is not
pleasant. She says it is pleasant. I doubt doubt it. If this is being
American I doubt it. If this is being making romance I doubt
it. If this is owning the earth I doubt it. If I doubt it it is
sometimes necessary to let this be all. Iowa is not Maine Maine
is not Iowa Louisiana is not either there are many states.

> In Spain there is no rain.
> Mr. Lewis.
> Mr. Lewis.

Page Mr. Wyndham Lewis on this page. Page on page. Why
does he rage and when. Not American being human Mr. Lewis
calls her Gerty and says she stammers. Who will be enemies because his name is not Gerty and he stammers. Being stammering
is being Mr. Lewis in one way and being stammering is being
Gerty in another way and it's all in the day. This way today.
Being stammering together is a chorus and a chorus being stammering together is thinking. Thinking being stammering. Many
rivers but only two rivers. There will be only a few two rivers
with furry edges. The cost is nothing. The cost is nothing much.
Much. Much is what you pay for. Only a few. Two by two
and one by one. Two is too few.

Now all together.
Repetition makes subways.
I know what I am saying and if you flatter me I am insulted.

❋

THE WOODEN UMBRELLA (1947)

. . . I want to say that just today I met Miss Hennessy
and she was carrying, she did not have it with her, but
she usually carried a wooden umbrella. This wooden umbrella is carved out of wood and looks like a real one
even to the little button and the rubber string that holds
it together. It is all right except when it rains. When it
rains it does not open and Miss Hennessy looks a little
foolish but she does not mind because it is after all the
only wooden umbrella in Paris. And even if there were
lots of others it would not make any difference.–
Gertrude Stein: *Everybody's Autobiography*.

When Kahnweiler the picture dealer told Miss Stein that Picasso
had stopped painting and had taken to writing poetry, she confessed that she had "a funny feeling" because "things belonged
to you and writing belonged to me. I know writing belongs
to me, I am quite certain," but still it was a blow. ". . . No
matter how certain you are about anything belonging to you
if you hear that somebody says it belongs to them it gives you
a funny feeling."

Later she buttonholed Picasso at Kahnweiler's gallery, shook
him, kissed him, lectured him, told him that his poetry was
worse than bad, it was offensive as a Cocteau drawing and in
much the same way, it was unbecoming. He defended himself
by reminding her that she had said he was an extraordinary
person, and he believed an extraordinary person should be able
to do anything. She said that to her it was a repellent sight
when a person who could do one thing well dropped it for
something else he could not do at all. Convinced, or defeated,
he promised to give back writing to its natural owner.

Writing was no doubt the dearest of Miss Stein's possessions,
but it was not the only one. The pavilion atelier in rue de

Fleurus was a catch-all of beings and created objects, and everything she looked upon was hers in more than the usual sense. Her weighty numerous divans and armchairs covered with dark, new-looking horsehair; her dogs, Basket and Pépé, conspicuous, special, afflicted as neurotic children; her clutter of small tables each with its own clutter of perhaps valuable but certainly treasured objects; her Alice B. Toklas; her visitors; and finally, ranging the walls from floor to ceiling, giving the impression that they were hung three deep, elbowing each other, canceling each other's best effects in the jealous way of pictures, was her celebrated collection of paintings by her collection of celebrated painters. These were everybody of her time whom Miss Stein elected for her own, from her idol Picasso (kidnaped bodily from brother Leo, who saw him first) to miniscule Sir Francis Rose, who seems to have appealed to the pixy in her.

Yet the vaguely lighted room where things accumulated, where they appeared to have moved in under a compulsion to be possessed once for all by someone who knew how to take hold firmly, gave no impression of disorder. On the contrary, an air of solid comfort, of inordinate sobriety and permanence, of unadventurous middle-class domesticity—respectability is the word, at last—settled around the shoulders of the guest like a Paisley shawl, a borrowed shawl of course, something to be worn and admired for a moment and handed back to the owner. Miss Stein herself sat there in full possession of herself, the scene, the spectators, wearing thick no-colored shapeless woolen clothes and honest woolen stockings knitted for her by Miss Toklas, looking extremely like a handsome old Jewish patriarch who had backslid and shaved off his beard.

Surrounded by her listeners, she talked in a slow circle in her fine deep voice, the word "perception" occurring again and again and yet again like the brass ring the children snatch for as their hobby horses whirl by. She was in fact at one period surrounded by snatching children, the literary young, a good many of them American, between two wars in a falling world. Roughly they were divided into two parties: those who were full of an active, pragmatic unbelief, and those who searched their own vitals and fished up strange horrors in the style of *transition*. The first had discovered that honor is only a word, and an embarrassing one, because it was supposed to mean something wonderful and was now exposed as meaning nothing at all. For them, nothing worked except sex and alcohol and pulling apart their lamentable Midwestern upbringings and scattering the pieces. Some of these announced that they wished their writings to be as free from literature as if they had never read a book, as indeed too many of them had not up to the time. The *transition* tone was even more sinister, for though it was supposed to be the vanguard of international experimental thought, its real voice was hoarse, anxious, corrupted mysticism speaking in a thick German accent. The editor, Eugene Jolas, had been born in the eternally disputed land of Alsace, bilingual in irreconcilable tongues, French and German, and he spoke both and English besides with a foreign accent. He had no mother tongue, nor even a country, and so he fought the idea of both, but his deepest self was German: he issued frantic manifestoes demanding that language be reduced to something he could master, crying aloud in "defense of the hallucinative forces," the exploding of the verb, the "occult hypnosis of language," "chthonian grammar"; reason he hated, and defended the voice of the blood, the disintegration of syntax—with a special grudge against English—preaching like an American Methodist evangelist in the wilderness for "the use of a language which is a mantic instrument, and which does not hesitate to adopt a revolutionary attitude toward word syntax, going even so far as to invent a hermetic language, if necessary." The final aim was "the illumination of a collective reality and a totalistic universe." Meanwhile Joyce, a man with a mother tongue if ever there was one, and a master of languages, was mixing them in strange new forms to the delight and enrichment of language for good and all.

Miss Stein had no problems: she simply exploded a verb as if it were a soap bubble, used chthonian grammar long before she heard it named (and she would have scorned to name it), was a born adept in occult hypnosis of language without even trying. Serious young men who were having a hard time learning to write realized with relief that there was nothing at all to it if you just relaxed and put down the first thing that came into your head. She gave them a romantic name, the Lost Generation, and a remarkable number of them tried earnestly if unsuccessfully to live up to it. A few of them were really lost, and disappeared, but others had just painted themselves into a very crowded corner. She laid a cooling hand upon their agitated brows and asked with variations, What did it matter? There were only a few geniuses, after all, among which she was one, only the things a genius said made any difference, the rest was "just there," and so she disposed of all the dark questions of life, art, human relations, and death, even eternity, even God, with perfect Stein logic, bringing the scene again into its proper focus, upon herself.

Some of the young men went away, read a book, began thinking things over, and became the best writers of their time. Humanly, shamefacedly, they then jeered at their former admiration, and a few even made the tactical error of quarreling with her. She enjoyed their discipleship while it lasted, and dismissed them from existence when it ended. It is easy to see what tremendous vitality and direction there was in the arts all over the world; for not everything was happening only in France; life was generated in many a noisy seething confusion in many countries. Little by little the legitimate line of succession appeared, the survivors emerged each with his own shape and meaning, the young vanguard became the Old Masters and even old hat.

In the meantime our heroine went on talking, vocally or on

paper, and in that slow swarm of words, out of the long drone
and mutter and stammer of her lifetime monologue, often there
emerged a phrase of ancient native independent wisdom, for she
had a shrewd deep knowledge of the commoner human motives. Her judgments were neither moral nor intellectual, and
least of all aesthetic, indeed they were not even judgments, but
simply her description from observation of acts, words, appearances giving her view; limited, personal in the extreme,
prejudiced without qualification, based on assumptions founded
in the void of pure unreason. For example, French notaries'
sons have always something strange about them—look at Jean
Cocteau. The Spaniard has a natural center of ignorance, all
except Juan Gris. On the other hand, Dali had not only the
natural Spanish center of ignorance, but still another variety,
quite malignant, of his own. Preachers' sons do not turn out
like other people—E. E. Cummings, just for one. Painters are
always little short round men—Picasso and a crowd of them.
And then she puts her finger lightly on an American peculiarity
of our time: ". . . so perhaps they are right the Americans
in being more interested in you than in the work you have
done, although they would not be interested in you if you had
not done the work you had done." And she remarked once to
her publisher that she was famous in America not for her
work that people understood but for that which they did not
understand. That was the kind of thing she could see through
at a glance.

It was not that she was opposed to ideas, but that she was not
interested in anybody's ideas but her own, except as material
to put down on her endless flood of pages. Like writing, opinion
also belonged to Miss Stein, and nothing annoyed her more—
she was easily angered about all sorts of things—than for anyone not a genius or who had no reputation that she respected,
to appear to be thinking in her presence. Of all those GI's who
swarmed about her in her last days, if anyone showed any
fight at all, any tendency to question her pronouncements, she

smacked him down like a careful grandmother, for his own good. Her GI heroes Brewsie and Willie are surely as near to talking zombies as anything ever seen in a book, and she loved, not them, but their essential zombiness.

Like all talkers, she thought other people talked too much, and there is recorded only one instance of someone getting the drop on her—who else but Alfred Stieglitz? She sat through a whole session at their first meeting without uttering one word, a feat which he mentioned with surprised approval. If we knew nothing more of Stieglitz than this we would know he was a great talker. She thought that the most distressing sound was that of the human voice, other people's voices, "as the hoot owl is almost the best sound," but in spite of this she listened quite a lot. When she was out walking the dogs, if workmen were tearing up the streets she would ask them what they were doing and what they would be doing next. She only stopped to break the monotony of walking, but she remembered their answers. When a man passed making up a bitter little song against her dog and his conduct vis-à-vis lamp posts and house walls, she put it all down, and it is wonderfully good reporting. Wise or silly or nothing at all, down everything goes on the page with the air of everything being equal, unimportant in itself, important because it happened to her and she was writing about it.

She had not always been exactly there, exactly that. There had been many phases, all in consistent character, each giving way in turn for the next, of her portentous being. Ford Madox Ford described her, in earlier Paris days, as trundling through the streets in her high-wheeled American car, being a spectacle and being herself at the same time. And this may have been near the time of Man Ray's photograph of her, wearing a kind of monk's robe, her poll clipped, her granite front and fine eyes displayed at their best period.

Before that, she was a youngish stout woman, not ever really young, with a heavy shrewd face between a hard round pom-

padour and a round lace collar, looking more or less like
Picasso's earliest portrait of her. What saved her then from
a good honest husband, probably a stockbroker, and a houseful of children? The answer must be that her envelope was a
tricky disguise of Nature, that she was of the company of
Amazons which nineteenth-century America produced among
its many prodigies: not-men, not-women, answerable to no function in either sex, whose careers were carried on, and how
successfully, in whatever field they chose: they were educators,
writers, editors, politicians, artists, world travelers, and international hostesses, who lived in public and by the public and
played out their self-assumed, self-created roles in such masterly
freedom as only a few early medieval queens had equaled.
Freedom to them meant precisely freedom from men and their
stuffy rules for women. They usurped with a high hand the
traditional masculine privileges of movement, choice, and the
use of direct, personal power. They were few in number and
they were not only to be found in America, and Miss Stein
belonged with them, no doubt of it, in spite of a certain tem-
peramental passivity which was Oriental, not feminine. With
the top of her brain she was a modern girl, a New Woman,
interested in scientific experiment, historical research, the rational view; for a time she was even a medical student, but
she could not deceive herself for long. Even during her four
years at Radcliffe, where the crisp theories of higher education battle with the womb-shaped female mind (and "they always afterward seemed foolish" to her at Radcliffe, she said,
meaning perhaps the promoters of these theories) she worried
and worried, for worrying and thinking were synonyms to
her, about the meaning of the universe, the riddle of human
life, about time and its terrible habit of passing, God, death,
eternity, and she felt very lonely in the awful singularity of
her confusions. Added to this, history taught her that whole
civilizations die and disappear utterly, "and now it happens
again," and it gave her a great fright. She was sometimes fright-

ened afterward, "but now well being frightened is something less frightening than it was," but her ambiguous mind faced away from speculation. Having discovered with relief that all knowledge was not her province, she accepted rightly, she said, every superstition. To be in the hands of fate, of magic, of the daemonic forces, what freedom it gave her not to decide, not to act, not to accept any responsibility for anything—one held the pen and let the mind wander. One sat down and somebody did everything for one.

Still earlier she was a plump solemn little girl abundantly upholstered in good clothes, who spent her allowance on the work of Shelley, Thackeray, and George Eliot in fancy bindings, for she loved reading and *Clarissa Harlowe* was once her favorite novel. These early passions exhausted her; in later life she swam in the relaxing bath of detective and murder mysteries, because she liked somebody being dead in a story, and of them all Dashiell Hammett killed them off most to her taste. Her first experience of the real death of somebody had taught her that it could be pleasant for her too. "One morning we could not wake our father." This was in East Oakland, California. "Leo climbed in by the window and called out that he was dead in his bed and he was." It seems to have been the first thing he ever did of which his children, all five of them, approved. Miss Stein declared plainly they none of them liked him at all: "As I say, fathers are depressing but our family had one," she confessed, and conveys the notion that he was a bore of the nagging, petty sort, the kind that worries himself and others into the grave.

Considering her tepid, sluggish nature, really sluggish like something eating its way through a leaf, Miss Stein could grow quite animated on the subject of her early family life, and some of her stories are as pretty and innocent as lizards running over tombstones on a hot day in Maryland. It was a solid, getting-on sort of middle-class Jewish family of Austrian origin, Keyser on one side, Stein on the other: and the Keysers came to Balti-

more about 1820. All branches of the family produced their
individual eccentrics—there was even an uncle who believed in
the Single Tax—but they were united in their solid understanding of the value of money as the basis of a firm stance in this
world. There were incomes, governesses, spending money,
guardians appointed when parents died, and Miss Stein was
fascinated from childhood with stories about how people earned
their first dollar. When, rather late, she actually earned some
dollars herself by writing, it changed her entire viewpoint about
the value of her work and of her own personality. It came to
her as revelation that the only difference between men and
four-footed animals is that men can count, and when they
count, they like best to count money. In her first satisfaction at
finding she had a commercial value, she went on a brief binge
of spending money just for the fun of it. But she really knew
better. Among the five or six of the seven deadly sins which
she practiced with increasing facility and advocated as virtues,
avarice became her favorite. Americans in general she found
to be rather childish about money: they spent it or gave it
away and enjoyed it wastefully with no sense of its fierce latent
power. "It is hard to be a miser, a real miser, they are as rare
as geniuses it takes the same kind of thing to make one, that
is time must not exist for them. . . . There must be a reality
that has nothing to do with the passing of time. I have it and
so had Hetty Green . . ." and she found only one of the
younger generation in America, a young man named Jay
Laughlin, who had, she wrote, praising him, avarice to that point
of genius which makes the true miser. She made a very true
distinction between avarice, the love of getting and keeping,
and love of money, the love of making and spending. There is
a third love, the love of turning a penny by ruse, and this was
illustrated by brother Michael, who once grew a beard to make
himself look old enough to pass for a G.A.R. veteran, and so
disguised he got a cut-rate railway fare for a visit home during

a G.A.R. rally, though all the men of his family fought on the Confederate side.

The question of money and of genius rose simultaneously with the cheerful state of complete orphanhood. Her mother disappeared early after a long illness, leaving her little nest of vipers probably without regret, for vipers Miss Stein shows them to have been in the most Biblical sense. They missed their mother chiefly because she had acted as a buffer between them and their father, and also served to keep them out of each other's hair. Sister Bertha and Brother Simon were simple-minded by family standards, whatever they were, Brother Leo had already started being a genius without any regard for the true situation, and after the death of their father, Brother Michael was quite simply elected to be the Goat. He had inherited the family hatred of responsibility—from their mother, Miss Stein believed, but not quite enough to save him. He became guardian, caretaker, business manager, handy-man, who finally wangled incomes for all of them, and set them free from money and from each other. It is pleasant to know he was a very thorny martyr who did a great deal of resentful lecturing about economy, stamping and shouting around the house with threats to throw the whole business over and let them fend for themselves if they could not treat him with more consideration. With flattery and persuasion they would cluster around and get him back on the rails, for his destiny was to be useful to genius, that is, to Miss Stein.

She had been much attached to her brother Leo, in childhood they were twin souls. He was two years older and a boy, and she had learned from Clarissa Harlowe's uncle's letter that older brothers are superior to younger sisters, or any boy to any girl in fact. Though she bowed to this doctrine as long as it was convenient, she never allowed it to get in her way. She followed her brother's advice more or less, and in turn he waited on her and humored and defended her when she was a selfish lazy little girl. Later he made a charming traveling com-

panion who naturally, being older and a man, looked after all
the boring details of life and smoothed his sister's path everywhere. Still, she could not remember his face when he was absent, and once was very nervous when she went to meet him
on a journey, for fear she might not recognize him. The one
thing wrong all this time was their recurring quarrel about who
was the genius of the two, for each had assumed the title and
neither believed for a moment there was room for more than
one in the family. By way of proving himself, brother Leo
took the pavilion and atelier in the rue de Fleurus, installed
himself well, and began trying hard to paint. Miss Stein, seeing
all so cozy, moved in on him and sat down and began to write
—no question of trying. "To try is to die," became one of her
several hundred rhyming aphorisms designed to settle all con-
ceivable arguments; after a time, no doubt overwhelmed by the
solid negative force of that massive will and presence, her
brother moved out and took the atelier next door, and went on
being useful to his sister, and trying to paint.

But he also went on insisting tactlessly that he, and not she,
was the born genius; and this was one of the real differences between them, that he attacked on the subject and was uneasy,
and could not rest, while his sister reasoned with him, patiently
at first, defending her title, regretting she could not share it.
Insist, argue, upset himself and her as much as he liked, she
simply, quietly knew with a Messianic revelation that she was
not only a genius, but *the* genius, and sometimes, she was certain, one of not more than half a dozen real ones in the world.
During all her life, whenever Miss Stein got low in her mind
about anything, she could always find consolation in this beautiful knowledge of being a born genius, and her brother's con-
tentiousness finally began to look like treason to her. She could
not forgive him for disputing her indivisible right to her
natural property, genius, on which all her other rights of possession were founded. It shook her—she worried about her work.
She had begun her long career of describing "how every one

who ever lived eats and drinks and loves and sleeps and talks and walks and wakes and forgets and quarrels and likes and dislikes and works and sits"—everybody's autobiography, in fact, for she had taken upon herself the immense task of explaining everybody to himself, of telling him all he needed to know about life, and she simply could not have brother Leo hanging around the edges of this grandiose scheme pinching off bits and holding them up to the light. By and by, too, she had Alice B. Toklas to do everything for her. So she and her brother drifted apart, but gradually, like one of Miss Stein's paragraphs. The separation became so complete that once, on meeting her brother unexpectedly, she was so taken by surprise she bowed to him, and afterward wrote a long poem about it in which her total confusion of mind and feeling were expressed with total incoherence: for once, form, matter and style stuttering and stammering and wallowing along together with the agitated harmony of roiling entrails.

There are the tones of sloth, of that boredom which is a low-pressure despair, of monotony, of obsession, in this portrait; she went walking out of boredom, she could drive a car, talk, write, but anything else made her nervous. People who were doing anything annoyed her: to be doing nothing, she thought, was more interesting than to be doing something. The air of deathly solitude surrounded her; yet the parade of names in her book would easily fill several printed pages, all with faces attached which she could see were quite different from each other, all talking, each taking his own name and person for granted—a thing she could never understand. Yet she could see what they were doing and could remember what they said. She only listened attentively to Picasso—for whose sake she would crack almost any head in sight—so she half-agreed when he said Picabia was the worst painter of all; but still, found herself drawn to Picabia because his name was Francis. She had discovered that men named Francis were always elegant, and though they might not know anything else, they always knew about themselves. This would remind her that she had never found out who she was. Again and again she would doubt her own identity, and that of everyone else. When she worried about this aloud to Alice B. Toklas, saying she believed it impossible for anyone ever to be certain who he was, Alice B. Toklas made, in context, the most inspired remark in the whole book. "It depends on who you are," she said, and you might think that would have ended the business. Not at all.

These deep-set, chronic fears led her to a good deal of quarreling, for when she quarreled she seems to have felt more real. She mentions quarrels with Max Jacob, Francis Rose, with Dali, with Picabia, with Picasso, with Virgil Thomson, with Braque, with Breton, and how many others, though she rarely says just why they quarreled or how they made it up. Almost nobody went away and stayed, and the awful inertia of habit in friendships oppressed her. She was sometimes discouraged at the prospect of having to go on seeing certain persons to the end, merely because she had once seen them. The world seemed smaller every day, swarming with people perpetually in movement, full of restless notions which, once examined by her, were inevitably proved to be fallacious, or at least entirely useless. She found that she could best get rid of them by putting them in a book. "That is very funny if you write about any one they do not exist any more, for you, so why see them again. Anyway, that is the way I am."

But as she wrote a book and disposed of one horde, another came on, and worried her afresh, discussing their ludicrous solemn topics, trying to understand things, and being unhappy about it. When Picasso was fretful because she argued with Dali and not with him, she explained that "one discusses things with stupid people but not with sensible ones." Her true grudge against intelligent people was that they talked "as if they were getting ready to change something." Change belonged to Miss Stein, and the duty of the world was to stand still so that she could move about in it comfortably. Her top flight of reasoning on the subject of intelligence ran as follows: "The most actively war-like nations could always convince the pacifists to become pro-German. That is because pacifists were such intelligent beings they could follow what any one is saying. If you follow what any one is saying then you are a pacifist you are a pro-German . . . therefore understanding is a very dull occupation."

Intellectuals, she said, always wanted to change things because they had an unhappy childhood. "Well, I never had an unhappy childhood, what is the use of having an unhappy anything?" Léon Blum, then Premier of France, had had an unhappy childhood, and she inclined to the theory that the political uneasiness of France could be traced to this fact.

There was not, of course, going to be another war (this was in 1937!), but if there was, there *would* be, naturally; and she never tired of repeating that dancing and war are the same thing "because both are forward and back," while revolution, on the contrary, is up and down, which is why it gets nowhere. Sovietism was even then going rapidly out of fashion in her circles, because they had discovered that it is very conservative, even if the Communists do not think so. Anarchists, being rarities, did not go out of fashion so easily. The most interesting thing that ever happened to America was the Civil War; but General Lee was severely to be blamed for leading his country into that war, just the same, because he must have known they could not win; and to her, it was absurd that any one should join battle in defense of a principle in face of certain defeat. For practical purposes, honor was not even a word. Still it was an exciting war and gave an interest to America which that country would never have had without it. "If you win you do not lose and if you lose you do not win." Even as she was writing these winged words, the Spanish Civil War, the Republicans against the Franco-Fascists, kept obtruding itself. And why? "Not because it is a revolution, but because I know so well the places they are mentioning and the things there they are destroying." When she was little in Oakland, California, she loved the big, nice American fires that had "so many horses and firemen to attend them," and when she was older, she found that floods, for one thing, always read worse in the papers than they really are; besides how can you care much about what is going on if you don't see it or know the people? For this reason she had Santa Teresa being indifferent to faraway Chinese while she was founding convents in Spain. William Seabrook came to see her to find out if she was as interesting as her books. She told him she was, and he discovered black magic in the paintings of Sir Francis Rose. And when she asked Dashiell Hammett why so many young men authors were writing novels about tender young male heroines instead of the traditional female ones, he explained that it was because as women grew more and more self-confident, men lost confidence in themselves, and turned to each other, or became their own subjects for fiction. This, or something else, reminded her several times that she could not write a novel, therefore no one could any more, and no one should waste time trying.

Somehow by such roundabouts we arrive at the important, the critical event in all this eventful history. Success. Success in this world, here and now, was what Miss Stein wanted. She knew just what it was, how it should look and feel, how much it should weigh and what it was worth over the counter. It was not enough to be a genius if you had to go on supporting your art on a private income. To be the center of a recondite literary cult, to be surrounded by listeners and imitators and seekers, to be mentioned in the same breath with James Joyce, and to have turned out bales of titles by merely writing a half-hour each day: she had all that, and what did it amount to? There was a great deal more and she must have it. As to her history of the human race, she confessed: "I have always been bothered . . . but mostly . . . because after all I do as simply as it can, as commonplacely as it can say, what everybody can and does do; I never know what they can do, I really do not know what they are, I do not think that any one can think because if they do, then who is who?"

It was high time for a change, and yet it occurred at hazard. If there had not been a beautiful season in October and part of November 1932, permitting Miss Stein to spend that season quietly in her country house, the *Autobiography of Alice B. Toklas* might never have been written. But it was written, and Miss Stein became a best-seller in America; she made real money. With Miss Toklas, she had a thrilling tour of the United States and found crowds of people eager to see her and listen to her. And at last she got what she had really wanted all along: to be published in the *Atlantic Monthly* and the *Saturday Evening Post*.

Now she had everything, or nearly. For a while she was afraid to write any more, for fear her latest efforts would not please her public. She had never learned who she was, and yet suddenly she had become somebody else. "You are you because your little dog knows you, but when your public knows you and does not want to pay you, and when your public knows you and does want to pay you, you are not the same you."

This would be of course the proper moment to take leave, as our heroine adds at last a golden flick of light to her self-portrait. "Anyway, I was a celebrity." The practical result was that she could no longer live on her income. But she and Alice B. Toklas moved into an apartment once occupied by Queen Christina of Sweden, and they began going out more, and seeing even more people, and talking, and Miss Stein settled every question as it came up, more and more. But who wants to read about success? It is the early struggle which makes a good story.

She and Alice B. Toklas enjoyed both the wars. The first one especially being a lark with almost no one getting killed where you could see, and it ended so nicely too, without changing anything. The second was rather more serious. She lived safely enough in Bilignin throughout the German occupation, and there is a pretty story that the whole village conspired to keep her presence secret. She had been a citizen of the world in the best European tradition; for though America was her native land, she had to live in Europe because she felt at home there. In the old days people paid little attention to wars, fought as they were out of sight by professional soldiers. She had always liked the notion, too, of the gradual Orientalization of the West, the peaceful penetration of the East into European culture. It had been going on a great while, and all Western geniuses worth mentioning were Orientals: look at Picasso, look at Einstein. Russians are Tartars, Spaniards are Saracens—had not all great twentieth-century painting been Spanish? And her cheerful conclusion was, that "Einstein was the creative philosophic mind of the century, and I have been the creative literary mind of the century also, with the Oriental mixing with the European." She added, as a casual afterthought, "Perhaps Europe is finished."

That was in 1938, and she could not be expected to know that war was near. They had only been sounding practice *alertes* in Paris against expected German bombers since 1935. She spoke out of her natural frivolity and did not mean it. She liked to prophesy, but warned her hearers that her prophecies never came out right, usually the very opposite, and no matter what happened, she was always surprised. She was surprised again: as the nations of Europe fell, and the Germans came again over the frontiers of France for the third time in three generations, the earth shook under her own feet, and not somebody else's. It made an astonishing difference. Something mysterious touched her in her old age. She got a fright, and this time not for ancient vanished civilizations, but for this civilization, this moment; and she was quite thrilled with relief and gay when the American army finally came in, and the Germans were gone. She did not in the least know why the Germans had come, but they were

gone, and so far as she could see, the American army had chased
them out. She remembered with positive spread-eagle patriotism
that America was her native land. At last America itself belonged
to Miss Stein, and she claimed it, in a formal published address
to other Americans. Anxiously she urged them to stay rich, to
be powerful and learn how to use power, not to waste themselves; for the first time she used the word "spiritual." Ours was
a spiritual as well as a material fight; Lincoln's great lucid words
about government of the people by the people for the people
suddenly sounded like a trumpet through her stammering confession of faith, she wanted nothing now to stand between her and
her newly discovered country. By great good luck she was born
on the winning side and she was going to stay there. And we were
not to forget about money as the source of power; "Remember
the depression, don't be afraid to look it in the face and find out
the reason why, if you don't find out the reason why you'll go
poor and my God, how I would hate to have my native land
go poor."

The mind so long shapeless and undisciplined could not now
express any knowledge out of its long willful ignorance. But
the heart spoke its crude urgent language. She had liked the
doughboys in the other war well enough, but this time she fell
in love with the whole American army below the rank of lieu-
tenant. She "breathed, ate, drank, lived GI's," she told them,
and inscribed numberless photographs for them, and asked them
all to come back again. After her flight over Germany in an
American bomber, she wrote about how, so often, she would
stand staring into the sky watching American war planes going
over, longing to be up there again with her new loves, in the
safe, solid air. She murmured, "Bless them, bless them." She had
been impatient with many of them who had still been naive
enough to believe they were fighting against an evil idea that
threatened everybody; some of them actually were simple
enough to say they had been—or believed they had been—fighting for democratic government. "What difference does it make

what kind of government you have?" she would ask. "All governments are alike. Just remember you won the war." But still, at the end, she warned them to have courage and not be just yes or no men. And she said, "Bless them, bless them."

It was the strangest thing, as if the wooden umbrella feeling the rain had tried to forsake its substance and take on the nature of its form; and was struggling slowly, slowly, much too late, to unfold.

Reflections on Willa Cather

❋

I never knew her at all, nor anyone who did know her; do not to this day. When I was a young writer in New York I knew she was there, and sometimes wished that by some charming chance I might meet up with her; but I never did, and it did not occur to me to seek her out. I had never felt that my condition of beginning authorship gave me a natural claim on the attention of writers I admired, such as Henry James and W. B. Yeats. Some proper instinct told me that all of any importance they had to say to me was in their printed pages, mine to use as I could. Still it would have been nice to have seen them, just to remember how they looked. There are three or four great ones, gone now, that I feel, too late, I should not have missed. Willa Cather was one of them.

There exist large numbers of critical estimates of her work, appreciations; perhaps even a memoir or two, giving glimpses of her personal history—I have never read one. She was not, in the popular crutch-word to describe almost any kind of sensation, "exciting"; so far as I know, nobody, not even one of the Freudian school of critics, ever sat up nights with a textbook in one hand and her works in the other, reading between the lines to discover how much sexual autobiography could be mined out of her stories. I remember only one photograph—Steichen's—made in middle life, showing a big plain smiling woman, her arms crossed easily over a girl-scout sort of white blouse, with a ragged part in her hair. She seemed, as the French say, "well seated" and not very outgoing. Even the earnestly amiable, finely shaped eyes, the left one faintly askew, were in some mysterious way not expressive, lacking as they did altogether that look of strangeness which a strange vision is supposed to give to the eye of any real artist, and very often does. One doesn't have to be a genius absolutely to get this look, it is often quite enough merely to believe one is a genius; and to have had the wild vision only once is enough—the after-light stays, even if, in such case, it is phosphorescence instead of living fire.

Well, Miss Cather looks awfully like somebody's big sister, or maiden aunt, both of which she was. No genius ever looked less like one, according to the romantic popular view, unless it was her idol, Flaubert, whose photographs could pass easily for those of any paunchy country squire indifferent to his appearance. Like him, none of her genius was in her looks, only in her works. Flaubert was a good son, adoring uncle of a niece, devoted to his friends, contemptuous of the mediocre, obstinate in his preferences, fiercely jealous of his privacy, unyielding to the death in his literary principles and not in the slightest concerned with what was fashionable. No wonder she loved him. She had been rebuffed a little at first, not by his astronomical standards in art—none could be too high for her—but by a certain coldness of heart in him. She soon got over that; it became for her only another facet of his nobility of mind.

Very early she had learned to reverence that indispensable faculty of aspiration of the human mind toward perfection called, in morals and the arts, nobility. She was born to the idea and brought up in it: first in a little crowded farmhouse in Virginia, and later, the eldest of seven children, in a little crowded ranch house in Nebraska. She had, as many American country people did have in those times and places, literate parents and grand-parents, soundly educated and deeply read, educated, if not always at schools, always at their own firesides. Two such, her grand-mothers, taught her from her infancy. Her sister, Mrs. Auld, in Palo Alto, California, told it like this:

"She mothered us all, took care of us, and there was a lot to do in such a big family. She learned Greek and Latin from our grandmothers before she ever got to go to school. She used to go, after we lived in Red Cloud, to read Latin and Greek with a little old man who kept a general store down the road. In the evenings for entertainment—there was nowhere to go, you know, almost nothing to see or hear—she entertained us, it was good as a theater for us! She told us long stories, some she made up herself, and some were her versions of legends and fairy tales she had read; she taught us Greek mythology this way, Homer; and tales from the Old Testament. We were all story tellers," said her sister, "all of us wanted to be the one to tell the stories, but she was the one who told them. And we loved to listen all of us to her, when maybe we would not have listened to each other."

She was not the first nor the last American writer to be formed in this system of home education; at one time it was the customary education for daughters, many of them never got to school at all or expected to; but they were capable of educating their grandchildren, as this little history shows. To her last day Willa Cather was the true child of her plain-living, provincial farming people, with their aristocratic ways of feeling and thinking; poor, but not poverty-stricken for a moment; rock-based in character, a character shaped in an old school of good manners, good morals, and the unchallenged assumption that classic culture was their birthright; the belief that knowledge of great art and great thought was a good in itself not to be missed for anything; she subscribed to it all with her whole heart, and in herself there was the vein of iron she had inherited from a long line of people who had helped to break wildernesses and to found a new nation in such faiths. When you think of the whole unbelievable history, how did anything like this survive? Yet it did, and this life is one of the proofs.

I have not much interest in anyone's personal history after the tenth year, not even my own. Whatever one was going to be was all prepared for before that. The rest is merely confirmation, extension, development. Childhood is the fiery furnace in which we are melted down to essentials and that essential shaped for good. While I have been reading again Willa Cather's essays and occasional papers, and thinking about her, I remembered a sentence from the diaries of Anne Frank, who died in the concentration camp in Bergen-Belsen just before she was sixteen years old. At less than fifteen, she wrote: "I have had a lot of sorrow, but who hasn't, at my age?"

In Miss Cather's superb little essay on Katherine Mansfield, she speaks of childhood and family life: "I doubt whether any contemporary writer has made one feel more keenly the many kinds of personal relations which exist in an everyday 'happy family' who are merely going on with their daily lives, with no crises or shocks or bewildering complications. . . . Yet every individual in that household (even the children) is clinging passionately to his individual soul, is in terror of losing it in the general family flavor . . . the mere struggle to have anything of one's own, to be oneself at all, creates an element of strain which keeps everybody almost at breaking point.

". . . Even in harmonious families there is this double life . . . the one we can observe in our neighbor's household, and, underneath, another—secret and passionate and intense—which is the real life that stamps the faces and gives character to the voices of our friends. Always in his mind each member is escaping, running away, trying to break the net which circumstances and his own affections have woven about him. One realizes that human relationships are the tragic necessity of human life; that they can never be wholly satisfactory, that every ego is half the time greedily seeking them, and half the time pulling away from them."

This is masterly and water-clear and autobiography enough for me: my mind goes with tenderness to the big lonely slow-moving girl who happened to be an artist coming back from reading Latin and Greek with the old storekeeper, helping with the housework, then sitting by the fireplace to talk down an assertive brood of brothers and sisters, practicing her art on them, refusing to be lost among them—the longest-winged one who would fly free at last.

I am not much given to reading about authors, or not until I have read what they have to say for themselves. I found Willa Cather's books for myself, early, and felt no need for intermediaries between me and them. My reading went on for a good many years, one by one as they appeared: *O Pioneers!*; *The Song of the Lark*; *My Antonia*; *Youth and the Bright Medusa*; *Death Comes for the Archbishop*; *Obscure Destinies*; just these, and no others, I do not know why, and never anything since, until I read her notebooks about two years ago. Those early readings began in Texas, just before World War I, before ever I left home; they ended in Paris, twenty years later, after the longest kind of journey.

With her first book I was reading also Henry James, W. B. Yeats, Joseph Conrad, my introduction to "modern" literature, for I was brought up on solid reading, too, well aged. About the same time I read Gertrude Stein's *Tender Buttons*, for sale at a little bookshop with a shoeshine stand outside; inside you could find magazines, books, newspapers in half-a-dozen languages, *avant-garde* and radical and experimental; this in a Texas coast town of less than ten thousand population but very polyglot and full of world travelers. I could make little headway with Miss Stein beyond the title. It was plain that she meant "tender buds" and I wondered why she did not say so. It was the beginning of my quarrel with a certain school of "modern" writing in which poverty of feeling and idea were disguised, but not well enough, in tricky techniques and disordered syntax. A year or two after *Tender Buttons* I was reading Joyce's *Dubliners*, and maybe only a young beginning writer of that time, with some preparation of mind by the great literature of the past, could know what a revelation that small collection of matchless stories could be. It was not a shock, but a revelation, a further unfolding of the deep world of the imagination. I had never heard of Joyce. By the pure chance of my roving curiosity, I picked up a copy of the book at that little shoeshine bookstore. It was a great day.

By the time I reached Paris, I had done my long apprenticeship, published a small book of my own, and had gone like a house afire through everything "new"—that word meant something peculiar to the times—absolutely everything "new" that was being published; also in music; also painting. I considered almost any painting with the varnish still wet, the artist standing by, so to speak, as more interesting than anything done even the year before. But some of the painters were Klee, Juan Gris, Modigliani. . . . I couldn't listen to music happily if it wasn't hot from the composer's brain, preferably conducted or played by himself. Still, some of the music was Stravinsky's. I was converted to the harpsichord by the first New York recital of Wanda Landowska. In the theater I preferred dress rehearsals, or even just rehearsals, to the finished performance; I was mad about the ballet and took lessons off and on with a Russian for two years; I even wrote a ballet libretto way back in 1920 for a young Mexican painter and scene designer who gave the whole thing to Pavlova, who danced it in many countries but not in New York, because the scenery was done on paper, was inflammable and she was not allowed to use it in New York. I saw photographs, however, and I must say they did not look in the least like anything I had provided for in the libretto. It was most unsatisfactory.

What has this to do with Willa Cather? A great deal. I had had time to grow up, to consider, to look again, to begin finding my way a little through the inordinate clutter and noise of my immediate day, in which very literally everything in the world was being pulled apart, torn up, turned wrong side out and upside down; almost no frontiers left unattacked, governments and currencies falling; even the very sexes seemed to be changing back and forth and multiplying weird, unclassifiable genders. And every day, in the arts, as in schemes of government and organized crime, there was, there had to be, something New.

Alas, or thank God, depending on the way you feel about it, there comes that day when today's New begins to look a little like yesterday's New, and then more and more so; you begin to suffer slightly from a sense of sameness or repetition: that painting, that statue, that music, that kind of writing, that way of thinking and feeling, that revolution, that political doctrine —is it really New? The answer is simply no, and if you are really in a perverse belligerent mood, you may add a half-truth —no, and it never was. Looking around at the debris, you ask has newness merely for its own sake any virtue? And you find that all along you had held and wound in your hand through the maze an unbreakable cord on which one by one, hardly knowing it, you had strung your life's treasures; it was as if they had come of themselves, while you were seeking and choosing and picking up and tossing away again, down all sorts of bypaths and up strange stairs and into queer corners; and there they were, things old and new, the things you loved first and those you loved last, all together and yours, and no longer old or new, but outside of time and beyond the reach of change, even your own; for that part of your life they belong to was in some sense made by them; if they went, all that part of your life would be mutilated, unrecognizable. While you hold and wind that cord with its slowly accumulating, weightless, unaccountable riches, the maze seems a straight road; you look back through all the fury you have come through, when it seemed so much, and so dismayingly, destruction, and so much just the pervasively trivial, stupid, or malignant-dwarfish tricks: fur-lined cups as sculpture, symphonies written for kitchen batteries, experiments on language very similar to the later Nazi surgical experiments of cutting and uniting human nerve ends never meant to touch each other: so many perversities crowding in so close you could hardly see beyond them. Yet look, you shared it, you were part of it, you even added to the confusion, so busy being new yourself. The fury and waste and clamor was, after all, just what you had thought it was in the first place, even if you had lost sight of it later—life, in a word, and great glory came of it, and splendid things that will go on living cleared of all the rubbish thrown up around their creation. Things you would have once thought incompatible to eternity take their right places in peace, in proper scale and order, in your mind—in your blood. They become that marrow in your bones where the blood is renewed.

I had liked best of all Willa Cather's two collections of short stories. They live still with morning freshness in my memory, their clearness, warmth of feeling, calmness of intelligence, an ample human view of things; in short the sense of an artist at work in whom one could have complete confidence: not even the prose attracted my attention from what the writer was saying—really saying, and not just in the words. Also I remember well my deeper impression of reserve—a reserve that was personal because it was a matter of temperament, the grain of the mind; yet conscious too, and practiced deliberately: almost a method, a technique, but not assumed. It was instead a manifesting, proceeding from the moral nature of the artist, morality extended to aesthetics—not aesthetics as morality but simply a development of both faculties along with all the others until the whole being was indivisibly one, the imagination and its expression fused and fixed.

A magnificent state, no doubt, at which to arrive; but it should be the final one, and Miss Cather seemed to be there almost from the first. What was it? For I began to have an image of her as a kind of lighthouse, or even a promontory, some changeless phenomenon of art or nature or both. I have a peculiar antipathy to thinking of anyone I know in symbols or mythical characters and this finally quietly alienated me from her, from her very fine books, from any feeling that she was a living, working artist in our time. It is hard to explain, for it was a question of tone, of implication, and what else? Finally, after a great while, I decided that Miss Cather's reserve amounted to a deliberate withholding of some vital part of herself as artist; not as if she had hidden herself at the center of her mystery but was still there to be disclosed at last; no, she had absented herself willfully.

I was quite wrong of course. She is exactly at the center of her own mystery, where she belongs. My immoderate reading of our two or three invaluably afflicted giants of contemporary literature, and their abject army of camp followers and imitators, had blurred temporarily my perception of that thin line separating self-reveal-ment from self-exhibition. Miss Cather had never any intention of using fiction or any other form of writing as a device for showing herself off. She was not Paul in travesty, nor the opera singer in "The Diamond Mine," nor that girl with the clear eyes who became an actress: above all, not the Lost Lady. Of course she was all of them. How not? She made all of them out of herself, where else could they have taken on life?

Her natural lack of picturesqueness was also a good protective coloring: it saved her from the invasive prying of hangers-on: and no "school" formed in her name. The young writers did not swarm over her with flattery, manuscripts in hand, meaning to use her for all she was worth; publishers did not waylay her with seductions the instant her first little book appeared; all S. S. Mc-Clure could think of to do for her, after he published *The Troll Garden*, was to offer her a job as one of his editors on *McClure's Magazine*, where she worked hard for six mortal years before it seems to have occurred to her that she was not being a writer, after all, which was what she had started out for. So she quit her job, and the next year, more or less, published *Alexander's Bridge*, of which she afterward repented, for reasons that were to last her a lifetime. The scene, London, was strange and delightful to her; she was trying to make a novel out of some interesting people in what seemed to her exotic situations, instead of out of something she really knew about with more than the top of her mind. "London is supposed to be more engaging than, let us say, Gopher Prairie," she remarks, "even if the writer knows Gopher Prairie very well and London very casually."

She realized at once that *Alexander's Bridge* was a mistake, her wrong turning, which could not be retraced too instantly and entirely. It was a very pretty success, and could have been her finish, except that she happened to be Willa Cather. For years she still found people who liked that book, but they couldn't fool her. She knew what she had done. So she left New York and went to Arizona for six months, not for repentance but for refreshment, and found there a source that was to refresh her for years to come. Let her tell of her private apocalypse in her own words: "I did no writing down there, but I recovered from the conventional editorial point of view."

She then began to write a book for herself—*O Pioneers!*—and it was "a different process altogether. Here there was no arranging or 'inventing'; everything was spontaneous and took its own place, right or wrong. This was like taking a ride through a familiar country on a horse that knew the way, on a fine morning when you felt like riding. The other was like riding in a park, with someone not altogether congenial, to whom you had to be talking all the time."

What are we to think? For certainly here is a genius who simply will not cater to our tastes for drama, who refuses to play the role in any way we have been accustomed to seeing it played. She wrote with immense sympathy about Stephen Crane: "There is every evidence that he was a reticent and unhelpful man, with no warmhearted love of giving out opinions." If she had said "personal confidences" she could as well have been writing about herself. But she was really writing about Stephen Crane and stuck to her subject. Herself, she gave out quite a lot of opinions, not all of them warmhearted, in the course of two short little books, the second a partial reprint of the first. You hardly realize how many and how firm and how cogent while reading her fine pure direct prose, hearing through it a level, well-tempered voice saying very good, sensible right things with complete authority—things not in fashion but close to here and now and always, not like a teacher or a mother—like an artist—until, after you have closed the book, her point of view begins to accumulate and take shape in your mind.

Freud had happened: but Miss Cather continued to cite the old Hebrew prophets, the Greek dramatists, Goethe, Shakespeare, Dante, Tolstoy, Flaubert, and such for the deeper truths of human nature, both good and evil. She loved Shelley, Wordsworth, Walter Pater, without any reference to their public standing at the time. In her essay, "The Novel Demeublé," she had the inspired notion to bring together for purposes of comparison Balzac and Prosper Merimée; she preferred Merimée on the ground quite simply that he was the better artist: you have to sort out Balzac's meanings from a great dusty warehouse of irrelevant vain matter—furniture, in a word. Once got at, they are as vital as ever. But Merimée is as vital, and you cannot cut one sentence without loss from his stories. The perfect answer to the gross power of the one, the too-finished delicacy of the other was, of course, Flaubert.

Stravinsky had happened; but she went on being dead in love with Wagner, Beethoven, Schubert, Gluck, especially *Orpheus*, and almost any opera. She was music-mad, and even Ravel's *La Valse* enchanted her; perhaps also even certain later music, but she has not mentioned it in these papers.

The Nude had Descended the Staircase with an epoch-shaking tread but she remained faithful to Puvis de Chavannes, whose wall paintings in the Panthéon of the legend of St. Genevieve inspired the form and tone of *Death Comes for the Archbishop*. She longed to tell old stories as simply as that, as deeply centered in the core of experience without extraneous detail as in the lives of the saints in *The Golden Legend*. She loved Courbet, Rembrandt, Millet and the sixteenth-century Dutch and Flemish painters, with their "warmly furnished interiors" but always with a square window open to the wide gray sea, where the masts of the great Dutch fleets were setting out to "ply quietly on all the waters of the globe. . . ."

Joyce had happened: or perhaps we should say, *Ulysses*, for the work has now fairly absorbed the man we knew. I believe that this is true of all artists of the first order. They are not magnified in their work, they disappear in it, consumed by it. That subterranean upheaval of language caused not even the barest tremor in Miss Cather's firm, lucid sentences. There is good internal evidence that she read a great deal of contemporary literature, contemporary over a stretch of fifty years, and think what contemporaries they were—from Tolstoy and Hardy and James and Chekhov to Gide and Proust and Joyce and Lawrence and Virginia Woolf, to Sherwood Anderson and Theodore Dreiser: the first names that come to mind. There was a regiment of them; it was as rich and fruitfully disturbing a period as literature has to show for several centuries. And it did make an enormous change. Miss Cather held firmly to what she had found for herself, did her own work in her own way as all the others were doing each in his unique way, and did help greatly to save and reassert and illustrate the validity of certain great and dangerously threatened principles of art. Without too much fuss, too—and is quietly disappearing into her work altogether, as we might expect.

Mr. Maxwell Geismar wrote a book about her and some others, called *The Last of the Provincials*. Not having read it I do not know his argument; but he has a case: she is a provincial; and I hope not the last. She was a good artist, and all true art is provincial in the most realistic sense: of the very time and place of its making, out of human beings who are so particularly limited by their situation, whose faces and names are real and whose lives begin each one at an individual unique center. Indeed, Willa Cather was as provincial as Hawthorne or Flaubert or Turgenev, as little concerned with aesthetics and as much with morals as Tolstoy, as obstinately reserved as Melville. In fact she always reminds me of very good literary company, of the particularly admirable masters who formed her youthful tastes, her thinking and feeling.

She is a curiously immovable shape, monumental, virtue itself in her art and a symbol of virtue—like certain churches, in fact, or exemplary women, revered and neglected. Yet like these again, she has her faithful friends and true believers, even so to speak her lovers, and they last a lifetime, and after: the only kind of bond she would recognize or require or respect.

1952

"It Is Hard to Stand in the Middle"

—E. P.: Canto XIII (Kung)

❋

In Mexico, many years ago, Hart Crane and I were reading again *Pavannes and Divisions*, and at some dogmatic statement in the text Crane suddenly burst out: "I'm tired of Ezra Pound!" And I asked him: "Well, who else is there?" He thought a few seconds and said: "It's true there's nobody like him, nobody to take his place." This was the truth for us then, and it is still the truth for many of us who came up, were educated, you might say, in contemporary literature, not at schools at all but by five writers: Henry James, James Joyce, W. B. Yeats, T. S. Eliot, and Ezra Pound. The beginning artist is educated by whoever helps him to learn how to work his own vein, who helps him to fix his standards, and who gives him courage. I believe I can speak for a whole generation of writers who acknowledge that these five men were in just this way, the great educators of their time.

The temptation in writing about *The Letters of Ezra Pound: 1907-1941* is to get down to individual letters, to quote endlessly, to lapse into gossip, to go into long dissertations on the state of society; the strange confusions of the human mind; music, sculpture, painting, war, economics; the menace of the American university; the weakness of having a private life; and finally the hell on earth it is to be at once a poet and a man of perfect judgment in all matters relating to art in a world of the deaf, dumb, and blind, of nitwits, numbskulls, and outright villains. One might go on for hours and pages citing instances, comparing letters, tracing change and development from year

74

to year, noting enthusiasms turning into abhorrence, admirations into contempt, splendid altruistic plans to foster the arts falling into ruin because almost nobody would help, and following the frantic pattern of the poet's relations with his assortment of friends, for such I suppose they must be called. Friendship with Pound seems to have been a very uncertain status.

It would all be false, and misleading from the main road. These letters are the most revealing documents I have read since those of Boswell or Jane Carlyle, but how differently revealing. For where nearly all letters we know are attempts to express personal feeling, to give private news, to entertain; or set-pieces on a subject, but still meant for one reader; these letters as published contain hardly one paragraph which does not relate in one way or another to one sole theme—the arts. Almost nothing about the weather, or how the writer is feeling that day; and a magnificent disregard for how the reader is feeling, except now and then: to William Carlos Williams, 1909, "I hope to God you have no feelings. If you have, burn this *before* reading." He then launches into a scarifying analysis of his dear friend's latest poetry.

There are very few landscapes; very little about health. The poet is married, a marriage that now has lasted nearly thirty-five years, so there must have been some sort of family life, but the reader would hardly guess it. Now and then he remarks on the difficulty of paying rent, but you understand at once that the difficulties of paying rent and being an artist are closely connected. He mentions once or twice that he is aging a trifle, or feels tired, but he is tired of fighting people who fight art, or he feels too old to take on a certain job of work. Once he mentions kittens in a letter to William Carlos Williams, but I feel sure he meant something else; it must have been a code.* To his father he

---

* W. B. Yeats told how Ezra Pound carried food scraps in his pockets for the hungry street cats who had so many enemies. Yeats doubted he really liked cats, though. "He never nurses the café cat," he observed. Of course not. The café cat was safe and comfortable.

writes literary gossip, and remarks that he is playing tennis that afternoon. To his mother he mentions the marriage of Hilda Doolittle and Richard Aldington, and later writes to her, "I am profoundly pained to hear that you prefer Marie Corelli to Stendhal, but I cannot help it." He remembers Yeats's father on an elephant at Coney Island; but that was Jack Yeats, after all, a painter—otherwise one knows he might have sat on an elephant all day without a glance from Pound.

No, this was not the point. Ezra Pound detested the "private life," denied that he ever had one, and despised those who were weak enough to need one. He was a warrior who lived on the battlefield, a place of contention and confusion, where a man shows all sides of himself without taking much thought for appearances. His own individual being is all the time tucked safely away within him, guiding his thoughts and feelings, as well as, at a long remove, his acts and words.

How right he was in so many things. The ferocious urge of his energy, his belief in himself with all his fears, his longing to be part of the world and his time, his curious lack of judgment of things outside his real interest now appear in these letters, and it is the truest document I have seen of that falling world between 1850 and 1950. We have been falling for a century or more, and Ezra Pound came along just at the right time to see what was happening.

He was a man concerned with public questions: specifically at first the question of the arts, the place of the artist in society, and he had a fanatical desire to force entire populations to respect art even if they could not understand it. (Indeed, he demanded reverence without understanding, for he sincerely did not believe that art was for the multitude. Whatever was too much praised he distrusted—even to the works of Sophocles. This is the inconsistency of his attitude all the way through: the attempt to force poetry upon people whom he believed not fitted to understand it.)

He believed himself to be the most patient soul alive, but he was not patient, he was tenacious, quite another thing. He was blowing up in wrath regularly from the very start, but he did not give up. He did not give up because he was incapable of abandoning a faith so furious it had the quality of religious fanaticism.

Witness his running fight, beginning in 1912, with Harriet Monroe, who controlled *Poetry; Poetry* was Pound's one hope in this country for a good number of years, so, some of the time, and at great cost to his nervous system, he controlled Miss Monroe. His exasperation with that innocent, unteachable, hard-trying woman came to the point where he was just the same as beating her over the head with a baseball bat. I should like to see the other side of this correspondence: her patience, or whatever it was, and her ability to absorb punishment, were equal to her inability to learn.

When Miss Monroe got really frightened at some of the things he sent her, he wrote: "Don't print anything of mine you think will kill the review, but . . . the public can go to the devil. It is the public's function to prevent the artist's expression by hook or by crook. . . . Given my head I'd stop any periodical in a week, only we are bound to run five years anyhow, we're in such a beautiful position to save the public's soul by punching its face that it seems a crime not to do so."

So it went for twenty-four long years, one of the most sustained literary wars on record, and yet it is hard to see what they would have done without each other. Harriet Monroe was his one instrument in this country, and continually she broke in his hands. She had some very genteel notions about language, and a schoolgirl taste for pretty verses that rhymed nicely and expressed delicate feelings, preferably about nature. ("No, most emphatically I will not ask Eliot to write down to any audience whatever," Pound wrote her in 1914. "I daresay my instinct was sound enough when I volunteered to quit the magazine a year ago. Neither will I send you Eliot's address in order that he may be insulted.") Bloody, Harriet's head undoubtedly was, but she would not let him go, and he would have been outraged if she had.

When after long years and in her old age, she tried at last to give up *Poetry*, to escape into private life with her family, he wrote: "The intelligence of the nation more important than the comfort or life of any one individual or the bodily life of a whole generation." That is truly the public spirit, the Roman senator speaking. Why did he take the trouble? For he adds, in contempt: "It is difficult enough to give the god damn amoeba a nervous system." Still, she had done her bit and could go, but she had no right to allow *Poetry* to die "merely because you have a sister in Cheefoo. . . ."

Pound was one of the most opinionated and unselfish men who ever lived, and he made friends and enemies everywhere by the simple exercise of the classic American constitutional right of free speech. His speech was free to outrageous license. He was completely reckless about making enemies. His so-called anti-Semitism was, hardly anyone has noted, only equaled by his anti-Christianism. It is true he hated most in the Catholic faith the elements of Judaism. It comes down squarely to anti-monotheism, which I have always believed was the real root of the difficulty between Judaism and the West. Pound felt himself to be in the direct line of Mediterranean civilization, rooted in Greece. Monotheism is simply not natural to the thought of such people and there are more of them than one might think without having looked into the question a little. Pound believed, rightly or wrongly, that Christianity was a debased cult composed of too many irreconcilable elements, and as the central power of this cult, he hated Catholicism worse than he did Judaism, and for many more reasons.

He was not a historian, and apparently did not know that religion flows from a single source, and that all are by now mingled and interrelated. Yet he did quote some things from ancient Chinese thought that are purely Christian in the sense that Christianity teaches the same ethics and morality, and so do the Jews, no matter from what earlier religion either of them derived it. So he was reckless and bitter and badly informed, but said what he thought, and in religious matters, in this period perhaps the most irreligious the world has ever known, it is still dangerous enough to be frank on that subject. "Anti-Semite" is a stupid, reprehensible word in that it does not mean what it says, for not only Semitic peoples have taught the doctrine of the One God, and it is used now largely for purposes of moral blackmail by irresponsible people.

Pound's lapses, his mistakes—and this would include his politics—occur when he deals with things outside his real interest, which was always art, literature, poetry. He was a lover of the sublime, and a seeker after perfection, a true poet, of the kind born in a hair shirt—a God-sent disturber of the peace in the arts, the one department of human life where peace is fatal. There was no peace in that urgent, overstimulated mind, where everything was jumbled together at once, a storehouse of treasure too rich ever to be sorted out by one man in one lifetime. And it was treasure.

It held exasperation, too; and related to the exasperation, but going deeper, are the cursing, and the backwoods spelling, and the deliberate illiteracy—at first humorous, high animal spirits, youthfully charming. They become obsessional, exaggerated, the tone of near-panic, the voice of Pound's deep fears. His fears were well founded; he was hard beset in a world of real and powerful enemies. I heard a stowaway on a boat once, cursing and shouting threats in that same monotonous, strained, desperate voice; in the end his captors only put him in the brig for the voyage. The artist Pound knew had become a kind of stowaway in society.

With the same kind of energy and obsessional faith Pound collided with the Douglas theory of social credit. He himself appears to have a basic principle of thought about economics:

"Debt is slavery." Ernestine Evans said she heard it on a gramophone record that got stuck, and Pound's voice repeated steadily at least fifty times: "Debt is slavery." She said the more often she heard it the more sense it made. This technique of repetition, in this case accidental, is known to the spreaders of lies. Maybe, though, it would be useful to repeat now and again a simple basic fact like that. "Debt is slavery." But for Pound even the Douglas plan was immediately drawn into the service of the arts.

Often in these letters there is in Pound a kind of socks-down, shirttail-out gracelessness which many will take delightedly for his true Americanism. In these moments he was a lout, and that is international. But he wore his loutishness with a difference. It is in his judgments, and his earlier judgments were much better than his later: though his pronouncements even on those he most admires run up and down like a panicky stock market. It is always praise or dispraise precisely according to what they have done in that present moment, and he is indignant when they do not always sit down quietly under it. He thundered not with just the voice of Jove, he was Jove. His judgments were indeed fallible, but his faith in them was not. "It isn't as if I were set in a groove. I read any number of masters, and recognize any number of kinds of excellence. But I'm sick to loathing of people who don't care for the master-work, who set out as artists with no intention of producing it, who make no effort toward the best, who are content with publicity and the praise of reviewers." His perfect assurance that he knew a work of art when he saw one, and his bent toward all kinds of excellence, led him into some lamentable errors which time little by little may correct.

As critic he was at his very best in the teacher-pupil relationship, when he had a manuscript under his eye to pull apart and put together again, or in simply stating the deep changeless principles of the highest art, relating them to each other and to their time and society. As one of the great poets of his time, his advice was unfathomably good and right in these things, and they are not outdated, and they cannot be unless the standard is simply thrown out.

Pound understood the nature of greatness: not that it voluntarily separates itself from the mass but that by its very being it is separate because it is higher. Greatness in art is like any other greatness: in religious experience, in love, it is great because it is beyond the reach of the ordinary, and cannot be judged by the ordinary, nor be accountable to it. The instant it is diluted, popularized, and misunderstood by the fashionable mind, it is no longer greatness, but window dressing, interior decorating, another way of cutting a sleeve. . . . Ezra Pound understood this simple law of natural being perfectly, and it is what redeems every fault and mitigates every failure and softens to the outraged ear of the mind and heart all that shouting and bullying and senseless obscenity—makes one respect all those wild hopeful choices of hopeless talents.

There is a doctrine that we should be patient in times of darkness and decline: but darkness and decline are the very things to fight, they are man-made, and can be unmade by man also. I am glad Pound was not patient in that sense, but obstinate and tenacious and obsessed and enraged. When you read these letters you will see what good sound reasons he had to be, if he was to make any headway against the obsessed tenacious inertia of his particular time. Most of the things and the kind of people he fought are still sitting about running things, fat and smug. That is true. And a great many of the talents he tried to foster came to nothing. Fighting the dark is a very unfashionable occupation now; but it is not altogether dead, and will survive and live again largely because of his life and example.

1950

The Art of Katherine Mansfield

This past fourteenth of October [1937] would have been Katherine Mansfield's forty-ninth birthday. This year is the fifteenth since her death. During her life she had a fabulous prestige among young writers in England and America. Her readers were not numerous but they were devoted. It must be a round dozen years since I have read any of her stories; reading them again in the collected edition, I am certain she deserved her fame, and I wonder why it was not greater.

Of late I find my interest diverted somewhat from her achievement as artist to the enigma of her personal history. Actually there is little in her work to justify this, since the work itself can stand alone without clues or notes as to its origins in her experience; a paper chase for autobiographical data in these stories may be interesting in itself, but it adds nothing to the value of the stories. They exist in their own right. Yet I find it impossible to make these few notes without a certain preoccupation with her personal life of constant flight and search with her perpetual longing for certainties and repose; her beginnings in New Zealand; going to London to find the kind of place and the kind of people she wanted; her life there first as musician and then as writer; the many influences upon her mind and emotions of her friends and enemies—who in effect seem to have been interchangeable; her prolonged struggle with illness; her insoluble religious dilemma; her mysterious loss of faith in her own gifts and faculties; the disastrous failure of her forces at thirty-three, and the slowly engulfing despair that brought her finally to die at Fontainebleau.

These things are of first importance in a study which is yet to

be done of the causes of Katherine Mansfield's own sense of failure in her work and in her life, but they do little to explain the
work itself, which is superb. This misplaced emphasis of my
attention I owe perhaps to her literary executor, who has edited
and published her letters and journals with a kind of merciless
insistence, a professional anxiety for her fame on what seems to
be the wrong grounds, and from which in any case his personal
relation to her might have excused him for a time. Katherine
Mansfield's work is the important fact about her, and she is in
danger of the worst fate that an artist can suffer—to be overwhelmed by her own legend, to have her work neglected for an
interest in her "personality."

There are eighty-eight stories in the collected edition, fifteen of
which, her last, were left unfinished. The matter for regret is in
these fifteen stories. Some of her best work is in them. She had
been developing steadily, along a straight and fairly narrow path,
working faithfully toward depth and concentration. Her handling
of her material was firmer, her style had reached the flexibility
of high tension and control, she had all her prime virtues and was
shedding her faults, but her work had improved strictly in kind
and not in difference. It is the same quick, ironic, perceptive
mind, the same (very sensual) emotional nature, at work here
from beginning to end.

In her the homely humility of the good craftsman toward his
medium deepened slowly into a fatal self-distrust, and she set up
for herself a standard of impossible perfection. It seems to have
been on the grounds of the morality of art and not aesthetics that
she began to desire a change in her own nature, who would have
had quite literally to be born again to change. But the point is,
she believed (or was persuaded that she believed) she could
achieve a spiritual and mental rebirth by the practice of certain
disciplines and the study of esoteric doctrines. She was innately
religious, but she had no point of reference, theologically speaking; she was unable to accept her traditional religion, and she did
finally, by what appears to have been an act of the will against

all her grain, adopt means to make her fatal experiment in purification. As her health failed, her fears grew, her religious impulse wasted itself in an anxious straining toward some unknown infinite source of strength, of energy-renewing power, from which she might at the cost of single-hearted invocation find some fulfillment of true being beyond her flawed mortal nature. Now for her help and counsel in this weighty matter she had all about her, at different periods, the advice and influence of John Middleton Murry, A. R. Orage, D. H. Lawrence, and, through Orage, Gurdjieff.

Katherine Mansfield has been called a mystic, and perhaps she was, but in the severe hierarchy of mysticism her rank cannot be very high. André Maurois only yesterday wrote of her "pure feminine mysticism." Such as it was, her mysticism was not particularly feminine, nor any purer than the mysticism of D. H. Lawrence; and that was very impure matter indeed. The secret of her powers did not lie in this domain of her mind, and that is the puzzle: that such a good artist could so have misjudged herself, her own capacities and directions. In that rather loosely defined and changing "group" of variously gifted persons with whom Katherine Mansfield was associated through nearly all her working years, Lawrence was the prophet, and the idol of John Middleton Murry. They all were nervously irritable, self-conscious, and groping, each bent on painting his own portrait (The Young Man as Genius), and Katherine Mansfield's nerves suffered too from the teaching and the preaching and the quarreling and the strange vocabulary of perverted ecstasy that threw a pall over any true joy of living.

She possessed, for it is in her work, a real gaiety and a natural sense of comedy; there were many sides to her that made her able to perceive and convey in her stories a sense of human beings living on many planes at once, with all the elements justly ordered and in right proportion. This is a great gift, and she was the only one among them who had it, or at least the only one able to express it. Lawrence, whose disciple she was not, was unjust to her as he was to no one else, and that is saying a good deal. He did his part to undermine her, and to his shame, for personal rather than other reasons. His long maudlin relationship with John Middleton Murry was the source of his malignance toward her.

Mr. Murry's words in praise of her are too characteristic of the time and the special point of view to be ignored. Even today he can write that "her art was of a peculiarly instinctive kind." I confess I cannot understand the use of this word. That she was born with the potentialities of an artist, perhaps? I judge her work to have been to a great degree a matter of intelligent use of her faculties, a conscious practice of a hard-won craftsmanship, a triumph of discipline over the unruly circumstances and confusions of her personal life and over certain destructive elements in her own nature. She was deliberate in her choice of material and in her methods of using it, her technical resources grew continually, she cleared away all easy effects and tricky turns of phrase; and such mastership is not gained by letting the instincts have it all their own way.

Again Mr. Murry, in his preface to the stories: "She accepted life . . . she gave herself . . . to life, to love . . . she loved life, with all its beauty and pain . . . she responded to life more completely than any writer I have known except D. H. Lawrence. . . ."

Life, love, beauty, pain, acceptance, response, these are great words and they should mean something, and their meaning depends upon their exact application and reference. Whose life? What kind of love? What sort of beauty? Pain from what cause? And so on. It was this kind of explicitness that Katherine Mansfield possessed and was able to use, when she was at her best and strongest. She was magnificent in her objective view of things, her real sensitiveness to climate, mental or physical, her genuinely first-rate equipment in the matter of the five senses, and my guess, based on the evidence of her stories, is that she by no means accepted everything, either abstractly or in detail, and that whatever her vague love of something called Life may have been, there was as much to hate as to love in her individual living. Mistakenly she fought in herself those very elements that combined to form her main virtue: a certain grim, quiet ruthlessness of judgment, an unsparing and sometimes cruel eye, a natural malicious wit, an intelligent humor; and beyond all she had a burning, indignant heart that was capable of great compassion. Read "The Woman at the Store," or "A Birthday," and "The Child-Who-Was-Tired," one of the most terrible of stories; read "The Fly," and then read "Millie," or "The Life of Ma Parker." With fine objectivity she bares a moment of experience, real experience, in the life of some one human being; she states no belief, gives no motives, airs no theories, but simply presents to the reader a situation, a place, and a character, and there it is; and the emotional content is present as implicitly as the germ is in the grain of wheat.

Katherine Mansfield has a reputation for an almost finicking delicacy. She was delicate as a surgeon's scalpel is delicate. Her choice of words was sure, a matter of good judgment and a good ear. Delicate? Read, in "A Married Man's Story," the passage describing the prostitute who has been beaten, coming into the shop of the evil little chemist for his famous "pick-me-up." Or such a scene as the fat man spitting over the balcony in "Violet"; or the seduction of Miss Moss in "Pictures." "An Indiscreet Journey" is a story of a young pair of lovers, set with the delicacy of sober knowledge against the desolate and brutalized scene of, not war, but a small village where there has been fighting, and the soldiers in the place are young Frenchmen, and the inn is "really a barn, set out with dilapidated tables and chairs." There are a few stories which she fails to bring off, quite, and these because she falls dangerously near to triviality or a sentimental wistfulness, of which she had more than a streak in certain moments and which she feared and fought in herself. But these are few, and far outweighed by her best stories, which are many. Her celebrated "Prelude" and "At the Bay," "The Doll's House," "The Daughters of the Late Colonel" keep their freshness and curious timelessness. Here is not her view of life but her many views of many kinds of lives, and there is no sign of even a tacit acquiescence in these sufferings, these conflicts, these evils deep-rooted in human nature. Mr. Murry writes of her adjusting herself to life as a flower, etc.; there is an elegiac poesy in this thought, but—and remember I am judging by her pages here under my eye—I see no sign that she ever adjusted herself to anything or anybody, except at an angle where she could get exactly the slant and the light she needed for the spectacle.

She had, then, all her clues; she had won her knowledge honestly, and she turned away from what she knew to pursue some untenable theory of personal salvation under a most dubious teacher. "I fail in my personal life," she wrote in her journal, and this sense of failure infected her life as artist, which is also personal. Her decision to go to Fontainebleau was no whim, no accident. She had long been under the influence of Orage, her first publisher and her devoted friend, and he was the chief disciple of Gurdjieff in England. In her last finished story, "The Canary," a deep parable of her confusion and despair, occurs the hopeless phrase: "Perhaps it does not so much matter what one loves in this world. But love something one must." It seems to me that St. Augustine knew the real truth of the matter: "It doth make a difference whence cometh a man's joy."

"The Canary" was finished in July 1922. "In the October following she deliberately abandoned writing for a time and went into retirement at Fontainebleau, where she died suddenly and unexpectedly on the night of January 9, 1923." And so joined that ghostly company of unfulfilled, unhappy English artists who died and are buried in strange lands.

October, 1937

Orpheus in Purgatory

✳

On his fiftieth birthday, "What a bore, what futility!" Rilke wrote to a friend about all the flowers and messages and visitors. ". . . Naturally, if one looks at it justly, there was something dear in it, but where is the love that does not make more trouble?"

It is hardly possible to exaggerate the lovelessness in which most people live, men or women: wanting love, unable to give it, or inspire it, unable to keep it if they get it, not knowing how to treat it, lacking the humility, or the very love itself that could teach them how to love: it is the painfullest thing in human life, and, since love is purely a creation of the human imagination, it is merely perhaps the most important of all the examples of how the imagination continually outruns the creature it inhabits. . . . Having imagined love, we are condemned to its perpetual disappointment; or so it seems.

"You know Rilke . . . you know how he is and how much he means to me. . . . You have never asked how it will end. . . . I . . . have not asked that question either, and perhaps that was wrong of me. I have been happy with him in the present . . . because of his noble and lofty spirit . . . because of his inexhaustible kindness. Every time I saw him was a gift of God to me. And I thought that if some day he had to withdraw, and be quite alone with his work, then I should be alone again . . . far away from him, not hearing from him any more but guarding his holy image in my heart. I should almost forbid myself to think of him."

This is Magda von Hattingberg, Rilke's Benvenuta (The Welcome One), writing to her sister when her curious association, whatever its real nature, with Rainer Maria Rilke was drawing to its close in 1914. It had been brief: two months of letters, three of living together; and strange: for by this account, the obvious conditions of such a relationship seem never to have existed. They traveled openly together for those three months, to Paris, to Berlin, Munich, Venice, besides visits to houses and castles of his friends. Yet Benvenuta says plainly (and she does wrap some plain things in the sustained fanatic rapture of her style) that when they parted forever they kissed for the first and last time. This statement comes as rather an anti-climax after the heroic if fevered effort of an apparently healthy, all-too-feminine young woman to grow wings for her god, devoted as he was to angels.

One hardly knows where to place *Rilke and Benvenuta* in the clutter of letters, memoirs, critical studies, and biographies so steadily accumulating around Rilke's name. As much hysterical nonsense has been written about him as about D. H. Lawrence, if that is possible. Like Lawrence, his personal attractiveness drew to him the parasitic kind of adorers who insist on feeding on the artist himself instead of on his work: who make mystification of the mysterious, and scandals instead of legends. But Rilke was luckier than Lawrence in this: that he also had many faithful good friends who anxiously and constantly for long years succeeded in defending and helping him, almost in spite of himself. For he demanded, and would have, and would content himself with nothing less than, the humanly impossible in all human relationships. As relatives, friends, publishers now dole out mangled fragments of his literary estate, the secret of their long enchantment with him seems lost, for a temperament rather less than enchanting is being revealed little by little. His after-life of fame is very similar to his former life in his restless, painful flesh: the perpetual unsatisfied guest, the helpless dependent, the alienated genius seeking silence and solitude to work out his destiny—Paul Valéry was shocked at the inhumanity of an "existence so separated . . . in such an abuse of the intimacy with silence, so much license given to one's dreams . . . ," the continuing stranger who claimed the veneration due to the poet, that is to say, prophet, priest, seer, one set apart by his tremendous mission. In the meantime: "One lives so badly one always comes into the present unready, unfit, and distraught for everything . . . only the ten days after Ruth's (his daughter's) birth, I think, did I live without the smallest waste; finding reality as indescribable, even to the smallest detail, as it doubtless always is." This to his wife in 1907.

By 1914 he had not yet discovered the truths of reality, indeed, it was not his goal; but after seven years of search and flight, of homelessness and poverty, added to his double sense of failure as human being and as poet—for the two warring beings were never to be reconciled in him—he was ready, or hoped he was ready, for "a more human and natural footing in life," and Magda von Hattingberg seemed to be the one who could provide it for him. She wrote him first, as women so often did, an adoring letter; he hastened to answer it, and thirty-five long years later, she publishes some of his letters—very interesting letters, too—some of hers, passages from her diary, some very valuable transcriptions of conversations they had, and for the rest, a rhapsodical, highflung, far-fetched romance which for style is an extraordinary blend of Marianna Alcoforado and The Duchess. . . .

In the best German Romantic tradition of the 1840's, not only all nature, and all society, but heaven itself, are tender accomplices in this transcendent episode. Nature especially assists with manifestations symbolically appropriate: the rains, the snows, the fogs, the sunshine, flowers of spring, arrive punctually; the moon is always obligingly full to witness a high encounter. They travel through enchanted landscapes like spirits in a dream, they even sit up all night outdoors somewhere at a crisis, she sleeps on his shoulder and the dawn finds them there, weary, a little stiff in their bones, but with exaltation undiminished. It is absurd, no other word for it. For the heroine was a young, beautiful, professional concert pianist, and too often, especially in the castles and drawing rooms, it is as if she played out her dream-romance on a grand piano, her costume always perfect, the moment perfect, the high-born spectators always on hand and attentive, the cultural ambience of the purest edelweiss.

But the fact that she has made herself so easy a target does not mean that she can be dismissed so easily. E. M. Butler, in her *Rilke*, tells her story in a few lines, and does not mention her name but quotes a letter from Rilke about her, written shortly after he had broken with her, broken with a decision and finality which shows plainly how dangerous to his future he considered her. For he was incapable of the kind of love she gave, and humanly wished to have from him; he could not endure the burden of her adoring warmth and energy and naturalness. After admitting that for years he had tried to flatter himself that his failures in love and in friendship had been the fault of others, that each in turn had violated, injured, wronged him, he writes: "I have entirely altered my opinion now after these last months of suffering. This time I have been obliged to recognize the fact that no one can help me, no one at all. And even if he (she) should come with the best and most loving of hearts, and should prove his worth to the very stars, . . . keeping his regard for me pure and untroubled, however often I broke the ray of his spirit with the cloudiness and density of my submarine world I would yet (I know it now) find the means to strip him of the fulness of his ever-renewed assistance, and to enclose him in a loveless vacuum, so that his useless succor would rot and wither and die a terrible death."

It is pleasant to know that none of this happened to his tenderly nicknamed Benvenuta; she had to a triumphant degree the womanly knack of starving gracefully on the thinnest ration of love, and yet at last spreads her own feast—a strange feast, but her food —out of that famine.

Only once had he succeeded in almost frightening her off. He was admiring some fantastic doll figure, and she protested that the virtue of a toy was in its effect on a child, and she could not imagine an innocent, healthy little girl not being repelled by this monster. Rilke proceeded to rip to shreds her notions of childish innocence, and to explain to her at length the innate corruptness of toys—and quoted also at length from his fierce essay against dolls, published shortly afterwards. She had unknowingly touched him on the quick: his mother had dressed him as a girl, and had given him dolls to play with.

The faithful and patient Princess Marie of Thurn and Taxis witnessed not only this love affair at one point, but many others with many other women. She was disconcerted, she wrote in her journal, at the attraction women had for Rilke. Rilke was equally disconcerted many times at the attraction he had for them: it seemed to him that what a man did only for God, a woman did always for a man. For a while he could impersonate a man, imitate his functions passably—provided the woman was infatuated enough, and most often she was, for women, of all sorts, and for all sorts of reasons, are flattered by the attentions of genius—even he could deceive himself into a plausible enough feeling, or a belief that he felt, or was capable of feeling, a natural, spontaneous sexual desire. But nothing of this could last: in no time at all he was faced with the terrible alternative: to go on with a eunuch-like sniffing and fumbling, or flight—flight in almost any direction, to any goal, even into another trap of womanly tenderness and incomprehension.

He depended in all faith and with good reason too, on the tenderness and sympathy of women: all of them high-minded, romantic, some of them very gifted, many nobly born and wealthy: but alas, seekers after a man-god rather than the God in man. By the simplest means, and without any method except that provided by the natural duplicity of his need to be adored and taken care of, Rilke wove his web about them for good. This web was the Word—the Word multiplied, an endless spinning of high, poetic, noble words, flowing easily as a melody carrying with it painless didactic counsel, and if they had not been so flattered, they might have read as we do now the warning between the lines: This is what I have to give, ask for nothing more.

He flattered the soul, or the intellect, or the heart, or all three at once; whatever the individual woman craved that words could supply, he gave her generously. There were more than enough words to go round. Not one of them had any real right to complain, for he was faithful to them all, and he paid them the highest compliment of never confusing one of them with another. . . . And he asked of them all the same thing—that they would save him for himself and from them.

1950

"The Laughing Heat of the Sun"

❉

Of all fine sights in the world to me, the best is that of an artist growing great, adding to his art with his years, as his life and his art are inseparable. Henry James's and W. B. Yeats's careers occur to mind first as spectacles in which I took delight, and Edith Sitwell, with *The Canticle of the Rose,* the collected volume of her work of more than thirty years, joins them. The true sign of this growth, in all alike, is the unfailing renewal, the freshness of every latest piece of work, the gradual, steady advance from phase to phase of increased power and direction, depth of feeling, and virtuosity, that laurel leaf added to technical mastery. Decade by decade, the familiar voice adds other notes to its range, a fuller tone, more sustained breath: an organic growth of the whole being.

Miss Sitwell's early work belonged to youth—it had the challenging note of natural arrogance, it was boldly experimental, inventive from a sense of adventure, full of high spirits and curiosity as to how many liberties the language would suffer to be taken without hitting back. There was sometimes also a certain artifice, the dew upon the rose turned out to be a crystal bead on a mother-of-pearl petal. Yet it was the work of a deft artificer, and a most ornamental rose, meant to amuse and charm, never intended to be mistaken for a natural flower.

It was the shimmer, the glancing light of this wit, this gaiety, one found so refreshing, for they were qualities markedly absent from the serious poetry of that long grim generation of censorious poets who were her contemporaries or later. Hardly anyone knew how to laugh, and those who did hardly dared to; it was

94

no time for frivolity, and laughter was frivolous in such a murderous time. Miss Sitwell dared: she laughed outright whenever she felt like it, and the reader laughed too: for plainly this laughter was not levity nor frivolity, it was the spontaneous merriment of a vital spirit, full of natural courage and confidence. The idea of death, which has paralyzed the humanity of so many poets for more than a century, affected her very differently. In the old robust way, she set out to make hay while her sun still shone. One felt this quality in her then, one is reassured of it now: "My poems are hymns in praise of the glory of life," she writes without any shade of apology for such an antique point of view. This praise is as clear in the early "Trio for Two Cats and a Trombone," or "Hornpipe," as it is in "Still Falls the Rain," written during a night raid in 1940.

The glory of life—the force of the affirmative passion of love in this poet, the feeling for glory in her, are the ground-virtues of her art, twin qualities almost lost for the present in the arts as in all human existence; as in her youth it sharpened her wit and her comedy, in middle life her sensuous celebration of the noble five human senses, in age her spiritual perceptions. This is such a progression as makes life and art worth practicing.

Her early poetry was, for me, associated, for all its "modern" speed and strepitation, with the old courtly music of Lully, Rameau, Purcell, Monteverdi, that I loved and do love: festival music, meant to be played in theaters, at weddings, christenings, great crystal-lighted banquets; or in the open air, in sweet-smelling gardens and the light of the full moon, with the torches waving their banners under the trees—gay music, serious great music, one can trust one's joy in it.

So with Edith Sitwell's poetry in those days between two wars, and so it is still. I am tempted to pick out here and there a few lines from some of those early things, but they do not take well to it. They are in full flight, it would be like plucking feathers from a bird. Pretty feathers, but they do not sing. Every word, every syllable does its part toward the final effect—her country

songs are fresh as country mornings; her kitchen songs are a welter of sooty pots, hard cold early light and tangle-haired sleepy
girls fighting with early cook-fires that will not catch. The beg-
gar maid is "that pink flower spike full of honey." Rain is rain in
these poems, it rains on the page and you can smell it and feel it.
There are "horses as fat as plums"—of course, I have seen them.
When witches are on the prowl, one ". . . hears no sound but
wind in trees; /One candle spills out thick gold coins, /Where
quilted dark with tree shade joins." Who does not remember
". . . the navy-blue ghost of Mr. Belaker /The allegro Negro
Cocktail shaker?" asking, at four in the morning, his violent, unanswerable question, "Why did the cock crow? Why am I lost?"
"The gaiety of some" (of her poems) "masks darkness," writes
Miss Sitwell.

Large numbers of the public felt lost, too. It all sounded hor-
ridly novel and they hated it. Miss Sitwell did not have an easy
time of it. The story has been told by her brother Sir Osbert Sitwell in his memoirs, so we need not go into it here. After all these
years, Time having brought it about that Miss Sitwell is now being called "classic" by the younger generation, she being famous,
a Doctor of Letters, at last she has time to sit down and explain
what she was doing in those days and why, and what she meant
by it.

She chooses many poems, those which caused the most dis-
turbance when they were new; line by line, syllable by syllable,
sometimes letter by letter, patiently she threads out meanings
and makes a design of them. It makes good sense—that good sense
the artist can always make of his intentions and methods after he
has done the work. It is an endearing habit artists have, and I find
nothing so enthralling as to hear or read a good artist telling how
he does it. For practical purposes he might as well try to communicate his breath for our use. For example, Miss Sitwell
chooses words not only for their meaning, but for sound, number of syllables, color, shape, texture, speed or slowness, thick-
ness, thinness, weight, and for the shadow they cast upon the

words near them. "Said King Pompey" is built on a scheme of R's for very good reasons. It is also "a poem about materialism and the triumphant dust."

Her introduction to *The Canticle* is good reading, and you can see, by the passages she cites, that whether or not it was so deliberate a thing as she now believes, she got her effects by just the means she says she did; a good deal more than most artists can prove. Beginning poets should be warned that this is not a ready-made technique, a bridge to anywhere. The live, inborn instinct for language, for the mother-tongue, must first be present, and whoever else has it to anywhere near this degree, will not get anything from Miss Sitwell except the pleasure of reading her poetry and an incitement to get on with his own work. This is about all that one artist can do for another, and it is really quite enough.

This poet's vision: "Seeing the immense design of the world, one image of wonder mirrored by another image of wonder—the pattern of fern and feather by the frost on the windowpane, the six rays of the snowflake mirrored in the rock-crystal's six-rayed eternity—seeing the pattern on the scaly legs of birds mirrored in the pattern of knot-grass, I asked myself, were those shapes molded by blindness? Are not these the correspondences, to quote a phrase of Swedenborg, whereby we speak with the angels?" Her theme: the eternal theme of saints and poets: the destiny of Man is to learn the nature of love and to seek spiritual rebirth. Her range of variations on this theme is endless. Every poem therefore is a love poem, even those towering songs of denunciation out of her counter-passion of hatred for the infamies of life and the willful wrong man does to the image of God in himself. So many peevish and obscene little writers of late have been compared to Swift I hesitate to set his name here even where I feel it is not out of place. In "Gold Coast Customs" I find for the first time in my contemporary reading a genius for invective as ferocious as Swift's own, invective in the high-striding authoritative

style, the same admirable stateliness of wrath, the savage indignation of a just mind and generous heart outraged to the far edge
of endurance. The mere natural murderousness of the human
kind is evil enough, but her larger rejection is of "the terrible
ideal of useless Suffering" symbolized by "Lazarus, the hero of
death and the mud, taking the place in men's minds of the Hero
of Life who was born in a stable."

This passage is from "Gold Coast Customs":

> But Lady Bamburgher's Shrunken Head
> Slum hovel, is full of the rat-eaten bones
> Of a fashionable god that lived not
> Ever, but still has bones to rot:
> A bloodless and an unborn thing
> That cannot wake, yet cannot sleep,
> That makes no sound, that cannot weep,
> That hears all, bears all, cannot move—
> It is buried so deep
> Like a shameful thing
> In that plague-spot heart, Death's last dust-heap.

Again: "Though Death has taken/And pig-like shaken/Rooted,
and tossed/the rags of me—"

"At one time," writes Miss Sitwell, "I wrote of the world
reduced to the Ape as mother, teacher, protector. But too, with
poor Christopher Smart, I blessed Jesus Christ with the Rose
and his people, a nation of living sweetness. My time of experiment was over."

This was later, and there is still the vast middle section of the
work, the rages, the revolts, the burning noon of drunkenness
on sensuous sound and image, the exaltation of the pagan myth,
the earth's fertility; the bold richness of the roving imagination
taking every land and every sea, every far-off and legendary
place, every dream and every nightmare of the blood, every
response of every human sense for its own. In this part, I find
my own favorites are all, one way or another, songs of mourning: "Colonel Fantock"; "Elegy on Dead Fashion"; "Three Rus-

tic Elegies"—"O perfumed nosegay brought for noseless death!"
She acknowledges his power over the suffering flesh, the betrayed heart: but he can plant only carrion which belongs to
his kingdom of the dust; Christ the Golden Wheat sows Himself perpetually for our perpetual resurrection. Rarely in the
poetry of our time is noseless death stared down so boldly.

"After 'Gold Coast Customs,'" writes Miss Sitwell, "I wrote
no poetry for several years, with the exception of a long poem
called 'Romance,' and one poem in which I was finding my
way. Then after a year of war, I began to write again—of the
state of the world, of the terrible rain" (of bombs). During this
long pause, she made the transition from the short, violently
accented line, to a long curving line, a changed tone and pace.
Of the late poems, the first one begins:

> I who was once a golden woman like those who walk,
> In the dark heavens—but am now grown old
> And sit by the fire, and see the fire grow cold,
> Watch the dark fields for a rebirth of faith and of wonder.

Again, in "Tattered Serenade":

> These are the nations of the Dead, their million-year-old
> Rags about them—these, the eternally cold,
> Misery's worlds, with Hunger, their long sun
> Shut in by polar worlds of ice, known to no other,
> Without a name, without a brother,
> Though their skin shows that they yet are men.

In these later poems, without exception tragic, a treasure of
distilled tragic experience, the mysterious earthly rapture is mingled with a strain of pure, Evangelical Christianity, raised to
the apocalyptic vision. Here, rightly, are some of the most
wonderful (wonderful, and I know the meaning of that word)
love songs in the English language: "Anne Boleyn's Song";
"Green Song"; "The Poet Laments the Coming of Old Age";
"Mary Stuart to James Bothwell"; and here begins the sustained use of the fire symbols, of gold the color of fire, the

sun, the sun's flame, the gold of wheat, of lion's manes, of foxes' pelts, of Judas' hair, fire of the hearth, molten gold, gold seed, the gold of corn, golden cheeks, golden eyelids; "the great gold planets, spangling the wide air," "gold-bearded thunders,"—a crescendo of rapture in celebration of fire after the ice-locked years of war when fire carried only death. As every symbol has many meanings, and is corruption or purification according to its relationships, so the sun, "the first lover of the earth," has been harnessed by man to his bloody purposes, and must be restored as the lover, as the giver of life:

And I who stood in the grave-clothes of my flesh
Unutterably spotted with the world's woes,
Cry, "I am Fire. See, I am the bright gold
That shines like a flaming fire in the night—the gold-trained planet,
The laughing heat of the Sun that was born from darkness."

In "The Song of the Cold," the cold which is the symbol of poverty, death, the hardened human heart, there is the final speech of marrow-frozen grief: "I will cry to the Spring to give me the birds' and the serpents' speech,/That I may weep for those who die of the cold—" but "The Canticle of the Rose" says:

The Rose upon the wall
Cries—"I am the voice of Fire:
And in me grows
The pomegranate splendor of Death, the ruby, garnet, almandine
Dews: Christ's wounds in me shine!"

This is the true flowering branch springing fresh from the old, unkillable roots of English poetry, with the range, variety, depth, fearlessness, the passion and elegance of great art.

1949

Eudora Welty and "A Curtain of Green"

❈

Friends of us both first brought Eudora Welty to visit me three years ago in Louisiana. It was hot midsummer, they had driven over from Mississippi, her home state, and we spent a pleasant evening together talking in the cool old house with all the windows open. Miss Welty sat listening, as she must have done a great deal of listening on many such occasions. She was and is a quiet, tranquil-looking, modest girl, and unlike the young Englishman of the story, she has something to be modest about, as *A Curtain of Green* proves.

She considers her personal history as hardly worth mentioning, a fact in itself surprising enough, since a vivid personal career of fabulous ups and downs, hardships and strokes of luck, travels in far countries, spiritual and intellectual exile, defensive flight, homesick return with a determined groping for native roots, and a confusion of contradictory jobs have long been the mere conventions of an American author's life. Miss Welty was born and brought up in Jackson, Mississippi, where her father, now dead, was president of a Southern insurance company. Family life was cheerful and thriving; she seems to have got on excellently with both her parents and her two brothers. Education, in the Southern manner with daughters, was continuous, indulgent, and precisely as serious as she chose to make it. She went from school in Mississippi to the University of Wisconsin, thence to Columbia, New York, and so home again where she lives with her mother, among her lifelong friends and acquaintances, quite simply and amiably. She tried a job or two because that seemed the next thing, and did

some publicity and newspaper work; but as she had no real
need of a job, she gave up the notion and settled down to writing.

She loves music, listens to a great deal of it, all kinds; grows
flowers very successfully, and remarks that she is "underfoot
locally," meaning that she has a normal amount of social life.
Normal social life in a medium-sized Southern town can become
a pretty absorbing occupation, and the only comment her friends
make when a new story appears is, "Why, Eudora, when did
you write that?" Not how, or even why, just when. They see
her about so much, what time has she for writing? Yet she spends
an immense amount of time at it. "I haven't a literary life at all,"
she wrote once, "not much of a confession, maybe. But I do feel
that the people and things I love are of a true and human world,
and there is no clutter about them. . . . I would not understand
a literary life."

We can do no less than dismiss that topic as casually as she
does. Being the child of her place and time, profiting perhaps
without being aware of it by the cluttered experiences, foreign
travels, and disorders of the generation immediately preceding
her, she will never have to go away and live among the Eskimos,
or Mexican Indians; she need not follow a war and smell death
to feel herself alive: she knows about death already. She shall
not need even to live in New York in order to feel that she is
having the kind of experience, the sense of "life" proper to a
serious author. She gets her right nourishment from the source
natural to her—her experience so far has been quite enough for
her and of precisely the right kind. She began writing spontane-
ously when she was a child, being a born writer; she continued
without any plan for a profession, without any particular encour-
agement, and, as it proved, not needing any. For a good number
of years she believed she was going to be a painter, and painted
quite earnestly while she wrote without much effort.

Nearly all the Southern writers I know were early, omnivo-
rous, insatiable readers, and Miss Welty runs reassuringly true

to this pattern. She had at arm's reach the typical collection of books which existed as a matter of course in a certain kind of Southern family, so that she had read the ancient Greek and Roman poetry, history and fable, Shakespeare, Milton, Dante, the eighteenth-century English and the nineteenth-century French novelists, with a dash of Tolstoy and Dostoievsky, before she realized what she was reading. When she first discovered contemporary literature, she was just the right age to find first W. B. Yeats and Virginia Woolf in the air around her; but always, from the beginning until now, she loved folk tales, fairy tales, old legends, and she likes to listen to the songs and stories of people who live in old communities whose culture is recollected and bequeathed orally.

She has never studied the writing craft in any college. She has never belonged to a literary group, and until after her first collection was ready to be published she had never discussed with any colleague or older artist any problem of her craft. Nothing else that I know about her could be more satisfactory to me than this; it seems to me immensely right, the very way a young artist should grow, with pride and independence and the courage really to face out the individual struggle; to make and correct mistakes and take the consequences of them, to stand firmly on his own feet in the end. I believe in the rightness of Miss Welty's instinctive knowledge that writing cannot be taught, but only learned, and learned by the individual in his own way, at his own pace and in his own time, for the process of mastering the medium is part of a cellular growth in a most complex organism; it is a way of life and a mode of being which cannot be divided from the kind of human creature you were the day you were born, and only in obeying the law of this singular being can the artist know his true directions and the right ends for him.

Miss Welty escaped, by miracle, the whole corrupting and destructive influence of the contemporary, organized tampering with young and promising talents by professional teachers who are rather monotonously divided into two major sorts: those theorists who are incapable of producing one passable specimen of the art they profess to teach; or good, sometimes first-rate, artists who are humanly unable to resist forming disciples and imitators among their students. It is all well enough to say that, of this second class, the able talent will throw off the master's influence and strike out for himself. Such influence has merely added new obstacles to an already difficult road. Miss Welty escaped also a militant social consciousness, in the current radical-intellectual sense, she never professed Communism, and she has not expressed, except implicitly, any attitude at all on the state of politics or the condition of society. But there is an ancient system of ethics, an unanswerable, indispensable moral law, on which she is grounded firmly, and this, it would seem to me, is ample domain enough; these laws have never been the peculiar property of any party or creed or nation, they relate to that true and human world of which the artist is a living part; and when he dissociates himself from it in favor of a set of political, which is to say, inhuman, rules, he cuts himself away from his proper society—living men.

There exist documents of political and social theory which belong, if not to poetry, certainly to the department of humane letters. They are reassuring statements of the great hopes and dearest faiths of mankind and they are acts of high imagination. But all working, practical political systems, even those professing to originate in moral grandeur, are based upon and operate by contempt of human life and the individual fate; in accepting any one of them and shaping his mind and work to that mold, the artist dehumanizes himself, unfits himself for the practice of any art.

Not being in a hurry, Miss Welty was past twenty-six years when she offered her first story, "The Death of a Traveling Salesman," to the editor of a little magazine unable to pay, for she could not believe that anyone would buy a story from her; the magazine was *Manuscript*, the editor John Rood, and he accepted it gladly. Rather surprised, Miss Welty next tried the

Southern Review, where she met with a great welcome and the enduring partisanship of Albert Erskine, who regarded her as his personal discovery. The story was "A Piece of News" and it was followed by others published in the *Southern Review,* the *Atlantic Monthly,* and *Harper's Bazaar.*

She has, then, never been neglected, never unappreciated, and she feels simply lucky about it. She wrote to a friend: "When I think of Ford Madox Ford! You remember how you gave him my name and how he tried his best to find a publisher for my book of stories all that last year of his life; and he wrote me so many charming notes, all of his time going to his little brood of promising writers, the kind of thing that could have gone on forever. Once I read in the *Saturday Review* an article of his on the species and the way they were neglected by publishers, and he used me as the example chosen at random. He ended his cry with 'What is to become of both branches of Anglo-Saxondom if this state of things continues?' Wasn't that wonderful, really, and typical? I may have been more impressed by that than would other readers who knew him. I did not know him, but I knew it was typical. And here I myself have turned out to be not at all the martyred promising writer, but have had all the good luck and all the good things Ford chided the world for withholding from me and my kind."

But there is a trap lying just ahead, and all short-story writers know what it is—The Novel. That novel which every publisher hopes to obtain from every short-story writer of any gifts at all, and who finally does obtain it, nine times out of ten. Already publishers have told her, "Give us first a novel, and then we will publish your short stories." It is a special sort of trap for poets, too, though quite often a good poet can and does write a good novel. Miss Welty has tried her hand at novels, laboriously, dutifully, youthfully thinking herself perhaps in the wrong to refuse, since so many authoritarians have told her that was the next step. It is by no means the next step. She can very well become a master of the short story, there are almost perfect stories in *A*

Curtain of Green. The short story is a special and difficult medium, and contrary to a widely spread popular superstition it has no formula that can be taught by correspondence school. There is nothing to hinder her from writing novels if she wishes or believes she can. I only say that her good gift, just as it is now, alive and flourishing, should not be retarded by a perfectly artificial demand upon her to do the conventional thing. It is a fact that the public for short stories is smaller than the public for novels; this seems to me no good reason for depriving that minority. I remember a reader writing to an editor, complaining that he did not like collections of short stories because, just as he had got himself worked into one mood or frame of mind, he was called upon to change to another. If that is an important objection, we might also apply it to music. We might compare the novel to a symphony, and a collection of short stories to a good concert recital. In any case, this complainant is not our reader, yet our reader does exist, and there would be more of him if more and better short stories were offered.

The stories in *A Curtain of Green* offer an extraordinary range of mood, pace, tone, and variety of material. The scene is limited to a town the author knows well; the farthest reaches of that scene never go beyond the boundaries of her own state, and many of the characters are of the sort that caused a Bostonian to remark that he would not care to meet them socially. Lily Daw is a half-witted girl in the grip of social forces represented by a group of earnest ladies bent on doing the best thing for her, no matter what the consequences. Keela, the Outcast Indian Maid, is a crippled little Negro who represents a type of man considered most unfortunate by W. B. Yeats: one whose experience was more important than he, and completely beyond his powers of absorption. But the really unfortunate man in this story is the ignorant young white boy, who had innocently assisted at a wrong done the little Negro, and for a most complex reason, finds that no reparation is possible, or even desirable to the victim. . . . The heroine of "Why I Live at the P.O." is a terrifying case of dementia praecox, when one reconsiders it. While reading, it is gorgeously funny. In this first group—for the stories may be loosely classified on three separate levels—the spirit is satire and the key grim comedy. Of these, "The Petrified Man" offers a fine clinical study of vulgarity—vulgarity absolute, chemically pure, exposed mercilessly to its final subhuman depths. Dullness, bitterness, rancor, self-pity, baseness of all kinds, can be most interesting material for a story provided these are not also the main elements in the mind of the author. There is nothing in the least vulgar or frustrated in Miss Welty's mind. She has simply an eye and an ear sharp, shrewd, and true as a tuning fork. She has given to this little story all her wit and observation, her blistering humor and her just cruelty; for she has none of that slack tolerance or sentimental tenderness toward symptomatic evils that amounts to criminal collusion between author and character. Her use of this material raises the quite awfully sordid little tale to a level above its natural habitat, and its realism seems almost to have the quality of caricature, as complete realism so often does. Yet, as painters of the grotesque make only detailed reports of actual living types observed more keenly than the average eye is capable of observing, so Miss Welty's little human monsters are not really caricatures at all, but individuals exactly and clearly presented: which is perhaps a case against realism, if we cared to go into it.

She does better on another level—for the important reason that the themes are richer—in such beautiful stories as "Death of a Traveling Salesman," "A Memory," "A Worn Path." Let me admit a deeply personal preference for this particular kind of story, where external act and the internal voiceless life of the human imagination almost meet and mingle on the mysterious threshold between dream and waking, one reality refusing to admit or confirm the existence of the other, yet both conspiring toward the same end. This is not easy to accomplish, but it is always worth trying, and Miss Welty is so successful at it, it would seem her most familiar territory. There is no blurring at the edges, but evidences of an active and disciplined imagination working firmly in a strong line of continuity, the waking faculty of daylight reason recollecting and recording the crazy logic of the dream. There is in none of these stories any trace of autobiography in the prime sense, except as the author is omnipresent, and knows each character she writes about as only the artist knows the thing he has made, by first experiencing it in imagination. But perhaps in "A Memory," one of the best stories, there might be something of early personal history in the story of the child on the beach, alienated from the world of adult knowledge by her state of childhood, who hoped to learn the secrets of life by looking at everything, squaring her hands before her eyes to bring the observed thing into a frame—the gesture of one born to select, to arrange, to bring apparently disparate elements into harmony within deliberately fixed boundaries. But the author is freed already in her youth from self-love, self-pity, self-preoccupation, that triple damnation of too many of the young and gifted, and has reached an admirable objectivity. In such stories as "Old Mr. Marblehall," "Powerhouse," "The Hitch-Hikers," she combines an objective reporting with great perception of mental or emotional states, and in "Clytie" the very shape of madness takes place before your eyes in a straight account of actions and speech, the personal appearance and habits of dress of the main character and her family.

In all of these stories, varying as they do in excellence, I find nothing false or labored, no diffusion of interest, no wavering of mood—the approach is direct and simple in method, though the themes and moods are anything but simple, and there is even in the smallest story a sense of power in reserve which makes me believe firmly that, splendid beginning that this is, it is only the beginning.

                                                                    1941

Homage to Ford Madox Ford

❋

Several years ago Ford Madox Ford remarked to a friend, with a real pride and satisfaction, that he had a book to show for every year of his life. Now he knew as well as anyone that no man can write sixty *good* books, he said himself there were books on that list he was willing to have out of print forever. But at the time of writing them, he had believed firmly each book was going to be good; in any case, each book was as good as he was capable of making it at that moment, that given circumstance; and in any case he could not have stopped himself from the enterprise, because he was a man of letters, born and bred. His life work and his vocation happened to be one and the same thing. A lucky man, in spite of what seems, sometimes, to the onlooker, as unlucky a life as was ever lived.

His labors were constant, his complicated seeking mind was never for one moment diverted from its speculations on the enduring topic of literature, the problems of creation, the fascinating pitfalls of technique, the moral, psychic, aesthetic aspects of art, all art, any one of the arts. He loved to live the life of the artist, he loved to discover, foster, encourage young beginners in what another admirer of his, Glenway Wescott, has described as "this severe and fantastic way of life." Toward the end, when he was at Olivet, Ford described himself as "an old man mad about writing." He was not really an old man—think of Hardy, think of Tolstoy, think of Yeats—and his madness was an illuminated sanity; but he had, when he wrote this, intimations of mortality in him, and he had always practiced, tongue in cheek, that "pride which apes humility." It pleased him to think of himself in that way; and indeed, when you consider his history, the tragic mischances of his life, his times of glory and success alternating with painful bouts with poverty and neglect, you might think, unless you were an artist, that he was a little mad to have run all the risks and to have taken all the punishment he did take at the hands of fortune,—and for what? I don't think he ever asked himself that question. I doubt greatly he ever seriously considered for one moment any other mode of life than the life he lived. I knew him for twelve years, in a great many places and situations, and I can testify that he led an existence of marvelous discomfort, of insecurity, of deep and pressing anxiety as to his daily bread; but no matter where he was, what his sufferings were, he sat down daily and wrote, in his crabbed fine hand, with pen, the book he was working on at the moment; and I never knew him when he was not working on a book. It is not the moment to estimate those books, time may reverse his own severe judgment on some of them, but any of you who have read the Tietjens cycle, or *The Good Soldier*, must have taken a long step forward in your knowledge of craftsmanship, of just what it takes to write a fine novel. His influence is deeper than we are able to measure, for he has influenced writers who never read his books; which is the fate of all masters.

There was in all something so typical, so classical in his way of life, his history, some phases of his career, so grand in the old manner of English men of letters, I think a reading of his books and a little meditation on his life and death might serve at once as guiding sign and a finger of warning to all eager people who thoughtlessly, perhaps, "want to write." You will learn from him what the effort really is; what the pains, and what the rewards, of a real writer; and if that is not enough to frighten you off, you may proceed with new confidence in yourself.

1942

Virginia Woolf

❋

Leonard Woolf, in selecting and publishing the shorter writings of his wife, Virginia Woolf, has taken occasion to emphasize, again and again, her long painstaking ways of working, her habit of many revisions and rewritings, and her refusal to publish anything until she had brought it to its final state. The four volumes to appear in the nine years since her death will probably be the lot, Mr. Woolf tells us. There seems to remain a certain amount of unfinished manuscripts—unfinished in the sense that she had intended still to reconsider them and would not herself have published them in their present versions. One cannot respect enough the devoted care and love and superb literary judgment of the executor of this precious estate.

"In the previous volumes," Mr. Woolf writes in his foreword to the latest collection, *The Captain's Death Bed*, "I made no attempt to select essays in accordance with what I thought to be their merit or importance; I aimed at including in each volume some of all the various kinds of essay."

It is easy to agree with him when he finds "The essays in this volume are . . . no different in merit and achievement from those previously published." Indeed, I found old favorites and new wonders in each of the earlier collections, finding still others again in this: the celebrated "Mr. Bennett and Mrs. Brown"; "Memories of a Working Woman's Guild"; "The Novels of Turgenev"; "Oliver Goldsmith." She speaks a convincing good word for Ruskin, such was her independence of taste, for surely this word is the first Ruskin has received in many a long year. She does a really expert taxidermy job on Sir

Walter Raleigh, poor man, though he certainly deserved it; does another on reviewing, so severe her husband feels he must modify it a little with a footnote.

The Captain's Death Bed contains in fact the same delicious things to read as always; apparently her second or third draft was as good as her ninth or fifteenth; her last would be a little different, but surely not much better writing, that is clear. Only she, the good artist, without self-indulgence, would have known how much nearer with each change she was getting to the heart of her thought. For an example of how near she could come to it, read the three and one-half pages called "Gas." It is about having a tooth out, in the same sense, as E. M. Forster once remarked, that *Moby Dick* is a novel about catching a whale.

Now it is to be supposed that with this final gathering up of her life's work the critics will begin their formal summings-up, analyses, exegeses; the various schools will attack or defend her; she will be "placed" here and there; Freud will be involved, if he has not been already; elegies will be written: Cyril Connolly has already shed a few mourning tears, and advised us not to read her novels for at least another decade: she is too painfully near to our most disastrous memories.

It turns out merely that Mr. Connolly wishes us to neglect her because she reminds him of the thirties, which he, personally, cannot endure. A great many of us who have no grudges against either the twenties or the thirties will find this advice mystifying. And there is a whole generation springing up, ready to read what is offered, who know and care nothing for either of those decades. My advice must be exactly the opposite: read everything of Virginia Woolf's now, for she has something of enormous importance to say at this time, here, today; let her future take care of itself.

I cannot pretend to be coldly detached about her work, nor, even if I were able, would I be willing to write a purely literary criticism of it. It is thirty-five years since I read her first novel,

The Voyage Out. She was one of the writers who touched the real life of my mind and feeling very deeply; I had from that book the same sense of some mysterious revelation of truth I had got in earliest youth from Laurence Sterne ("of all people!" jeers a Shandy-hating friend of mine), from Jane Austen, from Emily Brontë, from Henry James. I had grown up with these, and I went on growing with W. B. Yeats, the first short stories of James Joyce, the earliest novels of Virginia Woolf.

In the most personal way, all of these seemed and do seem to be my contemporaries; their various visions of reality, their worlds, merged for me into one vision, one world view that revealed to me little by little my familiar place. Living as I did in a world of readers devoted to solid, tried and true literature, in which unimpeachable moral grandeur and inarguable doctrine were set forth in balanced paragraphs, these writers were my own private discoveries. Reading as I did almost no contemporary criticism, talking to no one, still it did not occur to me that these were not great artists, who if only people could be persuaded to read them (even if by the light of Dr. Johnson) they would be accepted as simply and joyously as I accepted them.

In some instances I was to have rude surprises. I could never understand the "revival" of Henry James; I had not heard that he was dead. Rather suddenly Jane Austen came back into fashionable favor; I had not dreamed she had ever been out of it.

In much the same way I have been amazed at the career of Virginia Woolf among the critics. To begin with, there has been very little notice except of the weekly review variety. Compared to the libraries of criticism published about Joyce, Lawrence, Eliot and all her other fellow artists of comparable stature, she has had little consideration. In 1925 she puzzled E. M. Forster, whose fountain pen disappeared when he was all prepared in his mind to write about her early novels.

Almost everything has been said, over and over, about Virginia Woolf's dazzling style, her brilliant humor, her extraordinary sensibility. She has been called neurotic, and hyper-sensitive. Her style has been compared to cobwebs with dew drops, rainbows, landscapes seen by moonlight, and other un-substantial but showy stuff. She has been called a Phoenix, Muse, Sybil, a Prophetess, in praise, or a Feminist, in dispraise. Her beauty and remarkable personality, her short way with fools and that glance of hers, which chilled many a young literary man with its expression of seeing casually through a millstone—all of this got in the way. It disturbed the judgment and drew the attention from the true point of interest.

Virginia Woolf was a great artist, one of the glories of our time, and she never published a line that was not worth reading. The least of her novels would have made the reputation of a lesser writer, the least of her critical writings compare more than favorably with the best criticism of the past half-century. In a long, sad period of fear, a world broken by wars, in which the artists have in the most lamentable way been the children of their time, knees knocking, teeth chittering, looking for per-sonal salvation in the midst of world calamity, there appeared this artist, Virginia Woolf.

She was full of secular intelligence primed with the profane virtues, with her love not only of the world of all the arts created by the human imagination, but a love of life itself and of daily living, a spirit at once gay and severe, exacting and generous, a born artist and a sober craftsman; and she had no plan whatever for her personal salvation; or the personal salva-tion even of someone else; brought no doctrine; no dogma. Life, the life of this world, here and now, was a great mystery, no one could fathom it; and death was the end. In short, she was what the true believers always have called a heretic.

What she did, then, in the way of breaking up one of the oldest beliefs of mankind, is more important than the changes she made in the form of the novel. She wasn't even a heretic—

she simply lived outside of dogmatic belief. She lived in the naturalness of her vocation. The world of the arts was her native territory; she ranged freely under her own sky, speaking her mother tongue fearlessly. She was at home in that place as much as anyone ever was.

1950

E. M. Forster

❋

Dates memorable to me escape my mind, so I write them down on bits of paper. Bits of paper escape me, too; they love to hide themselves at the bottoms of large baskets of other papers marked "Miscellany." But E. M. Forster's volume of essays, called *Abinger Harvest*, until now my favorite book of his except *A Passage to India*, is never far from my reach, so by turning to a certain page in it, I am able to name exactly the time, the first and last time, that I ever saw Mr. Forster.

Mr. Forster sees so clearly the damage that Olympic Games, or any other form of commercialized, politicalized sport, does to everybody concerned I cannot help but hope that he sees through all those Cultural Fronts by now, too. We were nearly all of us taken in at least once. So it was one crowded, dusty evening, June 21, 1935, in Paris, that Mr. Forster appeared before a meeting of the International Congress of Writers. You can read about it in *Abinger Harvest*. I distrusted the whole thing for good reasons and attended only on the one evening when Mr. Forster was to speak. At that time, the Communists were busy dividing the whole world into two kinds of people: Fascist and Communist. They said you could tell Fascists by their abhorrence of culture, their racial prejudices, and their general inhumanity. This was true. But they said also that Communists were animated solely by a love of culture and the general good of their fellow man. Alas, this was not true.

But for great numbers of well-disposed persons, especially in France, England, and some of the Americas, it was dear, familiar talk and we fell for it like a ton of scrap iron. When

I say, then, that the evening Mr. Forster spoke in Paris was dusty and crowded, it was literally true: but it also is a way of saying that Communists in numbers running a show anywhere always gave me this sense of suffocation; and heaven knows they were there, with their usual solidarity of effrontery, efficiency and dullness, all over the place making muddlement, as ubiquitous and inescapable as a plague of June bugs in Texas.

Yet there were on the program as window-dressing a convincing number of artists not Communists, others just political geldings by Communist standards, and a few honest but uncommitted sympathizers. Among these last I suppose they counted Mr. Forster, and he did manage to get in a kind word for communism on the ground that its intentions were good; a high compliment, all considered. He also defended a mediocre book in the defense of free speech and the right to publish; restated his humane, liberal political views, and predicted that he and all his kind, including Aldous Huxley, should expect to be swept away by the next war.

I heard nothing of this at the time. I had to wait and read it in *Abinger Harvest*. I think it was just after André Malraux—then as dogmatic in communism as he is now in some other faith—had leaped to the microphone barking like a fox to halt the applause for Julien Benda's speech, that a little slender man with a large forehead and a shy chin rose, was introduced and began to read his paper carefully prepared for this occasion. He paid no attention to the microphone, but wove back and forth, and from side to side, gently, and every time his face passed the mouthpiece I caught a high-voiced syllable or two, never a whole word, only a thin recurring sound like the wind down a chimney as Mr. Forster's pleasant good countenance advanced and retreated and returned. Then, surprisingly, once he came to a moment's pause before the instrument and there sounded into the hall clearly but wistfully a complete sentence: "I DO believe in liberty!"

The applause at the end was barely polite, but it covered the

antics of that part of the audience near me; a whole pantomime
of malignant ridicule, meaning that Mr. Forster and all his kind
were already as extinct as the dodo. It was a discouraging moment.

Well, sixteen unbelievably long, painful years have passed, and
it is very reassuring to observe that, far from having been
swept away, Mr. Forster has been thriving in an admirable style
—that is to say, his own style, spare, unportentous but serious,
saying his say on any subject he chooses, as good a say as any
we are likely to have for a long time; fearless but not aggressive; candid without cruelty; and with that beautiful, purely
secular common sense which can hardly be distinguished in
its more inspired moments from a saintly idealism.

Indeed, Mr. Forster is an artist who lives in that constant
state of grace which comes of knowing who he is, where he
lives, what he feels and thinks about his world. Virginia Woolf
once wrote: "One advantage of having a settled code of morals
is that you know exactly what to laugh at." She knew, and so
does Mr. Forster. He pokes fun at things in themselves fatally
without humor, things oppressive and fatal to human happiness: megalomania, solemn-godliness, pretentiousness, self-love,
the meddlesome impulse which leads to the invasion and destruction of human rights. He disclaims a belief in Belief, meaning one can only suppose the kind of dogmatism promoted by
meddlesomeness and the rest; come right down to it, I hardly
know a writer with more beliefs than Mr. Forster; and all on
the side of the angels.

Two Cheers for Democracy, a collection of his short writings on a tremendous range of subjects, is his first book since
Abinger Harvest. It is an extension and enlargement of his
thought, a record of the life and feelings of an artist who has
been in himself an example of all he has defended from the
first: the arts as a civilizing force, civilization itself as the true
right aim of the human spirit, no matter what its failures may

have been; above all, his unalterable belief in the first importance of the individual relationships between human beings founded on the reality of love—not in the mass, not between nations, nonsense!—but between one person and another. This is of course much more difficult than loving just everybody and everything, for each one must really do something about it, and show his faith in works. He manages to raise two mild cheers for poor old misprized, blasphemed, abused Democracy, who took an awful thrashing lately, but may recover; and he hopes to be able honestly some day to give three. He has long since earned his three cheers, and a tiger.

1951

PERSONAL AND
PARTICULAR

Three Statements About Writing

❋

1939: THE SITUATION IN AMERICAN WRITING
Answers to Seven Questions

1. *Are you conscious, in your own writing, of the existence of a "usable past"? Is this mostly American? What figures would you designate as elements in it? Would you say, for example, that Henry James's work is more relevant to the present and future of American writing than Walt Whitman's?*

All my past is "usable," in the sense that my material consists of memory, legend, personal experience, and acquired knowledge. They combine in a constant process of re-creation. I am quite unable to separate the influence of literature or the history of literary figures from influences of background, upbringing, ancestry; or to say just what is American and what is not. On one level of experience and a very important one, I could write an autobiography based on my reading until I was twenty-five.

Henry James and Walt Whitman are relevant to the past and present of American literature or of any other literature. They are world figures, they are both artists, it is better not to mortgage the future by excluding either. Be certain that if the present forces and influences bury either of them, the future will dig him up again. The James-minded and the Whitman-minded people have both the right to their own kind of nourishment.

For myself I choose James, holding as I do with the conscious, disciplined artist, the serious expert against the expansive, indiscriminately "cosmic" sort. James, I believe, was the better workman, the more advanced craftsman, a better thinker, a man with a heavier load to carry than Whitman. His feelings are deeper and more complex than Whitman's; he had more confusing choices to make, he faced and labored over harder problems. I am always thrown off by arm-waving and shouting, I am never convinced by breast-beating or huge shapeless statements of generalized emotion. In particular, I think the influence of Whitman on certain American writers has been disastrous, for he encourages them in the vices of self-love (often disguised as love of humanity, or the working classes, or God), the assumption of prophetic powers, of romantic superiority to the limitations of craftsmanship, inflated feeling and slovenly expression.

Neither James nor Whitman is more relevant to the present and future of American literature than, say, Hawthorne or Melville, Stephen Crane or Emily Dickinson; or for that matter, any other first-rank poet or novelist or critic of any time or country. James or Whitman? The young writer will only confuse himself, neglect the natural sources of his education as artist, cramp the growth of his sympathies, by lining up in such a scrimmage. American literature belongs to the great body of world literature, it should be varied and free to flow into what channels the future shall open; all attempts to limit and exclude at this early day would be stupid, and I sincerely hope, futile. If a young artist must choose a master to admire and emulate, that choice should be made according to his own needs from the widest possible field and after a varied experience of study. By then perhaps he shall have seen the folly of choosing a master. One suggestion: artists are not political candidates; and art is not an arena for gladiatorial contests.

2. *Do you think of yourself as writing for a definite audience? If so, how would you describe this audience? Would you say that the audience for serious American writing has grown or contracted in the last ten years?*

In the beginning I was not writing for any audience, but spent a great while secretly and with great absorption trying to master a craft, to find a medium; my respect for this medium and the masters of it—no two of them alike—is very great. My search was all for the clearest and most arresting way to tell the things I wished to tell. I still do not write for any definite audience, though perhaps I have in mind a kind of composite reader.

It appears to me that the audience for serious American writing has grown in the past ten years. This opinion is based on my own observation of an extended reputation, a widening sphere of influence, an increasing number of readers, among poets, novelists, and critics of our first rank.

It is true that I place great value on certain kinds of perceptive criticism but neither praise nor blame affects my actual work, for I am under a compulsion to write as I do; when I am working I forget who approved and who dispraised, and why. The worker in an art is dyed in his own color, it is useless to ask him to change his faults or his virtues; he must, rather more literally than most men, work out his own salvation. No novelist or poet could possibly ask himself, while working: "What will a certain critic think of this? Will this be acceptable to my publisher? Will this do for a certain magazine? Will my family and friends approve of this?" Imagine what that would lead to. . . . And how much worse, if he must be thinking, "What will my political cell or block think of this? Am I hewing to the party line? Do I stand to lose my job, or head, on this?" This is really the road by which the artist perishes.

3. *Do you place much value on the criticism your work has received? Would you agree that the corruption of the literary supplements by advertising—in the case of the newspapers—and political pressures—in the case of the liberal weeklies—has made serious literary criticism an isolated cult?*

As to criticism being an isolated cult, for the causes you suggest or any other, serious literary criticism was never a crowded field; it cannot be produced by a formula or in bulk any more than can good poetry or fiction. It is not, any more than it ever was, the impassioned concern of a huge public. Proportionately to number, both of readers and publishers, there are as many good critics who have a normal audience as ever. We are discussing the art of literature and the art of criticism, and this has nothing to do with the vast industry of copious publishing, and hasty reviewing, under pressure from the advertising departments, or political pressure. It is a pernicious system: but I surmise the same kind of threat to freedom in a recently organized group of revolutionary artists who are out to fight and suppress if they can, all "reactionary" artists— that is, all artists who do not subscribe to their particular political faith.

4. *Have you found it possible to make a living by writing the sort of thing you want to, and without the aid of such crutches as teaching and editorial work? Do you think there is any place in our present economic system for literature as a profession?*

No, there has not been a living in it, so far. The history of literature, musical composition, painting shows there has never been a living in art, except by flukes of fortune; by weight of long, cumulative reputation, or generosity of a patron; a prize, a subsidy, a commission of some kind; or (in the American style) anonymous and shamefaced hackwork; in the English style, a tradition of hackwork, openly acknowledged if deplored. The grand old English hack is a melancholy spectacle perhaps, but a figure not without dignity. He is a man who sticks by his trade, does the best he can with it on its own terms, and abides by the consequences of his choice, with a kind of confidence in his way of life that has some merit, certainly.

Literature as a profession? It *is* a profession, and the professional literary man is on his own as any other professional man is.

If you mean, is there any place in our present economic system for the practice of literature as a source of steady income and economic security, I should say, no. There never has been, in any system, any guarantee of economic security for the artist, unless he took a job and worked under orders as other men do for a steady living. In the arts, you simply cannot secure your bread and your freedom of action too. You cannot be a hostile critic of society and expect society to feed you regularly. The artist of the present day is demanding (I think childishly) that he be given, free, a great many irreconcilable rights and privileges. He wants as a right freedoms which the great spirits of all time have had to fight and often to die for. If he wants freedom, let him fight and die for it too, if he must, and not expect it to be handed to him on a silver plate.

5. *Do you find, in retrospect, that your writing reveals any allegiance to any group, class, organization, region, religion, or system of thought, or do you conceive of it as mainly the expression of yourself as an individual?*

I find my writing reveals all sorts of sympathies and interests which I had not formulated exactly to myself; "the expression of myself as an individual" has never been my aim. My whole attempt has been to discover and understand human motives, human feelings, to make a distillation of what human relations and experiences my mind has been able to absorb. I have never known an uninteresting human being, and I have never known two alike; there are broad classifications and deep similarities, but I am interested in the thumbprint. I am passionately involved with these individuals who populate all these enormous migrations, calamities; who fight wars and furnish life for the future; these beings without which, one by one, all the "broad movements of history" could never take place. One by one—as they were born.

6. *How would you describe the political tendency of American writing as a whole since 1930? How do you feel about it yourself? Are you sympathetic to the current tendency toward what may be called "literary nationalism"—a renewed emphasis, largely uncritical, on the specifically "American" elements in our culture?*

Political tendency since 1930 has been to the last degree a confused, struggling, drowning-man-and-straw sort of thing, stampede of panicked crowd, each man trying to save himself—one at a time trying to work out his horrible confusions. How do I feel about it? I suffer from it, and I try to work my way out to some firm ground of personal belief, as the others do. I have times of terror and doubt and indecision, I am confused in all the uproar of shouting maddened voices and the flourishing of death-giving weapons. . . . I should like to save myself, but I have no assurance that I can, for if the victory goes as it threatens, I am not on that side.* The third clause of this question I find biased. Let me not be led away by your phrase "largely uncritical" in regard to the "emphasis on specifically American" elements in our culture. If we become completely uncritical and nationalistic, it will be the most European state of mind we could have. I hope we may not. I hope we shall have balance enough to see ourselves plainly, and choose what we shall keep and what discard according to our own needs; not be rushed into fanatic self-love and self-praise as a defensive measure against assaults from abroad. I think the "specifically American" things might not be the worst things for us to cultivate, since this is America, and we are Americans, and our history is not altogether disgraceful. The parent stock is Euro-

* At the time this was written it was clear enough that I was opposed to every form of authoritarian, totalitarian government or religion, under whatever name in whatever country. I still am.

pean, but this climate has its own way with transplantations, and I see no cause for grievance in that.

7. Have you considered the question of your attitude toward the possible entry of the United States into the next world war? What do you think the responsibilities of writers in general are when and if war comes?

I am a pacifist. I should like to say now, while there is still time and place to speak, without inviting immediate disaster (for I love life), to my mind the responsibility of the artist toward society is the plain and simple responsibility of any other human being, for I refuse to separate the artist from the human race: his prime responsibility "when and if war comes" is not to go mad. Madness takes many subtle forms, it is the old deceiver. I would say, don't be betrayed into all the old outdated mistakes. If you are promised something new and blissful at the mere price of present violence under a new master, first examine these terms carefully. New ideas call for new methods, the old flaying, drawing, and quartering for the love of God and the King will not do. If the method is the same, trust yourself, the idea is old, too. If you are required to kill someone today, on the promise of a political leader that someone else shall live in peace tomorrow, believe me, you are not only a double murderer, you are a suicide, too.

❄

1940*: INTRODUCTION TO "FLOWERING JUDAS"

It is just ten years since this collection of short stories first appeared. They are literally first fruits, for they were written and published in order of their present arrangement in this volume, which contains the first story I ever finished. Looking at them

---

* This was written on June 21, 1940, seven days after the fall of France.

again, it is possible still to say that I do not repent of them; if they were not yet written, I should have to write them still. They were done with intention and in firm faith, though I had no plan for their future and no notion of what their meaning might be to such readers as they would find. To any speculations from interested sources as to why there were not more of them, I can answer simply and truthfully that I was not one of those who could flourish in the conditions of the past two decades. They are fragments of a much larger plan which I am still engaged in carrying out, and they are what I was then able to achieve in the way of order and form and statement in a period of grotesque dislocations in a whole society when the world was heaving in the sickness of a millennial change. They were first published by what seems still merely a lucky accident, and their survival through this crowded and slowly darkening decade is the sort of fate no one, least of all myself, could be expected to predict or even to hope for.

We none of us flourished in those times, artists or not, for art, like the human life of which it is the truest voice, thrives best by daylight in a green and growing world. For myself, and I was not alone, all the conscious and recollected years of my life have been lived to this day under the heavy threat of world catastrophe, and most of the energies of my mind and spirit have been spent in the effort to grasp the meaning of those threats, to trace them to their sources and to understand the logic of this majestic and terrible failure of the life of man in the Western world. In the face of such shape and weight of present misfortune, the voice of the individual artist may seem perhaps of no more consequence than the whirring of a cricket in the grass; but the arts do live continuously, and they live literally by faith; their names and their shapes and their uses and their basic meanings survive unchanged in all that matters through times of interruption, diminishment, neglect; they outlive governments and creeds and the societies, even the very civilizations that produced them. They cannot be destroyed altogether because they represent the substance of faith and the only reality. They are what we find again when the ruins are cleared away. And even the smallest and most incomplete offering at this time can be a proud act in defense of that faith.

※

1942 : TRANSPLANTED WRITERS

One of the most disquieting by-products of the world disorders of the past few years has been the displacement of the most influential writers. The ablest German authors and journalists, for example, are no longer in Berlin and Leipzig, but in London and New York. The most articulate of the Spanish intelligentsia are not in Madrid but in Mexico City and Buenos Aires. This paradoxical situation must have far-reaching consequences, not only for the intellectuals themselves but for Germany, England and the United States, Spain, Mexico, and the Argentine. What, in your opinion, may these consequences be, immediate and remote, desirable and unfortunate?

The deepest harm in forced flight lies in the incurable wound to human pride and self-respect, the complete dislocation of the spiritual center of gravity. To be beaten and driven out of one's own place is the gravest disaster that can occur to a human being, for in such an act he finds his very humanity denied, his person dismissed with contempt, and this is a shock very few natures can bear and recover any measure of equilibrium.

Artists and writers, I think, do not suffer more than other people under such treatment, but they are apt to be more aware of the causes of their sufferings, they are better able to perceive what is happening, not only to them, but to all their fellow beings. I would not attempt to prophesy what the consequences of all this world displacement by violence of so many people might be; but I can only hope they will have learned something by it, and will leave in the grave of Europe their old quarrels and the old prejudices that have brought this catastrophe upon all of us. We have here enough of those things to fight without that added weight.

Americans are not going anywhere, and I am glad of it. Here we stay, for good or ill, for life or death; and my hope is that all those articulate intelligences who have been driven here will consent to stand with us, and help us put an end to this stampede of human beings driven like sheep over one frontier after another; I hope they will make an effort to understand what this place means in terms of the final battlefield. For the present, they must live here or nowhere, and they must share the responsibility for helping to make this a place where man can live as man and not as victim, pawn, a lower order of animal driven out to die beside the road or to survive in stealth and cunning.

The force at work in the world now is the oldest evil with a new name and new mechanisms and more complicated strategies; if the intelligentsia do not help to clarify the issues, maintain at least internal order, understand themselves and help others to understand the nature of what is happening, they hardly deserve the name. I agree with Mr. E. M. Forster that there are only two possibilities for any real order: in art and in religion. All political history is a vile mess, varying only in degrees of vileness from one epoch to another, and only the work of saints and artists gives us any reason to believe that the human race is worth belonging to.

Let these scattered, uprooted men remember this, and remember that their one function is to labor at preserving the humanities and the dignity of the human spirit. Otherwise they are lost and we are lost with them and whether they stay here or go yonder will not much matter.

No Plot, My Dear, No Story

✳

This is a fable, children, of our times. There was a great big little magazine with four and one half million subscribers, or readers, I forget which; and the editors sat up nights thinking of new ways to entertain these people who bought their magazine and made a magnificent argument to convince advertisers that $3,794.36 an inch space-rates was a mere gift at the price. Look at all the buying-power represented. Look at all the money these subscribers must have if they can afford to throw it away on a magazine like the one we are talking about. So the subscribers subscribed and the readers read and the advertisers bought space and everything went on ring-around-the-rosy like that for God knows how long. In fact, it is going on right now.

So the editors thought up something beautiful and sent out alarms to celebrated authors and the agents of celebrated authors, asking everybody to think hard and remember the best story he had ever read, anywhere, anytime, and tell it over again in his own words, and he would be paid a simply appalling price for this harmless pastime.

By some mistake a poor and only semi-celebrated author got on this list, and as it happened, that was the day the government had threatened to move in and sell the author's typewriter for taxes overdue, and a dentist had threatened to sue for a false tooth in the very front of the author's face; and there was also a grocery bill. So this looked as if Providence had decided to take a hand in the author's business, and he or she, it doesn't matter, sat down at once and remembered at least *one* of the most beautiful

stories he or she had ever read anywhere.* It was all about three
little country women finding a wounded man in a ditch, giving him cold water to drink out of his own cap, piling him into
their cart and taking him off to a hospital, where the doctors said
they might have saved their trouble for the man was as good
as dead.

The little women were just silly enough to be happy anyway
that they had found him, and he wasn't going to die by himself
in a ditch, at any rate. So they went on to market.

A month later they went back to the hospital, each carrying
a wreath to put on the grave of the man they had rescued and
found him there still alive in a wheel chair; and they were so
overcome with joy they couldn't think, but just dropped on their
knees in gratitude that his life was saved; this in spite of the fact
that he probably was not going to be of any use to himself or
anybody else for a long time if ever. . . . It was a story about
instinctive charity and selfless love. The style was fresh and clear
as the living water of their tenderness.

You may say that's not much of a story, but I hope you don't
for it would pain me to hear you agree with the editors of that
magazine. They sent it back to the author's agent with a merry
little note: "No plot, my dear—no *story*. Sorry."

So it looks as if the tax collector will get the author's typewriter, and the dentist the front tooth, and the crows may have
the rest; and all because the poor creature was stupid enough to
think that a short story needed *first* a *theme*, and then a point of
view, a certain knowledge of human nature and strong feeling
about it, and style—that is to say, his own special way of telling
a thing that makes it precisely his own and no one else's. . . .
The greater the theme and the better the style, the better the
story, you might say.

You might say, and it would be nice to think you would. Especially if you are an author and write short stories. Now listen

* "Living Water" by C. Sergeev-Tzensky, *The Dial*, July 1929.

carefully: except in emergencies, when you are trying to manufacture a quick trick and make some easy money, you don't really
need a plot. If you have one, all well and good, if you know what
it means and what to do with it. If you are aiming to take up the
writing *trade*, you need very different equipment from that
which you will need for the *art*, or even just the *profession* of
writing. There are all sorts of schools that can teach you exactly
how to handle the 197 variations on any one of the 37 basic plots;
how to take a parcel of characters you never saw before and
muddle them up in some difficulty and get the hero or heroine
out again, and dispose of the bad uns; they can teach you the
O. Henry twist; the trick of "slanting" your stuff toward this
market and that; you will learn what goes over big, what not so
big, what doesn't get by at all; and you will learn for yourself,
if you stick to the job, *why* all this happens. Then you are all set,
maybe. After that you have only to buy a pack of "Add-a-Plot"
cards (free ad.) and go ahead. Frankly, I wish you the luck you
deserve. You have richly earned it.

But there are other and surer and much more honest ways of
making money, and Mama advises you to look about and in-
vestigate them before leaping into such a gamble as mercenary
authorhood. Any plan to make money is a gamble, but grinding
out "slanted" stuff takes a certain knack, a certain willingness to
lose all, including honor; you will need a cold heart and a very
thick skin and an allowance from your parents while you are
getting started toward the big money. You stand to lose your
youth, your eyesight, your self-respect, and whatever potentialities
you may have had in other directions, and if the worst comes
to the worst, remember, nobody promised you anything. . . .
Well, if you are going to throw all that, except the self-respect,
into the ash can, you may as well, if you wish to write, be as
good a writer as you can, say what you think and feel, add a
little something, even if it is the merest fraction of an atom, to
the sum of human achievement.

First, have faith in your theme; then get so well acquainted with your characters that they live and grow in your imagination exactly as if you saw them in the flesh; and finally, tell their story with all the truth and tenderness and severity you are capable of; and if you have any character of your own, you will have a style of your own; it grows, as your ideas grow, and as your knowledge of your craft increases.

You will discover after a great while that you are probably a writer. You may even make some money at it.

One word more: I have heard it said, boldly and with complete sincerity by persons who should know better, that the only authors who do not write for the high-paying magazines are those who have not been able to make the grade; that any author who professes to despise or even disapprove of such writing and such magazines is a hypocrite; that he would be too happy to appear in those pages if only he were invited.

To such effrontery I have only one answer, based on experience and certain knowledge. It is simply not true.

1942

The Flower of Flowers

❈

Rose, O pure contradiction, bliss
To be the sleep of no one under so many eyelids.
                    —Rainer Maria Rilke: Epitaph

Its beginnings were obscure, like that of the human race whose history it was destined to adorn. The first rose was small as the palm of a small child's hand, with five flat petals in full bloom, curling in a little at the tips, the color red or white, perhaps even pink, and maybe sometimes streaked. It was a simple disk or wheel around a cup of perfume, a most intoxicating perfume, like that of no other flower. This perfume has been compared to that of many fruits: apricot, peach, melon; to animal substance: musk, ambergris; to honey (which has also many perfumes), to other flowers, to crushed leaves of the tea plant—this from China, naturally—and perhaps this is the secret of its appeal: it offers to the individual sense of smell whatever delights it most. For me, a rose smells like a rose, no one exactly like another, but still a rose and it reminds me of nothing else.

This rose grew everywhere in Africa and Asia, and it may have had many names, but they are lost.

This shall be a mere glimpse at some aspects of the life of the rose; it keeps the best company in the world, and the worst, and also the utterly mediocre: all with the same serenity, knowing one from the other; and all by name, but making, in the natural world, no difference between individuals, like any saint: which perhaps is a sign of its true greatness. In working miracles, as we shall see, it exercises the most scrupulous discrimination between one thing and another.

It was, and is, thorny by nature, for it detests the proximity of any other kind of plant, and serious botanists have deduced seriously that the rose was given its thorns as a weapon against other crowding vegetation. With such a perfume as it has, it needs more than thorns for its protection. It has no honey, yet even the bees and wasps who rob its generous pollen for food, get silly-drunk on the perfume, and may sometimes be seen swooping hilariously away at random, buzzing wildly and colliding with each other in air. For the sake of this perfume other great follies of extravagance have been committed. The Romans with their genius for gluttony devoured the roses of Egypt by the shipload, covering their beds and floors and banquet tables with petals; rose leaves dropped in their wine helped to prevent, or at least delay, drunkenness; heroes were crowned with them; and they were at last forced to bloom out of season by being grown in a network of hot water pipes.

The debasement of the rose may be said to have begun with this Roman invention of the hot house. After a long period in Europe when the rose fell into neglect, there came a gradual slow return in its popularity; and for the past century or so, in Europe and America, the rose has been cultivated extravagantly, cross-bred almost out of recognition, growing all the time larger, showier. The American Beauty rose—in the 1900's the rose of courtship, an expensive florist's item, hardly ever grown in good private gardens—in its hugeness, its coarse texture and vulgar color, its inordinate length of cane, still stands I believe as the dreariest example of what botanical experiment without wisdom or taste can do even to the rose. In other varieties it has been deprived of its thorns, one of its great beauties, and—surely this can never have been intended—its very perfume, the true meaning of the rose, has almost vanished. Yet they are all children of that precious first five-petaled rose which we call the Damask, the first recorded name of a rose.

It has been popularly supposed that the Crusaders brought the rose and the name back with them to Europe from Damascus,

where they saw it for the first time. Rosarians argue back and
forth, saying, *not* so, the Damask Rose was known in France
and by that name many centuries before the Crusades. It is very
likely, for the Christian penitential pilgrimages to Rome, to the
tombs and shrines of saints, and to the Holy Sepulchre, had begun
certainly as early as the eighth century. The most difficult and
dangerous and meritorious of these pilgrimages was, of course, to
the Holy Land, and the rose may very well have been among
the dear loot in the returning pilgrim's scrip, along with water
from the Jordan, bits of stone from the Sepulchre, fragments of
the True Cross, Sacred Nails, and a few Thorns; and, judging
by medieval European music, he had got a strange tune or two
fixed in his head, also. We know that more than this came into
Europe through long traffic and negotiation with the East, the
great threatening power which encroached steadily upon the
New World and above all, upon the new religion.

By the time of the troubadours, the rose was a familiar delight. In Richard the Lion-Hearted's day, Raoul, Sire de Coucy,
a famous poet, singer, soldier, nobleman, was writing poems
full of nightingales, morning dew, roses, lilies, and love to his
lady, the Dame de Fayel. He went with Richard on the Third
Crusade, and was killed by the Saracens at the battle of St.
Jean d'Acres, in 1191. The whole tone of his glittering little
songs, their offhand ease of reference, makes it clear that roses
and all those other charming things had long been the peculiar property of European poets. De Coucy names no species.
"When the rose and lily are born," he sings blithely, knowing
and caring nothing about Rosa Indica, Rosa Gallica, Rosa Centifolia, Eglantina; no, for the troubadour a rose was a rose. It
was beautiful to look at, especially with morning dew on it, a
lily nearby and a nightingale lurking in the shrubbery, all ready
to impale his bosom on the thorn; it smelled sweet and reminded
him of his lady, as well as of the Blessed Virgin, though never,
of course, at the same moment. That would have been sacrilege,
and the knight was nothing if not pious. Sacred and profane

love in the Western World had by then taken their places at opposite poles, where they have remained to this day; the rose was the favorite symbol of them both.

Woman has been symbolized almost out of existence. To man, the myth maker, her true nature appears unfathomable, a dubious mystery at best. It was thought proper to becloud the riddle still further by referring to her in terms of something else vaguely, monstrously, or attractively resembling her, or at least her more important and obvious features. Therefore she was the earth, the moon, the sea, the planet Venus, certain stars, wells, lakes, mines, caves; besides such other works of nature as the fig, the pear, the pomegranate, the shell, the lily, wheat or any grain, Night or any kind of darkness, any seed pod at all; above all, once for all, the Rose.

The Rose. What could be more flattering? But wait. It was the flower of Venus, of Aurora, a talisman against witchcraft, and the emblem, when white, and suspended over a banquet table, of friendly confidence: one spoke and acted freely under the rose, for all present were bound to silence afterward. It was the flower of the Blessed Virgin, herself the Mystical Rose; symbol of the female genitals, and the Gothic disk of celestial color set in the brows of great cathedrals. For Christian mystics the five red petals stood for the five wounds of Christ; for the pagans, the blood of Venus who stepped on a thorn while hurrying to the aid of Narcissus. It is the most subtle and aristocratic of flowers, yet the most varied of all within its breed, most easily corruptible in form, most susceptible to the changes of soil and climate. It is the badge of kings, and the wreath to crown every year the French girl chosen by her village as the most virtuous: *La Rosière. Le Spectre de la Rose*: a perverted image. No young girl ever dreamed of her lover in the form of a rose. She is herself the rose. . . .

The rose gives its name to the prayer-beads themselves slipped millions of times a day all over the world between prayerful fingers: these beads are still sometimes made of the dried hardened paste of rose petals. The simple flower is beloved of kings and peasants, children, saints, artists, and prisoners, and then all those numberless devoted beings who grow them so faithfully in little plots of gardens everywhere. It is a fragile flower that can survive for seventy-five years draped over a rail fence in a deserted farm otherwise gone to jungle; it blooms by the natural exaltation of pure being in a tin, with its roots strangling it to death; yet it is by nature the grossest feeder among flowers. With very few exceptions among wild roses, they thrive best, any good gardener will tell you, in deep trenches bedded with aged cow manure. One famous grower of Old Roses (Francis E. Lester, *My Friend the Rose*, 1942) advises one to bury a big beef bone, cooked or raw, deep under the new plant, so that its growing roots may in time descend, embrace and feed slowly upon this decayed animal stuff in the private darkness. Above, meanwhile, it brings to light its young pure buds, opening shyly as the breasts of virgins. (See: Lyric Poetry: Through the Ages.) Aside from the bloom, out of this tranced absorption with the rot and heat and moisture of the earth, there is distilled the perfume of perfumes from this flower of flowers.

(The nose is surely one of the most impressionable, if not positively erotic, of all our unruly members. I remember a kind old nun, rebuking me for my delight in the spectacle of this world saying, "Beware of the concupiscence of the eye!" I had never heard the word, but I knew what she meant. Then what about the ear? The pores of the skin, the tips of the fingers? We are getting on quicksand. Back, back to the rose, that tempts every mortal sense except the ear, lends itself to every pleasure, and helps by its presence or even its memory, to assuage every mortal grief.)

The rose: its perfume. It is—ten to one—the odor of sanctity that rises from the corpses of holy women, and the oil with which Laïs the Corinthian anoints herself after her bath. Saint Thérèse of Lisieux is shown holding a sheaf of roses, promising her faithful to shower them with roses—that is to say, blessings. The women in Minsky's old Burlesque Theater on the Bowery pinned large red cotton velvet roses over their abused breasts and public thighs, forming a triangle. They then waggled themselves as obscenely as they knew how; they did know how, and it was obscene; and the helpless caricatures of roses would waggle too: the symbol being brought to the final depths of aesthetic and moral imbecility.

"A rose said, 'I am the marvel of the universe. Can it be that a perfume maker shall have the courage to cause me suffering?' " Yes, it is possible. "A nightingale answered, 'One day of joy prepares a year of tears.' " (NOTE: My translation of a stanza of Omar Khayyam's from the French version.)

This divine perfume from the bone-devouring rose is sometimes got by distilling, a process of purification. The petals are mixed with the proper amount of water, put in the alembic, and the sweetness is sweated out, drop by drop, with death and resurrection for the rose in every drop. Or, and this must be a very old way of doing, one takes the sweet petals, picked tenderly in the morning unbruised, with the dew on them, and lays them gently on a thick bed of fat, beef fat, pork fat, or perhaps oil, just so it is pure, and fat. The perfume seeps from the veins of the rose into the fat, which in turn is mingled with alcohol which takes the fragrance to itself, and there you are. . . . Thinking it over, I am certain there is a great deal more to the art of extracting perfume from petals than this. I got my information from a small French household book, published in 1830, which gives receipts for making all sorts of fascinating messes: liqueurs, bleaching pastes for the complexion, waters of beauty—invariably based on rosewater or rose oil, hair dyes, lip salves, infusions of herbs and flowers, perfumes, heaven knows what. They look plausible on the page, while reading I trust them implicitly, and have never dared to try one of them. One important point the perfume receipt omitted: it did not say you must begin with Damask roses. In India, in the Balkans, in the south of France, wherever the art of making rosewater and attar of rose is still practiced, as in ancient Cyrenaica whose rose perfume was "the sweetest in the world," there is one only rose used: Rosa Damascena, five-petaled in the Balkans and in India, thirty-petaled in Grasse, and called the Provence Rose. In this Rose of Provence there is perhaps a mixture with Rosa Centifolia, native of the Caucasus—Cabbage Rose to us, to those of us who ever saw it, and smelled it—next to the Damask, the most deeply, warmly perfumed. Once in California, in a nursery, lost in a jungle of strange roses, I asked an old gardener, no doubt a shade too wistfully, "Haven't you a Cabbage Rose, or a Damask, or a Moss Rose?" He straightened up and looked at me wonderingly and said, "Why, my God, I haven't even heard those names for thirty years! Do you actually know those roses?" I told him yes, I did, I had been brought up with them. Slowly, slowly, slowly like moisture being squeezed out of an oak, his eyes filled with tears. "So was I," he said, and the tears dried back to their source without falling. We walked then among the roses, some of them very fine, very beautiful, of honorable breed and proved courage, but the roses which for me are the very heart of the rose were not there, nor had ever been.

They have as many pests as sheep, or bees, two notoriously afflicted races. Aphis, mildew, rust, caterpillars, saw-flies, leaf-cutting bees, thrips, canker worms, beetles, and so on. Spraying has become the bane of rose growers, for the new sorts of roses seem to be more susceptible than the old. I remember my grandmother occasionally out among her roses with a little bowl of soapy water and a small rag. She would wash the backs of a few leaves and dry them tenderly as if they were children's fingers. That was all I ever saw her do in that way, and her roses were celebrated.

Mankind early learned that the rose, except for its thorns, is a benevolent useful flower. It was good to eat, to drink, to smell, to wear, to cure many ailments, to wash and perfume with, to look at, to meditate upon, to offer in homage, piety, or love; in religion it has always been a practical assistant in the working of miracles. It was good to write poetry about, to paint, to draw, to carve in wood, stone, marble; to work in tapestry, plaster, clay, jewels, and precious metals. Besides rose-leaf jam, still made in England, one may enjoy candied rose leaves, rose honey, rose oil—good for the bath *or* for flavoring cakes and pastries; infusion of roses, a delicious tea once prescribed for many ills; above all, rose-hip syrup, an old valuable remedy in medieval pharmacies, manufactured by monks, and housewives. The Spanish Mission fathers brought the Damask Rose—which they called the Rose of Castile—to America and planted it in their dispensary gardens. Rose-hip syrup was one of their great remedies. It was known to cure aches and pains, collywobbles in the midriff, a pallid condition, general distemper, or ill-assortedness. And why not? Modern medical science has in this instance proved once more that ancient herbalists were not just old grannies out pulling weeds and pronouncing charms over them. Rose-hip syrup, say British medical men, contains something like four hundred times more of vitamin C, measure for measure, than oranges or black currants, and whoever drinks freely of it will be largely benefited, if he needs vitamin C, as most of us do, no doubt. They needed it in medieval times, too, and it is pleasant to think that quite large numbers of them got it.

Bear's grease mixed with pounded rose petals made a hopeful hair restorer. The ancient Persians made a rose wine so powerful yet so benign it softened the hardest heart, and put the most miserable wretch to sleep. In Elizabethan England they made a rose liqueur warranted to "wash the mulligrubs out of a moody brain." Mulligrubs is a good word yet in my part of the country, the South, to describe that state of lowered resistance to life now known generally as the "blues." In turn, "blues," in its exact present sense, was a good word in seventeenth-century England, and was brought to America by the early Virginia settlers. Whether they brought roses at first I do not know, nor whether they found any here; but there is a most beautiful rose, single, large-petaled, streaked red and white, called the Cherokee Rose, of a heavenly perfume, which is perfectly at home here. It came from Asia by way of England, however, a long time ago, and has not a drop of Indian blood in it. Maybe the Virginians did bring it—it flourishes best in the Southern states.

The celebrated botanists, rose growers, collectors, hybridizers, perfume makers, as well as the scientific or commercial exploiters of the rose, have all been men; so far as I know, not a woman among them. And naturally in such a large company we find a few who labor restlessly to grow a rose with a six-foot stem; with a thousand petals, and a face broad as a plate; to color them blue, or black, or violet. The rose being by nature a bush, they could not rest until they made a tree of it. In the same spirit, there are those who embalm them in wax, dip them in dye-stuffs, manufacture them in colored paper, and sprinkle them with synthetic perfume. This is not real wickedness but something worse, sheer poverty of feeling and misdirected energy with effrontery, a combination found in all vulgarizers. The "arrangers" of great music, the "editors" of literary masterpieces, the re-painters of great pictures, the falsifiers of noble ideas—that whole race of the monkey-minded and monkey-fingered "adapters"; the rose too has been their victim. Remy de Gourmont cursed all women in the name of the rose, with the ferocity of perverted love; and aesthetic hyper-sensibility turned not to hatred but to something even more painful, disgust, nausea, at the weight of false symbol, the hypocritical associations, the sickly sentiment which appeared to have overwhelmed it. With the wild logic of bitterness and disillusion, he cursed the rose, that is, woman, and through it, all those things which had degraded it in his eyes, concluding that the rose itself is vile by nature, and attracts vileness. Only a disappointed lover behaves so unreasonably. He got a brilliant poem out of it, however (*"Litanies de la Rose"*).

Women have been the treasurers of seedlings and cuttings; they are the ones who will root a single slip in a bottle of water in the corner of a closet; or set out, as the pioneer American women did, on their bitter journeys to the Carolinas, to Kentucky, to Texas, to California, the Middle West, the Indian territories, guarding who knows how their priceless little store of seeds and roots of apples, plums, pears, grapes, and roses— always roses. China Rose, Bengal Rose, Musk Rose, Moss Rose, Briar Rose, Damask Rose—in how many places those very same pioneer rose bushes are blooming yet. But where did all those hedges of wild roses spring from? Were they always there? Gloire de Dijon, Cup of Hebe, Old Blush, Roger Lambelin, Cherokee, Maréchal Niel, Cramoisy—these are some names I remember from gardens I knew; and Noisette, a small perfect rose, result of the first cross-breeding in this country, a century and a quarter ago. . . . Where did I see that little story about someone advertising a place for sale as an earthly paradise, "the only drawbacks being the litter of rose petals and the noise of nightingales"?

The rose is sacred to religion, to human love, and to the arts. It is associated with the longing for earthly joy, and for eternal life. There is a noticeable absence of them, or flowers of any kind in the textbooks of magic, witchcraft, the Black Arts by any name. The world of evil is mechanistic, furnished with alembics, retorts, ovens, grinding stones; herbs, mainly poisonous; the wheel, but not the rose; hollow circles, zones of safety for the conjuror. The alchemist with his madness for gold—for what did they devote all that hermetic wisdom, that moral grandeur, that spiritual purity they professed but to the dream of making gold? Or of turning pebbles into jewels, as St. John was said to have done? A slander, I do believe, unless taken symbolically. But the evidence is against this: the alche-

mists meant to make real gold. It is the most grotesquely materialistic of all ends. The witch, with her blood vows and her
grave robbing and her animal rites and transformations, how
stupid and poor her activities and aims! Where can pictures
more coarse and gross and debased be found than in books of
magic: they cannot even rouse horror except in the offended
eye.

Evil is dull, that is the worst of it, and black magic is the
dullest of all evils. . . . Only when the poor metamorphosed
Ass can find and eat of good Venus's roses may he be restored
again to his right form, and to the reassuring, purely human
world of love and music and poetry, reclaimed by the benign
sweetness of its petals and leaves from the subhuman mechanistic domain of evil.

And then, the rose of fire: that core of eternal radiance in
which Dante beheld the Beatific Vision; this rose still illuminates
the heart of Poets:

> '. . . From my little span
> I cry of Christ, Who is the ultimate Fire
> Who will burn away the cold in the heart of Man. . . .'
> Springs come, springs go. . . .
> 'I was reddere on Rode than the Rose in the rayne.'
> 'This smel is Crist, clepid the plantynge of the Rose in Jerico.'
>   (Edith Sitwell, "The Canticle of the Rose")

And:

> All shall be well and
> All manner of thing shall be well
> When the tongues of flame are in-folded
> Into the crowned knot of fire
> And the fire and the rose are one.
>   (T. S. Eliot, "Little Gidding")

※

A NOTE ON PIERRE-JOSEPH REDOUTÉ
(1750-1840)

For the reproductions of his water colors, he invented
a process of printing in colors which he never consented
to perfect to the point where it would be completely
mechanical. Each one of these prints had further to be
retouched by hand. They owe to these light but indispensable retouchings the capricious illusion and movement of life—a life prolonged beyond its term. In effect,
the greater part of the roses who posed for Redouté no
longer exist today, in nature. Rosarians are not conserva-
tors. They have come to create a race of roses, they do
not care whether they shall endure, but only that they,
the creators, shall give shape to a new race. So the old
species disappear little by little; or if they survive, it is
not in famous rosaries, which disdain them, but in old
gardens, scattered, forgotten, where there is no concern
for fashions in flowers.—Jean-Louis Vaudoyer: *Les Roses
de Bagatelle*.

Here is an eye-witness description of Pierre-Joseph Redouté:
"A short thick body, with the members of an elephant, a face
heavy and flat as a Holland cheese, thick lips, a dull voice,
crooked fat fingers, a repellent aspect altogether; and under
this rind, an extreme fineness of tact, exquisite taste, a profound
sense of the arts, great delicacy of feeling, with the elevation
of character and constancy in his work necessary to develop
his genius: such was Redouté, the painter of flowers, who had
as his students all the pretty women in Paris." This is by
Joseph-François Grillé, a lively gossip in his day.

A writer of our own time, looking at Redouté's portraits, by
Gérard and others, concludes: "In spite of the solid redingote,
the ample cravat and the standing collar of the bourgeois, his

portraits make one think of some old gardener weathered and wrinkled like a winter apple."

Dear me: I have seen only the engraving after a painting by Gérard, and can find nothing at all strange, much less monstrous, in it. He seems a man of moderate build, in the becoming dress of his age, though plainer than most; with a very good face indeed with rather blunt features, and pleasant, candid, attentive eyes. Perhaps Gérard loved the man who lived inside that unpromising but useful rind, and showed him as he really was.

He was born in Saint-Hubert, Belgium, the son and grandson of artisan-painters, decorators of churches and municipal buildings. His two brothers became also painter-decorators. In the hardy fashion of the times, after a solid apprenticeship to his father, at the age of thirteen he was turned out in the world to make his own way. Dreaming of fame, riches, glory, he roamed all Belgium and Flanders looking for jobs and starving by the way. He took a year of hard work at Liège in the ateliers of famous painters and was sent to Luxembourg to paint portraits of his first royalties, the Princess de Tornaco and others. The Princess was so pleased with his work she gave him letters to present to certain persons of quality residing in Versailles.

In Flanders he studied deeply the painters of the ancient Flemish school. After ten years of this laborious apprenticeship, he joined his elder brother Antoine-Ferdinand in Paris; Antoine-Ferdinand had all that time been unadventurously earning a good living as painter-decorator. Pierre-Joseph helped his brother decorate the Italian Theater, and painted flowers wherever he was allowed. He learned the art of engraving, and he managed to get into the King's Garden, a botanical wonder, in that time, of royal and noble gardens, in order to study, draw and paint plants and flowers. There he met Charles-Louis

L'Héritier of Belgium, a man of great wealth, an impassioned botanist and adherent of the classical methods of Linnaeus.

From this time Redouté's history is the straight road to fame, fortune, and the happy life of a man capable of total constancy to his own gifts; who had the great good fortune to be born at the right hour in time, in the right place, and with the pure instinct which led him infallibly to the place where he could flourish and the people who needed and wanted precisely the thing that he could do. The rage for botanical gardening which had been growing for nearly two centuries had reached its climax. Only the royal, the noble, only the newly rich could afford these extravagant collections of rare shrubs, trees, flowers. There were no more simple adorers of flowers, but collectors of rarities and amateur botanists. It was an age of nature lovers, whose true god was science. Redouté was a botanist and a scientist, a decorator with a superior talent for painting. He stepped into the whole company of such combination scientists and decorator-artisans which surrounded and lived by the bounty of rich amateurs. Armed with brush, pencil, microscope, copper plates, stains, colors and acids, they adhered mightily and single-mindedly to their sources of benefits—intellectual bees, they were. Nothing could have been more touching than their indifference to social significance: they hadn't got the faintest notion where the times were driving them, or why; theirs only to pursue their personal passions and pleasures with scientific concentration, theirs to invent new processes of engraving, coloring, more exact representations of the subject in hand. The gardeners were concerned only to invent new roses, the botanists to botanize them, the artist-artisans to anatomize and engrave them. They were good workmen to whom the employment and not the employer was important.

It is astonishing how a world may turn over, and a whole society fall into ruin, and yet there is always a large population which survives, and hardly knows what has happened; indeed, can with all good faith write as a student in Paris did to his anxious father in Bordeaux, at the very height of the troubles of 1792: "All is quiet here," he declared, mentioning casually an execution or so. Later, he gave most painful descriptions of seeing, at every step in the street, the hideous bleeding rags of corpses piled up, uncovered; once he saw seven tumbrils of them being hauled away, the wheels leaving long tracks of blood. Yet there was dancing in the streets (he did not like to dance), bonfires at the slightest pretext (he hated bonfires), and all public places of entertainment were going at full speed. A craze for a new game called Coblentz, later Yo-yo, came to the point that everybody played it no matter where, all the time. When the King was beheaded, in January 1793, Mercier tells how people rushed to dip handkerchiefs, feathers, bits of paper in his blood, like human hyenas: one man dipped his finger in it, tasted it, and said: "It's beastly salty!" (*Il est bougrement salé!*) Yet no doubt there were whole streets and sections where no terror came. Our student, an ardent Republican and stern moralist, got his four years of tutoring and college, exactly as planned. The Collège de France opened its doors promptly every autumn the whole time he was there.

Redouté, in the center of the royal family, as private painting teacher to the Queen, later appointed as "Designer of the Royal Academy of Sciences," designer in Marie Antoinette's own Cabinet, seemed destined to go almost as untouched by political disasters as the student writing to his father. On the very eve of the revolution, he was called before the royal family in the Temple, to watch the unfolding of a particularly ephemeral cactus bloom, and to paint it at its several stages.

When the Queen was put to death in October 1793, it was David, patriot-painter, who made the terrible little sketch of her in the cart on her way to the scaffold: a sunken-faced old woman with chopped-off hair, the dress of a fishwife, hands bound behind her, eyes closed: but her head carried as high, her spine as straight, as if she were on her throne. We see for the first time

clearly the long curved masculine-looking nose, the brutal Haps-
burg jaw. But something else that perhaps David did not mean
to show comes through his sparse strokes: as if all the elements
of her character in life had been transmuted in the hour of her
death—stubbornness to strength, arrogance to dignity, recklessness to courage, frivolity to tragedy. It is wonderful what strange
amends David, moved by hatred, made to his victim.*

Her friendly, but preoccupied, painter-decorator happened to
be in England with L'Héritier, who had done some very fancy
work indeed getting away with a treasure of botanical specimens
against a capricious government order. The two sat poring over
their precious loot in perfect peace while France was being put
together again. They returned, and went on with their work under
the National Convention, which took great pride in the embellish-
ment of the King's Garden, re-named the Garden of Natural
History. (By 1823, after four overturns of the French government, this garden settled down for a good while under the name
of the Museum of Natural History of the King's Garden.)

Josephine Bonaparte of course had the most lavish, extravagant
collection of rare plants, trees, and flowers at Malmaison, and
Redouté became her faithful right hand as painter, decorator,
straight through her career as Empress, and until her death. In
the meantime he was teacher of painting to Empress Marie-
Louise; went on to receive a gold medal from the hand of
Louis XVIII for his invention of color printing from a single
plate; the ribbon of the Legion of Honor was bestowed upon
him by Charles X, in 1825; he painted the portrait of the rose
named for Queen Marie Amélie; and lived to see his adored
pupil Princess Marie-Louise, elder daughter of Louis-Philippe,
become Queen of the Belgians.

---

* In 1790, the Queen's lover, Count Fersen, wrote to his sister: "She
is an angel of courage, of conduct, of sensibility: no one ever knew how
to love as she does." He had known her since they were both eighteen
years old, and had been her lover for more than five years. He had himself
all the qualities he found in her, and more.

During one upset or another, his beautiful house and garden at Fleury-sous-Meudon, were almost destroyed; he seems to have invested all the handsome fortune he had made in this place. Yet he simply moved into Paris with his family and went on working. In 1830 again there were the crowds milling savagely in the gardens of the Royal Palace, this time roaring: "Long live the Charter. Down with Charles X! Down with the Bourbons!" Charles went down and Louis-Philippe came in, the last king Redouté was to see. While royal figures came and went in the Tuileries, "that inn for crowned transients," as Béranger remarked, the painters Gérard, Isabey, and Redouté remained a part of the furniture of the Crown, no matter who wore it.

Such a charmed life! Only one of that huge company of men living in the tranced reality of science and art, was for a moment in danger. L'Héritier almost got his head cut off during the first revolution; in 1805 he was killed in the street near his own door—I have seen no account which says why. Did even those who murdered him know why they did it? Did L'Héritier himself know?

The story of Redouté's labors, his teaching, painting, engraving, his valuable discoveries in methods of engraving, coloring plates, and printing, is overwhelming. He worked as he breathed, with such facility, fertility of resources, and abundant energy, he was the wonder of his colleagues, themselves good masters of the long hard day's work. Redouté is said to have painted more than one thousand pictures of roses alone, many of them now vanished; it is on these strange, beautiful portrait-anatomies that his popular fame endures. He loved fame, and was honestly eager for praise, like a good child; but he took no short cuts to gain them, nor any unworthy method. When he invented a certain process of printing in colors, he saw its danger, and stopped short of perfecting it; he did not want any work to become altogether mechanical. All his prints made by this process required to be retouched by hand, for as a good artist he understood, indeed had learned from nature itself, the divine law of uniqueness: that no two leaves on the same tree are ever exactly alike.

His life had classical shape and symmetry. It began with sound gifts in poverty, labor and high human aspirations, rose to honestly won fame and wealth, with much love, too, and admiration without envy from his fellow artists and his students. It went on to very old age in losses and poverty again, with several friends and a royalty or two making ineffectual gestures toward his relief. But then, his friends, both artist and royal, were seeing hard times too. On the day of his death he received a student for a lesson. The student brought him a lily, and he died holding it.

1950

Portrait: Old South

❊

I am the grandchild of a lost War, and I have blood-knowledge of what life can be in a defeated country on the bare bones of privation. The older people in my family used to tell such amusing little stories about it. One time, several years after the War ended, two small brothers (one of them was my father) set out by themselves on foot from their new home in south Texas, and when neighbors picked them up three miles from home, hundreds of miles from their goal, and asked them where they thought they were going, they answered confidently, "To Louisiana, to eat sugar cane," for they hadn't tasted sugar for months and remembered the happy times in my grandmother's cane fields there.

Does anyone remember the excitement when for a few months we had rationed coffee? In my grandmother's day, in Texas, everybody seemed to remember that man who had a way of showing up with a dozen grains of real coffee in his hand, which he exchanged for a month's supply of corn meal. My grandmother parched a mixture of sweet potato and dried corn until it was black, ground it up and boiled it, because her family couldn't get over its yearning for a dark hot drink in the mornings. But she would never allow them to call it coffee. It was known as That Brew. Bread was a question, too. Wheat flour, during the period euphemistically described as Reconstruction, ran about $100 a barrel. Naturally my family ate corn bread, day in, day out, for years. Finally Hard Times eased up a little, and they had hot biscuits, nearly all they could eat, once a week for Sunday breakfast. My father never forgot the taste of those biscuits, the big, crusty tender kind made with butter-milk and soda, with melted butter and honey, every blessed Sunday that came. "They almost made a Christian of me," he said.

My grandfather, a soldier, toward the end of the War was riding along one very cold morning, and he saw, out of all reason, a fine big thick slice of raw bacon rind lying beside the road. He dismounted, picked it up, dusted it off and made a hearty breakfast of it. "The best piece of bacon rind I ever ate in my life," said my grandfather. These little yarns are the first that come to mind out of hundreds; they were the merest sur-face ripples over limitless deeps of bitter memory. My elders all remained nobly unreconstructed to their last moments, and my feet rest firmly on this rock of their strength to this day.

The woman who made That Brew and the soldier who ate the bacon rind had been bride and groom in a Kentucky wedding somewhere around 1850. Only a few years ago a cousin of mine showed me a letter from a lady then rising ninety-five who remembered that wedding as if it had been only yesterday. She was one of the flower girls, carrying a gilded basket of white roses and ferns, tied with white watered-silk ribbon. She couldn't remember whether the bride's skirt had been twenty-five feet or twenty-five yards around, but she inclined to the latter figure; it was of white satin brocade with slippers to match.

The flower girl was allowed a glimpse of the table set for the bridal banquet. There were silver branched candlesticks every-where, each holding seven white candles, and a crystal chan-delier holding fifty white candles, all lighted. There was a white lace tablecloth reaching to the floor all around, over white satin. The wedding cake was tall as the flower girl and of astonishing circumference, festooned all over with white sugar roses and green leaves, actual live rose leaves. The room, she wrote, was a perfect bower of southern smilax and white dogwood. And there was butter. This is a bizarre note, but there was an enormous silver butter dish, *with feet* (italics mine), containing at least ten pounds of butter. The dish had cupids and some sort of fruit around the rim, and the butter was molded or carved, to resemble a set-piece of roses and lilies, every petal and leaf standing out sharply, natural as life. The flower girl, after the lapse of nearly a century, remembered no more than this, but I think it does well for a glimpse.

That butter. She couldn't get over it, and neither can I. It seems as late-Roman and decadent as anything ever thought up in Hollywood. Her memory came back with a rush when she thought of the food. All the children had their own table in a small parlor, and ate just what the grownups had: Kentucky ham, roast turkey, partridges in wine jelly, fried chicken, dove pie, half a dozen sweet and hot sauces, peach pickle, watermelon pickle and spiced mangoes. A dozen different fruits, four kinds of cake and at last a chilled custard in tall glasses with whipped cream capped by a brandied cherry. She lived to boast of it, and she lived along with other guests of that feast to eat corn pone and bacon fat, and yes, to be proud of that also. Why not? She was in the best of company, and quite a large gathering too.

In my childhood we ate, my father remarked, "as if there were no God." By then my grandmother, her brocaded wedding gown cut up and made over to the last scrap for a dozen later brides in the connection, had become such a famous cook it was mentioned in her funeral eulogies. There was nobody like her for getting up a party, for the idea of food was inseparably connected in her mind with social occasions of a delightful nature, and though she loved to celebrate birthdays and holidays, still any day was quite good enough to her. Several venerable old gentlemen, lifelong friends of my grandmother, sat down, pen in hand, after her death and out of their grateful recollection of her bountiful hospitality—their very words—wrote long accounts of her life and works for the local

newspapers of their several communities, and each declared
that at one time or another he had eaten the best dinner of his
life at her table. The furnishings of her table were just what
were left over from times past, good and bad; a mixture of thin
old silver and bone-handled knives, delicate porcelain, treasured
but not hoarded, and such crockery as she had been able to
replace with; fine old linen worn thin and mended, and stout
cotton napery with fringed borders; no silver candlesticks at
all, and a pound of sweet butter with a bouquet of roses stamped
upon it, in a plain dish—plain for the times; it was really a
large opal-glass hen seated on a woven nest, rearing aloft her
scarlet comb and beady eye.

Grandmother was by nature lavish, she loved leisure and calm,
she loved luxury, she loved dress and adornment, she loved to
sit and talk with friends or listen to music; she did not in the
least like pinching or saving and mending and making things
do, and she had no patience with the kind of slackness that
tried to say second-best was best, or half good enough. But the
evil turn of fortune in her life tapped the bottomless reserves
of her character, and her life was truly heroic. She had no such
romantic notion of herself. The long difficulties of her life she
regarded as temporary, an unnatural interruption to her normal
fate, which required simply firmness, a good deal of will-power
and energy and the proper aims to re-establish finally once
more. That no such change took place during her long life did
not in the least disturb her theory. Though we had no money
and no prospects of any, and were land-poor in the most typical
way, we never really faced this fact as long as our grandmother
lived because she would not hear of such a thing. We had been
a good old family of solid wealth and property in Kentucky,
Louisiana and Virginia, and we remained that in Texas, even
though due to a temporary decline for the most honorable reasons, appearances were entirely to the contrary. This accounted

for our fragmentary, but strangely useless and ornamental education, appropriate to our history and our station in life, neither
of which could be in the least altered by the accident of straitened
circumstances.

Grandmother had been an unusually attractive young woman,
and she carried herself with the graceful confidence of a natural
charmer to her last day. Her mirror did not deceive her, she
saw that she was old. Her youthful confidence became matri-
archal authority, a little way of knowing best about almost
everything, of relying upon her own experience for sole guide,
and I think now she had earned her power fairly. Her bountiful
hospitality represented only one of her victories of intelligence
and feeling over the stubborn difficulties of life. Her mind and
her instinct ran in flashes of perception, and she sometimes had
an airy, sharp, impatient way of speaking to those who didn't
keep up with her. She believed it was her duty to be a stern
methodical disciplinarian, and made a point of training us as
she had been trained even to forbidding us to cross our knees,
or to touch the back of our chair when we sat, or to speak
until we were spoken to: love's labors lost utterly, for she
had brought up a houseful of the worst spoiled children in
seven counties, and started in again hopefully with a long series
of motherless grandchildren—for the daughters of that after-
war generation did not survive so well as their mothers, they
died young in great numbers, leaving young husbands and children—who were to be the worst spoiled of any. She never
punished anyone until she was exasperated beyond all endurance, when she was apt to let fly with a lightning, long-armed
slap at the most unexpected moments, usually quite unjustly
and ineffectually.

Truth was, when she had brought her eleven children into
the world, she had had a natural expectation of at least as many
servants to help her bring them up; her gifts were social, and
she should never have had the care of children except in leisure,

for then she was delightful, and communicated some of her graces to them, and gave them beautiful memories. We loved the smell of her face powder and the light orange-flower perfume she wore, the crinkled waves of her hair, the knot speared through with a small pointed Spanish comb. We leaned upon her knee, and sniffed in the sweetness of her essential being, we nuzzled her face and the little bit of lace at her collar, enchanted with her sweetness.

Her hands were long since ruined, but she was proud of her narrow feet with their high insteps, and liked to dress them in smooth black kid boots with small spool-shaped heels. When she went "abroad"—that is, shopping, calling, or to church—she wore her original mourning gowns, of stiff, dull, corded silks, made over and refurbished from time to time, and a sweeping crape veil that fell from a peaked cap over her face and to the hem of her skirt in the back. This mourning had begun for her husband, dead only twenty-five years, but it went on for him, and for her daughters and for grandchildren, and cousins, and then brothers and sisters, and, I suspect, for an old friend or so. In this garb, holding up her skirt in front with one black-gloved hand, she would walk with such flying lightness her grandchild would maintain a heated trot to keep pace with her.

She loved to have us say our prayers before bedtime in a cluster around her knees, and in our jealousy to be nearest, and to be first, we often fell fighting like a den of bear cubs, instead of christened children, and she would have to come in among us like an animal trainer, the holy hour having gone quite literally to hell. "Birds in their little nests agree, and 'tis a shameful sight," she would remark on these occasions, but she never finished the rhyme, and for years I wondered why it was a shameful sight for little birds to agree, when Grandmother was rather severe with us about our quarreling. It was "vulgar," she said, and for her, that word connoted a peculiarly detestable form of immorality, that is to say, bad manners. Inappropriate conduct was bad manners, bad manners were bad morals, and bad morals led to bad manners, and there you were, ringed with fire, and no way out.

She was an individual being if ever I knew one, and yet she never did or said anything to make herself conspicuous; there are no strange stories to tell, no fantastic gestures. She rode horseback at a gallop until the year of her death, but it seemed only natural. Her sons had to restrain her from an engineering project, which seemed very simple to her and perhaps was really simple: she had wished to deflect the course of a small river which was encroaching on her land in Louisiana; she knew exactly how it should be done, and it would have made all the difference, she felt. She smoked cubeb cigarettes, for her throat, she would say, and add that she had always imagined she would enjoy the taste of tobacco. She and my father would sit down for a noggin of hot toddy together on cold evenings, or just a drop of good Bourbon before dinner because they enjoyed it. She could not endure to see a horse with its head strung up in a checkrein, and used to walk down a line of conveyances drawn up around the church, saying amiably to the dozing Negro drivers, "Good morning, Jerry; good morning, Uncle Squire," reaching up deftly and loosing the checkrein. The horses hung their heads and so did the drivers, and the reins stayed unfastened for that time, at any rate.

In a family full of willful eccentrics and headstrong characters and unpredictable histories, her presence was singularly free from peaks and edges and the kind of color that leaves a trail of family anecdotes. She left the lingering perfume and the airy shimmer of grace about her memory.

1944

Audubon's Happy Land

❋

The center of St. Francisville is ugly as only small towns trying frantically to provide gasoline and sandwiches to passing
motorists can be, but its lane-like streets unfold almost at once
into grace and goodness. On the day of our visit, the only sign
of special festivity was a splendid old Negro, in top hat, frock
coat with nosegay in buttonhole, a black cotton umbrella shad-
ing his venerable head, seated before the casually contrived
small office where we bought our tickets for the Audubon pilgrimage and were joined by our guide. The old Negro rose,
bowed, raised his hat at arm's length to an angle of forty-five
degrees more or less, playing his role in the ceremonies not
only as a detail of the scene, but as part also of its history. Our
guide appeared in a few minutes, tying a flowered kerchief
under her chin, *babushka* fashion, as she came. She was dark
and thin and soft-voiced, so typically Louisiana French that we
thought she must be from New Orleans, or the Bayou Teche
country. It turned out that she was from Idaho, lately married
to a cousin of the Percys at "Greenwood." No matter; she belonged also, by virtue of love and attachment, as well as appearance, to the scene and its history.

Saint Francis, who preached to the birds, and Audubon, who
painted them as no one before or since, are both commemorated
in this place. In 1779, the monks of Saint Francis founded the
town and christened it. Spain ruled the territory then, though
the brothers Le Moyne—Iberville and Bienville—had claimed it
three-quarters of a century before for France. The Spanish government made a classical error with the classical result. It in-

vited wealthy foreign investors to help settle the country, and the foreign investors ended by taking final possession. These particular foreigners bore such names as Ratliff, Barrow, Wade, Hamilton, Percy; they were all men of substance and of worldly mind, mostly from Virginia and the Carolinas, who obtained by Spanish grant splendid parcels of land of about twelve thousand acres each. These acres formed a subtropical jungle to the very banks of the Mississippi. A man could not, said an old woodsman, sink his hunting knife to the hilt in it anywhere.

The newcomers had on their side the strong arm of slave labor, and definite views on caste, property, morals, and manners. They pushed back the Louisiana jungle mile by mile, uncovered rich lands, and raised splendid crops. They built charming houses and filled them with furniture from France and England. Their silver and porcelain and linen were such as befitted their pride, which was high, and their tastes, which were delicate and expensive. Their daughters sang, danced, and played the harpsichord; their sons played the flute and fought duels; they collected libraries, they hunted and played chess, and spent the winter season in New Orleans. They traveled much in Europe, and brought back always more and more Old World plunder. Everywhere, with ceaseless, intensely personal concern, they thought, talked, and played politics.

In a few short years, these wealthy, nostalgic Americans were, in the phrase of the day, "groaning under the galling yoke of Spain." They forgathered evening after evening in one or another of their mansions and groaned; that is to say, discussed the matter with shrewdness, realism, and a keen eye to the possibilities. They called upon President Madison to lend a hand in taking this territory from Spain, which continued to hold it for some reason long after the Louisiana Purchase. "President Madison," says a local historian of that day, "remained deaf to their cries." The Feliciana planters then stopped crying, organized a small army, and marched on the Spanish capital, Baton Rouge. Harsh as it sounds in such a gentlemanly sort of argument, they caused the Spanish Commandant to be killed as proof of the seriousness of their intentions. They then declared for themselves the Independent Republic of West Florida, with St. Francisville as its capital. A certain Mr. Fulwar Skipwith was elected President. All was done in form, with a Constitution, a Body of Laws, and a flag designed for the occasion. The strategy was a brilliant success. President Madison sent friendly troops to annex the infant republic to the United States of America. This Graustarkian event took place in 1810.

The next year, a Roosevelt (Nicholas), partner in an Eastern steamship company, sent the first steamboat into the Mississippi, straight past St. Francisville and her sister town, Bayou Sara. The days of opulence and glory began in earnest, based solidly on land, money crops, and transportation, to flourish for just half a century.

It is quite finished as to opulence, and the glory is now a gentle aura, radiating not so much from the past as from the present, for St. Francisville lives with graceful competence on stored wealth that is not merely tangible. The legend has, in fact, magnified the opulence into something more than it really was, to the infinite damage of a particular truth: that wealth in the pre-War South was very modest by present standards, and it was not ostentatious, even then. The important thing to know about St. Francisville, as perhaps a typical survivor of that culture, is this: no one there tells you about steamboat wealth, or wears the air of poverty living on its memories, or (and this is the constant, rather tiresome accusation of busy, hasty observers) "yearns for the good old days."

The town's most treasured inhabitant was Audubon, and its happiest memory. This is no afterthought, based on his later reputation. And it is the more interesting when we consider what kind of reputation Audubon's was, almost to the end; nothing at all that a really materialistic society would take seriously. He was an artist, but not a fashionable one, never successful by any worldly standards; but the people of St. Francisville loved him, recognized him, took him to themselves when he was unknown and almost in despair. And now in every house, they will show you some small souvenir of him, some record that he was once a guest there. The Pirries, of New Orleans and Oakley, near St. Francisville, captured him in New Orleans at the moment when he was heading East, disheartened, and brought him to Oakley for the pleasant employment of teaching their young daughter, Miss Eliza, to dance and draw, of mornings. His afternoons, and some of his evenings, he spent in the Feliciana woods, and we know what he found there.

The Feliciana country is not a jungle now, nor has it been for a great while. The modest, occasional rises of earth, called hills, are covered with civilized little woods, fenced grazing-fields for fine cattle, thatches of sugar cane, of corn, and orchards. Both Felicianas, east and west, are so handsome and amiable you might mistake them for one, instead of twins. For fear they will be confounded in the stranger's eye, the boundaries are marked plainly along the highway. The difference was to me that West Feliciana was holding a spring festival in honor of Audubon, and I, a returned Southerner, in effect a tourist, went straight through East Feliciana, which had not invited visitors, to West Feliciana, which had.

You are to think of this landscape as an April garden, flowering with trees and shrubs of the elegant, difficult kind that live so securely in this climate: camellias, gardenias, crêpe myrtle, fine old-fashioned roses; with simpler things, honeysuckle, dogwood, wisteria, magnolia, bridal-wreath, oleander, redbud, leaving no fence or corner bare. The birds of Saint Francis and of Audubon fill the air with their light singing and their undisturbed flight. The great, dark oaks spread their immense branches fronded with moss; the camphor and cedar trees add their graceful shapes and their dry, spicy odors; and yes, just as you have been told, perhaps too often, there are the white, pillared houses seated in dignity, glimpsed first at a distance through their park-like gardens.

The celebrated oak *allées* are there at "Live Oak," at "Waverly," at "Rosedown," perhaps the finest grove of all at "Highland"—the wide, shaded driveways from the gate to the great door, all so appropriately designed for the ritual events of life, a wedding or a funeral procession, the christening party, the evening walks of betrothed lovers. W. B. Yeats causes one of his characters to reflect, in face of a grove of ancient trees, "that a man who planted trees, knowing that no descendant nearer than his great-grandson could stand under their shade, had a noble and generous confidence." That kind of confidence created this landscape, now as famous, as banal, if you like, as the horse-chestnuts along the Champs Elysées, as the perfume gardens of Grasse, as the canals of Venice, as the lilies-of-the-valley in the forest of Saint-Cloud. It possesses, too, the appeal of those much-visited scenes, and shares their nature, which is to demand nothing by way of arranged tribute; each newcomer may discover it for himself; but this landscape shares its peculiar treasure only with such as know there is something more here than mere hungry human pride in mahogany staircases and silver doorknobs. The real spirit of the place planted those oaks, and keeps them standing.

The first thing that might strike you is the simplicity, the comparative smallness of even the largest houses (in plain figures, "Greenwood" is one hundred feet square; there is a veranda one hundred and ten feet long at "The Myrtles," a long, narrow house), compared not only to the grandeur of their legend, but to anything of corresponding fame you may have seen, such as the princely houses of Florence or the Spanish palaces in Mexico, or, as a last resort, the Fifth Avenue museums of the fantastically rich of two or three generations ago. Their importance is of another kind—that of the oldest New York houses, or the Patrizieren houses in Basel; with a quality nearly akin to the Amalienburg in the forest near Munich, quite the loveliest house I ever saw, or expect to see. These St. Francisville houses are examples of pure domestic architecture, somehow urban in style, graceful, and differing from city houses in this particular, that they sit in landscapes designed to show them off; they are meant to be observed from every point of view. No two of them are alike, but they were all built to be lived in, by people who had a completely aristocratic sense of the house as a dwelling-place.

They are ample and their subtle proportions give them stateliness not accounted for in terms of actual size. They are placed in relation to the south wind and the morning sun. Their ceilings are high, because high ceilings are right for this kind of architecture, and this kind of architecture is right for a hot climate. Their fireplaces are beautiful, well placed, in harmony with the rooms, and meant for fine log fires in the brief winters. Their windows are many, tall and rightly spaced for light and air, as well as for the view outward. All of them, from "Live Oak," built in 1779, to "The Myrtles," built in the 1840's, have in common the beauty and stability of cypress, blue poplar, apparently indestructible brick made especially for the chimneys and foundations, old methods of mortising and pinning, handforged nails.

"Live Oak" stands on a green knoll, and, from the front door, one looks straight through the central room to the rolling meadow bordered with iris in profuse bloom. This house is really tired, worn down to the bare grain, the furniture just what might have been left from some remote disaster, but it is beautiful, a place to live in, with its wide, double porches and outside staircase in the early style of the Spanish in Louisiana, its dark paneling, and its air of gentle remoteness.

"Waverly" is another sort of thing altogether, a bright place full of color, where the old furniture is set off with gaily flowered rugs, and the heavy old Louisiana four-poster beds—of a kind to be found nowhere else—are dressed sprucely in fresh curtains. The white pillars of "Waverly" are flat and slender, and the graceful fan-lights of the front door are repeated on the second floor, with an especially airy effect. The vestiges of the old boxwood maze are being coaxed back to life there, and gardenias grow in hedges, as they should.

At "The Myrtles," the flowery iron grille of the long veranda sets the Victorian tone; the long dining-room still wears, between the thin moldings, its French wallpaper from 1840—sepia-colored panels from floor to ceiling of game birds and flowers. The cypress floor is honey-colored, the Italian marble mantel-piece was that day banked with branches of white dogwood. All the rooms are long, full of the softest light lying upon the smooth surfaces of old fruitwood and mahogany. From the back veranda, an old-fashioned back yard, full of country living, lay in the solid shade of grape arbors and trees rounded like baskets of flowers. Chickens roamed and picked there; there was a wood-pile with a great iron wash-pot up-ended against it, near the charred spot where the fire is still built to heat the water.

At "Virginia," we saw George Washington's account-book, made, I believe, at Valley Forge, with all the detailed outlay of that troublesome episode. "Virginia" is by way of being an inn now—that is to say, if travelers happen along they will be put up in tall, canopied beds under fine old quilted coverlets. The large silver spoons in the dining-room came from an ancestor of the Fisher family—Baron de Würmser, who had them as a gift from Frederick the Great. Generous-sized ladles they are, too, paper-thin and flexible. Like so many old coin silver spoons, they appear to have been chewed, and they have been. A thin silver spoon was once considered the ideal object for an infant to cut his teeth upon. But there were dents in a de Würmser soup ladle which testified that some Fisher infant must have been a saber-toothed tiger. "Surely no teething child did that," I remarked. "No," said the hostess, a fleeting shade of severity on her brow. "It was thrown out with the dish-water once, and the pigs got it." Here is the French passport for a Fisher grand-father, dated 1836. It was then he brought back the splendid flowered wallpaper, even now fresh in its discreet colors, the hand-painted mauve linen window-shades on rollers, then so fashionable, replacing the outmoded Venetian blinds; the ornate, almost morbidly feminine drawing-room chairs and sofas.

At "Greenwood," the host was engaged with a group of oil prospectors, for, beneath their charming, fruitful surfaces, the Felicianas are suspected of containing the dark, the sinister new treasure more powerful than gold. If so, what will become of the oaks and the flourishing fields and the gentle cattle? What will become of these lovely houses? "They make syrup and breed cattle here," said our guide; "that keeps 'Greenwood' going very well. Some people (she named them) wanted Mr. Percy to make a dude ranch of this place, but he wouldn't hear of it."

We mentioned our premonitions about St. Francisville if oil should be discovered. Our guide spoke up with the quiet reck-lessness of faith. "It wouldn't do any harm," she said. "The Feliciana people have had what money can buy, and they have something money can't buy, and they know it. They have nothing to sell. Tourists come here from all over and offer them thousands of dollars for their little things, just little things they don't need and hardly ever look at, but they won't sell them."

"Greenwood" is the typical Southern mansion of too many songs, too many stories—with the extravagant height of massive, round pillar, the too-high ceiling, the gleaming sweep of central hall, all in the 1830 Greek, gilded somewhat, but lightly. There is bareness; space dwarfing the human stature and breathing a faint bleakness. Yet the gentle groves and small hills are framed with overwhelming effect between those columns; effect grandi-ose beyond what the measuring eye knows is actually there.

It seems now that the builders should have known that this

house was the end, never the beginning. It is quite improbable that anyone should again build a house like "Greenwood" to live in. But there it is, with the huge beams of the gallery being replaced, oil prospectors roaming about, and the hostess sitting in her drawing-room with the green-and-gold chairs, the lace curtains fine as bride veils drifting a little; the young girls in jodhpurs are going out to ride. Here, as everywhere else, there were no radios or gramophones going, no telephones visible or ringing; and it seemed to me suddenly that this silence, the silence of a house in order, of people at home, the silence of leisure, is the most desirable of all things we have lost.

At "Highland," descendants in the fourth generation stand in the shade of the oaks planted, as the old House Book records, in January 1832. The house is older. It has its share of drum tables, fiddle-backed chairs, carved door-frames and wainscoting, but its real beauty lies in the fall of light into the ample, square rooms, the rise of the stair tread, the energy and firmness of its structure. The paneled doors swing on their hand-forged hinges as they did the day they were hung there; the edge of the first doorstep—an immense log of cypress square-hewn—is as sharp as though feet had not stepped back and forth over it for one hundred and forty years.

"Rosedown" is more formal, with its fish pool and eighteenth-century statuary set along the *allée*, and in a semicircle before the conventionally planted garden. The office still stands there, and the "slave bell" in its low wooden frame. The "slave bell" was the dinner-bell for the whole plantation. Above all, at "Rosedown," the Ancestors still rule, still lend their unquenchable life to a little world of fabulous old ladies and a strange overgrowth of knickknacks sprouting like small, harmless fungi on a tree-trunk. Their portraits—Sully seems to have been the preferred painter—smile at you, or turn their attentive heads toward one another; as handsome and as gallant and elegantly dressed a set of young men and women as you would be apt to find blood-kin under one roof. "My great-great-grandfather," said the old, old lady, smiling back again at the high-headed, smooth-cheeked young beau in the frilled shirt-bosom and deep blue, sloping-shouldered coat. His eyes are the same bright hazel as her own. This was the only house in which the past lay like a fine dust in the air.

Steamboats brought wealth and change to St. Francisville once, and oil may do it again. In that case, we are to suppose that new grand pianos would replace the old, square, black Steinways of 1840, as they had in turn replaced the harpsichords. There would be a great deal of shoring up, replacement, planting, pruning, and adding. There would be travel again, and humanistic education. The young people who went away cannot, alas, come back young, but the young there now would not have to go away.

And what else would happen to this place, so occupied, so self-sufficient, so reassuringly solid and breathing? St. Francisville is not a monument, nor a *décor*, nor a wailing-wall for mourners for the past. It is a living town, moving at its own pace in a familiar world. But it was comforting to take a last glance backward as we turned into the main highway, at Audubon's Happy Land, reflecting that, for the present, in the whole place, if you except the fruits of the earth and the picture postcards at "Rosedown," there was nothing, really nothing, for sale.

1939

A House of My Own

❋

Not long ago, my sister returned to me a bundle of my letters to her, dated from my nineteenth year. My life has been, to say the least, varied: I have lived in five countries and traveled in several more. But at recurring intervals I wrote, in all seriousness: "Next year I shall find a little house in the country and settle there." Meantime I was looking at little houses in the country, all sorts of houses in all sorts of countries.

I shopped with friends in Bucks County long before that place became the fashion. I chose a perfect old stone house and barn sitting on a hill there, renovated it splendidly, and left it forever, all in one fine June morning. In this snapshot style, I have also possessed beautiful old Texas ranch houses; a lovely little Georgian house in Alexandria, Virginia; an eighteenth-century Spanish-French house in Louisiana.

I have stood in a long daydream over an empty, roofless shell of white coral in Bermuda; in several parts of my native South, I admired and would have been glad to live in one of those little, sloping-roofed, chimneyed houses the Negroes live in, houses quite perfectly proportioned and with such dignity in their desolation. In Mexico, I have walked through empty, red-tiled houses, in their patios, and under their narrow, arched cloisters, living a lifetime there in a few hours. In Switzerland, my house was tall, steep-roofed, the very one I chose was built in 1390. It was still occupied, however, with lace curtains at the window and a cat asleep on the window sill. In France, it was a peasant house, standing flush to the village street, with a garden in back. Indeed, I have lived for a few hours in any number of the most lovely houses in the world.

There was never, of course, much money, never quite enough; there was never time, either; there was never permanency of any sort, except the permanency of hope.

This hope had led me to collect an unreasonable amount of furniture and books, unreasonable for one who had no house to keep them in. I lugged them all with me from Mexico to Paris to New York to Louisiana and back to New York, then stored them, and accepted an invitation to Yaddo, in Saratoga Springs. Yaddo invites artists with jobs to finish to come, and work quietly in peace and great comfort, during summers. My invitation was for two months. That was a year ago, and I am still here, seemingly having taken root at North Farm on the estate. Several times I went away for a few weeks, and when I returned, as the train left Albany, I began to have a sense of homecoming. One day, hardly knowing when it happened, I knew I was going to live here, for good and all, and I was going to have a house in the country. I began to move my personal equivalent of heaven and earth to make it possible. As travelers in Europe make it a point of *gourmandise* to drink the wine of the country, so I had always chosen the house of the country. Here, the house of the country is plain, somewhat prim, not large, late Colonial; perhaps modified Georgian would be a useful enough description.

Some friends recommended to me an honest man who knew every farm within miles around. "You can believe every word he says," they assured me. On the first of January, in zero weather and deep snow, I explained to him what I was looking for, and we started touring the countryside. My house must be near Saratoga Springs, my favorite small town of all America that I had seen.* It must be handsomely located in a good, but domestic landscape, with generous acres, well-watered and wooded, and it must not cost above a certain modest sum.

Nodding his head understandingly, he drove me at once sixty miles away into Vermont and showed me a nineteen-room

* That was *then!*

house on a rock-bound spot. He showed me, within the next eighteen days, every sort of house from pink brick mansions on a quarter acre to shingle camp bungalows in wild places far from human habitation. We slogged through snow to our knees to inspect Victorian Gothic edifices big enough to house a boarding school. We crept into desolate little shacks where snow and leaves were piled in the corners of the living-room.

Between each wild goose chase, I repeated, patiently and monotonously as a trained crow, my simple wants, my unalterable wishes. At last I reminded him that our friends had told me I could believe every word he said, but until he believed every word I said, too, we could make no progress whatever. And I said good-by, which seemed to make no impression. Two days later he called again and said perhaps he had a house for me, after all.

That was January 21, 1941. As our car turned into the road, a hen pheasant flew up and struck lightly against the radiator-cap and lost a few breast-feathers. With desperate superstition I got out and picked them up and put them in my handbag, saying they might bring me luck.

We drove for a few miles around Saratoga Lake, turned into an inclined road between a great preserve of spruce and pine, turned again to the right on a small rise, and my honest man pointed into the valley before us. I looked at an old Colonial house, rather small, modified Georgian, with a red roof and several cluttery small porches and sheds clinging to its sides. It sat there in a modest state, surrounded by tall, bare trees, against a small hill of evergreen.

"But that is my house," I told him. "That's mine."

We struggled around it again knee-deep in snowdrifts, peering through windows.

"Let's not bother," I said. "I'll take it."

"But you must see inside first," he insisted.

"I know what's inside," I said. "Let's go to see the owner."

The owner, a woman of perhaps fifty who looked incapable

of surprise, had to be told several times, in different phrases, that her house was sold at last, really sold. My honest man had had it on his list for seven long years. Her hopes were about exhausted. I gave him a look meant to be terrible, but he missed it, somehow.

She wanted to tell the history of her house. It was one of the first built in this part of the country, by first settlers, related to Benedict Arnold. It had been lived in since the day it was finished; her own family had been there for eighty-five years. She was the last of her immediate family. With a difficult tear, she said that she had buried all her nearest and dearest from that house; and living there alone as she had been, there were times in the winter evenings when it seemed they were all in the same room with her.

In no time at all, it seems now, the transaction was complete, and I was well seized of my property. I had always thought that was a mere picturesque phrase. It is simply a statement of fact. I am seized of my property, and my property is well seized of me. It is described as having one hundred and five acres of meadow and woodland, with two brooks, a spring, and an inexhaustible well. Besides all this, there are forty acres of molding sand, of which eighteen are under contract to a sand dealer. However, I should not mind this, as the land to be mined for sand lay far away; the operations would be conducted safely out of sight. Of this more later.

I remembered a remark of Mr. E. M. Forster on taking possession of his woods: the first thing he noticed was that his land made him feel heavy. I had become almost overnight a ton weight of moral, social, and financial responsibility, subject to state and county tax, school tax, and an astonishing variety of insurance. Besides the moral, legal, and financial aspects peculiar to myself, the affair had become a community interest. My new-found friends gave me any amount of advice, all seriously good. They were anxious about me. They told me how pleased they were I was going to live there. Other friends drove out to visit, inspect, and approve. My house was solid as a church, in foundation, beams, walls, and roof, and the cellar was an example to all cellars.

Friends came up in the spring from New York, strolled in the meadows, picked flowers, and advised me to practice virtue and circumspection in every act of my new life. There began arriving presents, such as five incredibly elegant very early Victorian chairs and settles, Bohemian mirror glass lamps with crystal-beaded shades, cranberry glass bowls.

My life began to shape itself to fit a neighborhood, and that neighborhood included everybody who came near my house or knew that I had got it. All this is strange new pleasure.

And almost at once I encountered some strange new troubles, oh, a sea of them, some of them surprising, yet once encountered, nothing that does not seem more or less in the natural order of being. For example, the inexhaustible well. It was that for a family who drew water by the pailful, but not enough for two little baths and a new kitchen. I went out the other day to look again at my lovely landscape and my beloved house, indeed I can hardly bear to stay away from them, and there were three strange men pulling up the pump, dropping plumb-lines into the well, and sinking points in the earth here and there. They had also with them a rosy-colored, forked, hazel wand, and they almost blushed their heads off when I knew what it was and asked them if it worked.

"Naw, it's all just a lot of nonsense," said the one who was trying to make it work. They all agreed there was nothing in it, but each of them knew several well-diggers who had seen it work or who could even work it themselves. "There are actually men," said one of them, "who just walk around holding it like this, and when he comes to where there is water, it turns and twists itself right out of his hands." But there wasn't anything to it, just the same, and just the same they never go to look for water without taking one along. They haven't found a well yet, but I do not let my mind dwell on this.

The sand man, thinking that the place was vacated and nobody would know or care, came and leveled over the entire slope of my east meadow within a few steps of the house, before I got into action and persuaded him he was, to say it mildly, not within his rights. There is a great and dreadful scar four feet deep and seventy-five feet long, where I had meant to plant the rose hedge, which must be filled in with tons of soil.

I have a tenant house, which a Southern friend described as something transplanted from *Tobacco Road*. Be that as it may. There are broad plans afoot for it, and I am looking for a tenant farmer. With this in view, I bought, of the best and sturdiest, the following implements: one metal rake, one wooden rake, one hoe, one ax (of the kind used by champion woodcutters in contests), one handsaw, one spading fork, one mattock, one spade, one brush hook, one snath and blade (medium), one wheelbarrow, one long, dangerous-looking scythe blade, one hammer, one ten-inch file, one grindstone, one four-gallon water-pail, and this is the merest beginning. But I have no tenant farmer.

There is a half-ton of old lumber thrown down on a bed of flowers whose name I do not know, but who were just getting ready to bloom. The sand men hacked a road through my pine woods, taking off great branches of fine trees. Contractors came and went in series. Through the years I have collected a small library of architectural magazines, photographs of old houses before and after, plans for remodeling, and a definite point of view of my own. The first man on the ground looked everything over, listened patiently to my plans and hopes, asked me, "Why take all that trouble for an old house?" and disappeared, never to be seen again. The second was magnificently sympathetic and competent, but he was used to building houses for the Whitneys and Vanderbilts and other racing people in Saratoga, and it was impossible to scale down his ideas.

Others went out, pried up the old random-width floors, tore chunks out of the plaster, knocked bricks out of the chimney, pumped out the well, tested beams, ripped slates off the roof, pulled down sheds and porches, and one by one disappeared. . . . I have a contractor, though. He is Swedish, he has been in this country seventeen years, he is an authority on American Colonial houses, and I decided he should do the work when he went through my house, looked around once, nodded his head, and remarked gently, "Ah, yes, I know just what is here." The house and the furniture are only about ten miles apart now. There remains nothing except to draw them together.

It seems a very long ten miles, perhaps the longest I shall ever travel. I am saving the pheasant feathers to burn, for luck, on the first fire I light in the fine old fireplace with its bake oven and graceful mantelpiece. It will be high time for fires again, no doubt, when I get there.

1941

Note, July 1952: I lived there just thirteen months.

The Necessary Enemy

❋

She is a frank, charming, fresh-hearted young woman who married for love. She and her husband are one of those gay, good-looking young pairs who ornament this modern scene rather more in profusion perhaps than ever before in our history. They are handsome, with a talent for finding their way in their world, they work at things that interest them, their tastes agree and their hopes. They intend in all good faith to spend their lives together, to have children and do well by them and each other—to be happy, in fact, which for them is the whole point of their marriage. And all in stride, keeping their wits about them. Nothing romantic, mind you; their feet are on the ground.

Unless they were this sort of person, there would be not much point to what I wish to say; for they would seem to be an example of the high-spirited, right-minded young whom the critics are always invoking to come forth and do their duty and practice all those sterling old-fashioned virtues which in every generation seem to be falling into disrepair. As for virtues, these young people are more or less on their own, like most of their kind; they get very little moral or other aid from their society; but after three years of marriage this very contemporary young woman finds herself facing the oldest and ugliest dilemma of marriage.

She is dismayed, horrified, full of guilt and forebodings because she is finding out little by little that she is capable of hating her husband, whom she loves faithfully. She can hate him at times as fiercely and mysteriously, indeed in terribly

179

much the same way, as often she hated her parents, her brothers
and sisters, whom she loves, when she was a child. Even then
it had seemed to her a kind of black treacherousness in her, her
private wickedness that, just the same, gave her her only private
life. That was one thing her parents never knew about her,
never seemed to suspect. For it was never given a name. They
did and said hateful things to her and to each other as if by
right, as if in them it was a kind of virtue. But when they said
to her, "Control your feelings," it was never when she was
amiable and obedient, only in the black times of her hate. So
it was her secret, a shameful one. When they punished her,
sometimes for the strangest reasons, it was, they said, only because they loved her—it was for her good. She did not believe
this, but she thought herself guilty of something worse than
ever they had punished her for. None of this really frightened
her: the real fright came when she discovered that at times her
father and mother hated each other; this was like standing on
the doorsill of a familiar room and seeing in a lightning flash
that the floor was gone, you were on the edge of a bottomless
pit. Sometimes she felt that both of them hated her, but that
passed, it was simply not a thing to be thought of, much less
believed. She thought she had outgrown all this, but here it was
again, an element in her own nature she could not control,
or feared she could not. She would have to hide from her
husband, if she could, the same spot in her feelings she had
hidden from her parents, and for the same no doubt disreputable,
selfish reason: she wants to keep his love.

Above all, she wants him to be absolutely confident that she
loves him, for that is the real truth, no matter how unreasonable
it sounds, and no matter how her own feelings betray them both
at times. She depends recklessly on his love; yet while she is
hating him, he might very well be hating her as much or even
more, and it would serve her right. But she does not want to
be served right, she wants to be loved and forgiven—that is, to
be sure he would forgive her anything, if he had any notion

of what she had done. But best of all she would like not to have anything in her love that should ask for forgiveness. She doesn't mean about their quarrels—they are not so bad. Her feelings are out of proportion, perhaps. She knows it is perfectly natural for people to disagree, have fits of temper, fight it out; they learn quite a lot about each other that way, and not all of it disappointing either. When it passes, her hatred seems quite unreal. It always did.

Love. We are early taught to say it. I love you. We are trained to the thought of it as if there were nothing else, or nothing else worth having without it, or nothing worth having which it could not bring with it. Love is taught, always by precept, sometimes by example. Then hate, which no one meant to teach us, comes of itself. It is true that if we say I love you, it may be received with doubt, for there are times when it is hard to believe. Say I hate you, and the one spoken to believes it instantly, once for all.

Say I love you a thousand times to that person afterward and mean it every time, and still it does not change the fact that once we said I hate you, and meant that too. It leaves a mark on that surface love had worn so smooth with its eternal caresses. Love must be learned, and learned again and again; there is no end to it. Hate needs no instruction, but waits only to be provoked . . . hate, the unspoken word, the unacknowledged presence in the house, that faint smell of brimstone among the roses, that invisible tongue-tripper, that unkempt finger in every pie, that sudden oh-so-curiously *chilling* look—could it be boredom?—on your dear one's features, making them quite ugly. Be careful: love, perfect love, is in danger.

If it is not perfect, it is not love, and if it is not love, it is bound to be hate sooner or later. This is perhaps a not too exaggerated statement of the extreme position of Romantic Love, more especially in America, where we are all brought up on it, whether we know it or not. Romantic Love is changeless, faithful, passionate, and its sole end is to render the two lovers happy. It has no obstacles save those provided by the hazards of fate (that is to say, society), and such sufferings as the lovers may cause each other are only another word for delight: exciting jealousies, thrilling uncertainties, the ritual dance of courtship within the charmed closed circle of their secret alliance; all *real* troubles come from without, they face them unitedly in perfect confidence. Marriage is not the end but only the beginning of true happiness, cloudless, changeless to the end. That the candidates for this blissful condition have never seen an example of it, nor ever knew anyone who had, makes no difference. That is the ideal and they will achieve it.

How did Romantic Love manage to get into marriage at last, where it was most certainly never intended to be? At its highest it was tragic: the love of Héloïse and Abélard. At its most graceful, it was the homage of the trouvère for his lady. In its most popular form, the adulterous strayings of solidly married couples who meant to stray for their own good reasons, but at the same time do nothing to upset the property settlements or the line of legitimacy; at its most trivial, the pretty trifling of shepherd and shepherdess.

This was generally condemned by church and state and a word of fear to honest wives whose mortal enemy it was. Love within the sober, sacred realities of marriage was a matter of personal luck, but in any case, private feelings were strictly a private affair having, at least in theory, no bearing whatever on the fixed practice of the rules of an institution never intended as a recreation ground for either sex. If the couple discharged their religious and social obligations, furnished forth a copious progeny, kept their troubles to themselves, maintained public civility and died under the same roof, even if not always on speaking terms, it was rightly regarded as a successful marriage. Apparently this testing ground was too severe for all but the stoutest spirits; it too was based on an ideal, as impossible in its way as the ideal Romantic Love. One good thing to be said for it is that society took responsibility for the conditions of marriage, and the sufferers within its bonds could always blame the system, not themselves. But Romantic Love crept into the marriage bed, very stealthily, by centuries, bringing its absurd notions about love as eternal springtime and marriage as a personal adventure meant to provide personal happiness. To a Western romantic such as I, though my views have been much modified by painful experience, it still seems to me a charming work of the human imagination, and it is a pity its central notion has been taken too literally and has hardened into a convention as cramping and enslaving as the older one. The refusal to acknowledge the evils in ourselves which therefore are implicit in any human situation is as extreme and unworkable a proposition as the doctrine of total depravity; but somewhere between them, or maybe beyond them, there does exist a possibility for reconciliation between our desires for impossible satisfactions and the simple unalterable fact that we also desire to be unhappy and that we create our own sufferings; and out of these sufferings we salvage our fragments of happiness.

Our young woman who has been taught that an important part of her human nature is not real because it makes trouble and interferes with her peace of mind and shakes her self-love, has been very badly taught; but she has arrived at a most important stage of her re-education. She is afraid her marriage is going to fail because she has not love enough to face its difficulties; and this because at times she feels a painful hostility toward her husband, and cannot admit its reality because such an admission would damage in her own eyes her view of what love should be, an absurd view, based on her vanity of power. Her hatred is real as her love is real, but her hatred has the advantage at present because it works on a blind instinctual level, it is lawless; and her love is subjected to a code of ideal conditions, impossible by their very nature of fulfillment, which prevents its free growth and deprives it of its right to recognize its human limitations and come to grips with them. Hatred is natural in a sense that love, as she conceives it, a young person brought up in the tradition of Romantic Love, is not natural at all. Yet it did not come by hazard, it is the very imperfect expression of the need of the human imagination to create beauty and harmony out of chaos, no matter how mistaken its notion of these things may be, nor how clumsy its methods. It has conjured love out of the air, and seeks to preserve it by incantations; when she spoke a vow to love and honor her husband until death, she did a very reckless thing, for it is not possible by an act of the will to fulfill such an engagement. But it was the necessary act of faith performed in defense of a mode of feeling, the statement of honorable intention to prac- tice as well as she is able the noble, acquired faculty of love, that very mysterious overtone to sex which is the best thing in it. Her hatred is part of it, the necessary enemy and ally.

1948

"*Marriage Is Belonging*"

❋

Having never written a word about marriage, so far as I remember,* and being now at the point where I have learned better than to have any theories about it, if I ever had; and believing as I do that most of the stuff written and talked about it is more or less nonsense; and having little hope that I shall add luster to the topic, it is only logical and natural that I should venture to write a few words on the subject.

My theme is marriage as the art of belonging—which should not be confused with possessing—all too often the art, or perhaps only the strategy, and a risky one, of surrendering gracefully with an air of pure disinterestedness as much of your living self as you can spare without incurring total extinction; in return for which you will, at least in theory, receive a more than compensatory share of another life, the life in fact presumably dearest to you, equally whittled down in your favor to the barest margin of survival. This arrangement with variations to suit the circumstances is of course the basis of many contracts besides that of marriage; but nowhere more than in marriage does the real good of the relationship depend on intangibles not named in the bond.

The trouble with me is—always was—that if you say "marriage" to me, instantly the word translates itself into "love," for only in such terms can I grasp the idea at all, or make any sense of it. The two are hopelessly associated, or rather identified, in my mind; that is to say, love is the only excuse for marriage, if any excuse is necessary. I often feel one should be offered. Love without marriage can sometimes be very awkward for all concerned;

* See preceding. So much for memory.

but marriage without love simply removes that institution from the territory of the humanly admissible, to my mind. Love is a state in which one lives who loves, and whoever loves has given himself away; love then, and not marriage, is belonging. Marriage is the public declaration of a man and a woman that they have formed a secret alliance, with the intention to belong to, and share with each other, a mystical estate; mystical exactly in the sense that the real experience cannot be communicated to others, nor explained even to oneself on rational grounds.

By love let me make it clear, I do not refer only to that ecstatic reciprocal cannibalism which goes popularly under the name, and which is indeed commonly one of the earliest biological symptoms (Boy Eats Girl and vice versa), for, like all truly mystical things, love is rooted deeply and rightly in this world and this flesh. This phase is natural, dangerous but not necessarily fatal; so remarkably educational it would be a great pity to miss it; further, of great importance, for the flesh in real love is one of the many bridges to the spirit; still, a phase only, which being passed is too often mistaken for the whole thing, and the end of it. This is an error based on lack of imagination, or the simple incapacity for further and deeper exploration of life, there being always on hand great numbers of people who are unwilling or unable to grow up, no matter what happens to them. It leads to early divorce, or worse. Like that young man whose downward career began with mere murder, this error can lead to infidelity, lying, eavesdropping, gambling, drinking, and finally to procrastination and incivility. These two last can easily have destroyed more marriages than any amount of murder, or even lying.

Let us recall a few generalities about marriage in its practical aspects which are common knowledge, such as: it is one of the most prevalent conditions of the human adult, heading the list of vital statistics, I believe. It has been made very easy to assume, and fairly easy in the legal sense, at least, to abandon; and it is famous for its random assortment of surprises of every kind—leaf-covered booby traps, spiders lurking in cups, pots of gold under rainbows, triplets, poltergeists in the stair closet, and flights of cupids lolling on the breakfast table—anything can happen. Every young married pair believes their marriage is going to be quite different from the others, and they are right—it always is. The task of regulating its unruly impulses is a thorn in the souls of theologians, its social needs and uses the insoluble riddle of law-makers. Through all ages known to man almost everybody, even those who wouldn't be seen dead wearing a wedding ring, have agreed that somehow, in some way, at some time or another, mar-riage has simply got to be made to work better than it does, or ever has, for that matter. Yet on the whole, my guess is that it works about as well as any other human institution, and rather better than a great many. The drawback is, it is the merciless revealer, the great white searchlight turned on the darkest places of human nature; it demands of all who enter it the two most diffi-cult achievements possible: that each must be honest with himself, and faithful to another. I am speaking here only of the internal reality of marriage, not its legal or even its social aspects.

In its present form it is comparatively modern. As an idea, it must have begun fairly soon after the human male discovered his highly important role in the bringing forth of young. For countless aeons, we are told by those who pretend to know, it was believed that the powers of generation were vested in women alone, people having never been very bright about sex, right from the start. When men at last discovered, who knows how? that they were fathers, their pride in their discovery must have been equaled only by their indignation at having worshiped women as vessels of the Great Mystery when all along they should have been worshiping themselves. Pride and wrath and no doubt the awful new problem of what to do with the children, which had never bothered them before, drove them on to an infinite number of complicated and contradictory steps toward getting human affairs on a sounder basis. And, after all this time (skipping lightly over the first few hundred thousand years of total confusion), in our fine big new busy Western world, we have succeeded in establishing not only as the ideal, but in religious and legal fact (if not altogether in practice), as the very crown and glory of human ties, a one-man-one-woman-until-death sort of marriage, rivaling the swans for purity, with a ritual oath exchanged not only to stick to each other through thick and thin, to practice perfect fidelity, flawless forbearance, a modified bodily servitude, but to love each other dearly and kindly to the end.

All this is to be accomplished in a physical situation of the direst intimacy, in which all claims to the most ordinary privacy may be disregarded by either, or both. I shall not attempt to catalogue the daily accounting for acts, words, states of feeling and even thoughts, the perpetual balance and check between individual wills and points of view, the unbelievable amount of tact, intelligence, flexibility, generosity, and God knows what, it requires for two people to go on growing together and in the same directions instead of cracking up and falling apart.

Take the single point of fidelity: It is very hard to be entirely faithful, even to things, ideas, above all, persons one loves. There is no such thing as perfect faithfulness any more than there is perfect love or perfect beauty. But it is fun trying. And if I say faithfulness consists of a great many things beside the physical, never let it be dreamed that I hold with the shabby nonsense that physical infidelity is a mere peccadillo beneath the notice of en-lightened minds. Physical infidelity is the signal, the notice given, that all the fidelities are undermined. It is complete betrayal of the very principle on which love and marriage are based, and be-sides, a vulgar handing over of one's partner to public shame. It is exactly as stupid as that, to say nothing more.

Yet every day quite by the thousands delightfully honest young couples, promising, capable, sometimes gifted, but in no way superhuman, leap gaily into marriage—a condition which, for even reasonable success and happiness (both words seem rather trivial in this connection), would tax the virtues and resources and staying powers of a regiment of angels. But what else would you suggest that they do?

Then there come the children. Gladly, willingly (if you do not think so, I refer you to the birth records of this country for the past ten years. There haven't been so many young wives having so many babies so fast for at least four generations!) these pairs proceed to populate their houses, or flats—often very small flats, and mother with a job she means to keep, too—with perfect strangers, often hostile, whose habits even to the most adoring gaze are often messy and unattractive. They lie flat on their noses at first in what appears to be a drunken slumber, then flat on their backs kicking and screaming, demanding impossibilities in a foreign language. They are human nature in essence, without conscience, without pity, without love, without a trace of consideration for others, just one seething cauldron of primitive appetites and needs; and what do they really need? We are back where we started. They need love, first; without it everything worth saving is lost or damaged in them; and they have to be taught love, pity, conscience, courage—everything. And what becomes of them? If they are lucky, among all the million possibilities of their fates, along with the innumerable employments, careers, talents, ways of life, they will learn the nature of love, and they will marry and have children.

If this all sounds a little monotonous, and gregarious, well, sometimes it is, and most people like that sort of thing. They always have. It is hardly possible to exaggerate the need of a human being, not a madman, or a saint, or a beast, or a self-alienated genius who is all of these in one, and therefore the scapegoat for all the rest, to live at peace—and by peace I mean in reconciliation, not easy contentment—with another human being, and with that one in a group or society where he feels he belongs. The best, the very best, of all these relationships is that one in marriage between a man and a woman who are good lovers, good friends, and good parents; who belong to each other, and to their children, and whose children belong to them: that is the meaning of the blood tie that binds them, and may bind them sometimes to the bone. Children cut their teeth on their parents and their parents cut their wisdom teeth

on each other: that is what they are there for. It is never really
dull, and can sometimes be very memorably exciting for everybody. In any case, the blood-bond, however painful, is the condition of human life in this world, the absolute point of all de-
parture and return. The ancient biological laws are still in force,
the difference being merely in the way human beings regard them,
and though I am not one to say all change is progress, in this one
thing, a kind of freedom and ease of mind between men and
women in marriage—or at least the possibility of it, change has
been all for the better. At least they are able now to fight out
their differences on something nearer equal terms.

We have the bad habit, some of us, of looking back to a time—
almost any time will do—when society was stable and orderly,
family ties stronger and deeper, love more lasting and faithful,
and so on. Let me be your Cassandra prophesying after the fact,
and a long study of the documents in the case: it was never true,
that is, no truer than it is now. Above all, it was not true of
domestic life in the nineteenth century. Then, as now, it was just
as good in individual instances as the married pairs involved were
able to make it, privately, between themselves. The less attention
they paid to what they were expected to think and feel about marriage, and the more attention to each other as loved and loving,
the better they did, for themselves and for everybody. The laws
of public decorum were easy to observe, for they had another
and better understanding. The Victorian marriage feather bed
was in fact set upon the shaky foundation of the wavering human
heart, the inconsistent human mind, and was the roiling hotbed
of every dislocation and disorder not only in marriage but all
society, which we of the past two generations have lived through.
Yet in love—this is what I have been talking about all the time—
a certain number of well-endowed spirits, and there are surprisingly quite a lot of them in every generation, have always been
able to take their world in stride, to live and die together, and
to keep all their strange marriage vows not because they spoke

them, but because like centuries of lovers before them, they were prepared to live them in the first place.

Example: A certain woman was apparently a prisoner for life in several ways: already thirty-five or -six years old, supposed to be an incurable invalid, whose father had forbidden any of his children to marry; and above all, a poet at a time when literary women were regarded as monsters, almost. Yet she was able to write, in the first flush of a bride's joy: "He preferred . . . of free and deliberate choice, to be allowed to sit only an hour a day by my side, to the fulfillment of the brightest dream which should exclude me in any possible world."

This could be illusion, but the proof of reality came fifteen years later. Just after her death her husband wrote to a friend: "Then came what my heart will keep till I see her again and longer—the most perfect expression of her love to me within my whole knowledge of her. Always smilingly, and happily, and with a face like a girl's; and in a few minutes she died in my arms, her head on my cheek."

If you exclaim that this is not fair, for after all, these two were, of course, the Robert Brownings, I can only reply that it is because I sincerely believe they were not so very special that I cite them. Don't be thrown off by that lyrical nineteenth-century speech, nor their fearless confidence not only in their own feelings, but the sympathy of their friends; it is the kind of love that makes real marriage, and there is more of it in the world than you might think, though the ways of expressing it follow the fashions of the times; and we certainly do not find much trace of it in our contemporary literature. It is *very* old-style, and it was, long before the Brownings. It is new, too, it is the very newest thing, every day renewed in an endless series of those fortunate people who may not have one point in common with the Brownings except that they know, or are capable of learning, the nature of love, and of living by it.

1951

American Statement: 4 July 1942

❋

Since this war began I have felt sometimes that all our good words had been rather frayed out with constant repetition, as if they were talismans that needed only to be spoken against the evil and the evil would vanish; or they have been debased by the enemy, part of whose business is to disguise fascism in the language of democracy. And I have noticed that the people who are doing the work and the fighting and the dying, and those who are doing the talking, are not at all the same people.

By natural sympathy I belong with those who are not talking much at present, except in the simplest and straightest of terms, like the young Norwegian boy who escaped from Norway and joined the Canadian forces. When asked how he felt about Norway's fate, he could say only, "It is hard to explain how a man feels who has lost his country." I think he meant it was impossible; but he had a choice, to accept defeat or fight, and he made the choice, and that was his way of talking. There was the American boy going into the navy, who answered the same foolish question: "It's too serious a thing to be emotional about." And the young American wife who was one of the last civilians to escape, by very dangerous and exhausting ways, from a bombarded island where her husband was on active duty. She was expecting her first baby. "Oh yes, I had the baby," she said, matter-of-factly, "a fine healthy boy." And another girl, twenty-one years old, has a six-month-old girl baby and a husband who will be off to the army any day now. She wrote: "I'm glad I have that job. Her Daddy won't have to worry about us."

While the talkers have been lecturing us, saying the American people have been spoiled by too much prosperity and made slack of fiber by too much peace and freedom, and gloating rather over the painful times we are about to endure for our own good, I keep my mind firmly on these four young ones, not because they are exceptional but precisely because they are not. They come literally in regiments these days, though not all of them are in uniform, nor should be. They are the typical millions of young people in this country, and they have not been particularly softened by prosperity; they were brought up on the depression. They have not been carefully sheltered: most of them have worked for a living when they could find work, and an astonishing number of them have helped support their families. They do their jobs and pay their taxes and buy War Savings Stamps and contribute to the Red Cross and China Relief and Bundles for Britain and all the rest. They do the work in factories and offices and on farms. The girls knit and nurse and cook and are learning to replace the boys in skilled work in war production. The boys by the thousand are getting off to camp, carrying their little two-by-four suitcases or bundles. I think of this war in terms of these people, who are my kind of people; the war they are fighting is my war, and yes, it is hard to find exactly the right word to say to them. I wait to hear what they will have to say to the world when this war is won and over and they must begin their lives again in the country they have helped to save for democracy.

I wait for that with the most immense and deep longing and hope and belief in them.

In the meantime let us glance at that theory, always revived in the heat and excitement of war, that peace makes spirits slothful and bodies flabby. In this season, when Americans are celebrating the birthday of our Republic, its most important birthday since that first day of our hard-won beginnings, we might remember that the men who wrote the Constitution and compiled the Body of Liberties were agreed on the revolutionary theory that peace was a blessing to a country—one of the greatest blessings, and they were careful to leave recorded their opinions on this subject. And they were right. Peace is good, and the arts of peace, and its fruits. The freedom we may have only in peace is good. It was never true there was too much of either; the truth is, there was never enough, never rightly exercised, never deeply enough understood. But we have been making a fairly steady headway this century and a half in face of strong and determined opposition from enemies within as well as from without. We have had poverty in a country able to support in plenty more than twice its present population, yet by long effort we were arriving at an increasing standard of good living for greater and greater numbers of people. One of the prime aims of the democratic form of government was to create an economy in which all the people were to be allowed access to the means and materials of life, and to share fairly in the abundance of the earth. This has been the hardest fight of all, the bitterest, but the battle is by no means lost, and it is not ended, and it will be won in time.

Truth is, the value of peace to us was that it gave us time, and the right to fight for our liberties as a people, against our internal enemies, using those weapons provided for us within our own system of government; and the first result of war with an external enemy is that this right is suspended, and there is the danger that, even if the foreign war is won, the gains at home may be lost, and must be fought for all over again.

It has been the habit and the principle of this people to think in terms of peace, and perhaps to live in rather a too-optimistic faith that peace could be maintained when all the plainest signs pointed in the opposite direction; but they have fought their wars very well, and they will fight this one well, too. And it is no time to be losing our heads and saying, or thinking, that in the disciplines and the restrictions and the heavy taxes and the restraint on action necessary to concerted effort, we have already lost the freedoms we are supposed to be fighting for. If we lose the war, there will be nothing left to talk about; the blessed and sometimes abused American freedom of speech will have vanished with the rest. But we are not going to lose this war, and the people of this country are going to have the enormous privilege of another chance to make of their Republic what those men who won and founded it for us meant for it to be. We aren't going anywhere, that is one great thing. Every single soul of us is involved personally in this war; this is the last stand, and this is our territory. Here is the place and now is the time to put a stop, once and for all, to the stampede of the human race like terrorized cattle over one world frontier after another. We stay here.

And during this period of suspension of the humanities, in the midst of the outrage and the world horror staggering to the imagination, we might find it profitable to examine the true nature of our threatened liberties, and their political, legal, and social origins and meanings, and decide exactly what their value is, and where we should be without them. They were not accidental by any means; they are implicit in our theory of government, which was in turn based on humanistic concepts of the importance of the individual man and his rights in society. They are not mere ornaments on the façade, but are laid in the foundation stone of the structure, and they will last so long as the structure itself but no longer. They are not inalienable: the house was built with great labor and it is made with human hands; human hands can tear it down again, and will, if it is not well loved and defended. The first rule for any effective defense is: Know your enemies. Blind, fanatical patriotism which shouts and weeps is no good for this war. This is another kind of war altogether. I trust the quiet coldness of the experienced fighters, I like their knowing that words are wasted in this business.

The Future Is Now

❋

Not so long ago I was reading in a magazine with an enormous circulation some instructions as to how to behave if and when we see that flash brighter than the sun which means that the atom bomb has arrived. I read of course with the intense interest of one who has everything to learn on this subject; but at the end, the advice dwindled to this: the only real safety seems to lie in simply being somewhere else at the time, the farther away the better; the next best, failing access to deep shelters, bombproof cellars and all, is to get under a stout table—that is, just what you might do if someone were throwing bricks through your window and you were too nervous to throw them back.

This comic anticlimax to what I had been taking as a serious educational piece surprised me into real laughter, hearty and carefree. It is such a relief to be told the truth, or even just the facts, so pleasant not to be coddled with unreasonable hopes. That very evening I was drawn away from my work table to my fifth-story window by one of those shrill terror-screaming sirens which our excitement-loving city government used then to affect for so many occasions: A fire? Police chasing a gangster? Somebody being got to the hospital in a hurry? Some distinguished public guest being transferred from one point to another? Strange aircraft coming over, maybe? Under the lights of the corner crossing of the great avenue, a huge closed vehicle whizzed past, screaming. I never knew what it was, had not in fact expected to know; no one I could possibly ask would know. Now that we have bells clamoring away instead for such events, we all have one doubt less, if perhaps one expectancy more. The single siren's voice means to tell us only one thing.

But at that doubtful moment, framed in a lighted window level with mine in the apartment house across the street, I saw a young man in a white T-shirt and white shorts at work polishing a long, beautiful dark table top. It was obviously his own table in his own flat, and he was enjoying his occupation. He was bent over in perfect concentration, rubbing, sandpapering, running the flat of his palm over the surface, standing back now and then to get the sheen of light on the fine wood. I am sure he had not even raised his head at the noise of the siren, much less had he come to the window. I stood there admiring his workmanlike devotion to a good job worth doing, and there flashed through me one of those pure fallacies of feeling which suddenly overleap reason: surely all that effort and energy so irreproachably employed were not going to be wasted on a table that was to be used merely for crawling under at some unspecified date. Then why take all those pains to make it beautiful? Any sort of old board would do.

I was so shocked at this treachery of the lurking Foul Fiend (despair *is* a foul fiend, and this was despair) I stood a moment longer, looking out and around, trying to collect my feelings, trying to think a little. Two windows away and a floor down in the house across the street, a young woman was lolling in a deep chair, reading and eating fruit from a little basket. On the sidewalk, a boy and a girl dressed alike in checkerboard cotton shirts and skin-tight blue denims, a costume which displayed acutely the structural differences of their shapes, strolled along with their arms around each other. I believe this custom of lovers walking enwreathed in public was imported by our soldiers of the First World War from France, from Paris indeed. "You didn't see that sort of thing here before," certain members of the older generation were heard to remark quite often, in a tone of voice. Well, one sees quite a lot of it now, and it is a very pretty, reassuring sight. Other citizens of all sizes and kinds and ages were crossing back and forth; lights flashed red and green, punctually. Motors zoomed by, and over the great city—but where am I going? I never read other peoples' descriptions of great cities, more particularly if it is a great city I know. It doesn't belong here anyway, except that I had again that quieting sense of the continuity of human experience on this earth, its perpetual aspirations, set-backs, failures and re-beginnings in eternal hope; and that, with some appreciable differences of dress, customs and means of conveyance, so people have lived and moved in the cities they have built for more millennia than we are yet able to account for, and will no doubt build and live for as many more.

Why did this console me? I cannot say; my mind is of the sort that can often be soothed with large generalities of that nature. The silence of the spaces between the stars does not affright me, as it did Pascal, because I am unable to imagine it except poetically; and my awe is not for the silence and space of the endless universe but for the inspired imagination of man, who can think and feel so, and turn a phrase like that to communicate it to us. Then too, I like the kind of honesty and directness of the young soldier who lately answered someone who asked him if he knew what he was fighting for. "I sure do," he said, "I am fighting to live." And as for the future, I was once reading the first writings of a young girl, an apprentice author, who was quite impatient to get on with the business and find her way into print. There is very little one can say of use in such matters, but I advised her against haste—she could so easily regret it. "Give yourself time," I said, "the future will take care of itself." This opinionated young person looked down her little nose at me and said, "The future is now." She may have heard the phrase somewhere and liked it, or she may just have naturally belonged to that school of metaphysics; I am sure she was too young to have investigated the thought deeply. But maybe she was right and the future does arrive every day and it is all we have, from one second to the next.

So I glanced again at the young man at work, a proper-looking candidate for the armed services, and realized the plain, homely fact: he was not preparing a possible shelter, something to cower

under trembling; he was restoring a beautiful surface to put his
books and papers on, to serve his plates from, to hold his cocktail
tray and his lamp. He was full of the deep, right, instinctive,
human belief that he and the table were going to be around together for a long time. Even if he is off to the army next week,
it will be there when he gets back. At the very least, he is doing
something he feels is worth doing now, and that is no small thing.

At once the difficulty, and the hope, of our special time in this
world of Western Europe and America is that we have been
brought up for many generations in the belief, however tacit, that
all humanity was almost unanimously engaged in going forward,
naturally to better things and to higher reaches. Since the eight-
eenth century at least when the Encyclopedists seized upon the
Platonic theory that the highest pleasure of mankind was pursuit
of the good, the true, and the beautiful, progress, in precisely the
sense of perpetual, gradual amelioration of the hard human lot,
has been taught popularly not just as theory of possibility but as
an article of faith and the groundwork of a whole political doctrine. Mr. Toynbee has even simplified this view for us with picture diagrams of various sections of humanity, each in its own
cycle rising to its own height, struggling beautifully on from
craggy level to level, but always upward. Whole peoples are
arrested at certain points, and perish there, but others go on.
There is also the school of thought, Oriental and very ancient,
which gives to life the spiral shape, and the spiral moves by nature
upward. Even adherents of the circular or recurring-cycle school,
also ancient and honorable, somehow do finally allow that the
circle is a thread that spins itself out one layer above another,
so that even though it is perpetually at every moment passing
over a place it has been before, yet by its own width it will have
risen just so much higher.

These are admirable attempts to get a little meaning and order
into our view of our destiny, in that same spirit which moves the
artist to labor with his little handful of chaos, bringing it to co-

herency within a frame; but on the visible evidence we must admit that in human nature the spirit of contradiction more than holds its own. Mankind has always built a little more than he has hitherto been able or willing to destroy; got more children than he has been able to kill; invented more laws and customs than he had any intention of observing; founded more religions than he was able to practice or even to believe in; made in general many more promises than he could keep; and has been known more than once to commit suicide through mere fear of death. Now in our time, in his pride to explore his universe to its unimaginable limits and to exceed his possible powers, he has at last produced an embarrassing series of engines too powerful for their containers and too tricky for their mechanicians; millions of labor-saving gadgets which can be rendered totally useless by the mere failure of the public power plants, and has reduced himself to such helplessness that a dozen or less of the enemy could disable a whole city by throwing a few switches. This paradoxical creature has committed all these extravagances and created all these dangers and sufferings in a quest—we are told—for peace and security.

How much of this are we to believe, when with the pride of Lucifer, the recklessness of Icarus, the boldness of Prometheus and the intellectual curiosity of Adam and Eve (yes, intellectual; the serpent promised them wisdom if . . .) man has obviously outreached himself, to the point where he cannot understand his own science or control his own inventions. Indeed he has become as the gods, who have over and over again suffered defeat and downfall at the hands of their creatures. Having devised the most exquisite and instantaneous means of communication to all corners of the earth, for years upon years friends were unable even to get a postcard message to each other across national frontiers. The newspapers assure us that from the kitchen tap there flows a chemical, cheap and available, to make a bomb more disturbing to the imagination even than the one we so appallingly have; yet no machine has been invented to purify that water so that it will not spoil even the best tea or coffee. Or at any rate, it is not in use. We are the proud possessors of rocket bombs that go higher and farther and faster than any ever before, and there is some talk of a rocket ship shortly to take off for the moon. (My plan is to stow away.) We may indeed reach the moon some day, and I dare predict that will happen before we have devised a decent system of city garbage disposal.

This lunatic atom bomb has succeeded in rousing the people of all nations to the highest point of unanimous moral dudgeon; great numbers of persons are frightened who never really had much cause to be frightened before. This world has always been a desperately dangerous place to live for the greater part of the earth's inhabitants; it was, however reluctantly, endured as the natural state of affairs. Yet the invention of every new weapon of war has always been greeted with horror and righteous indignation, especially by those who failed to invent it, or who were threatened with it first . . . bows and arrows, stone cannon balls, gunpowder, flintlocks, pistols, the dumdum bullet, the Maxim silencer, the machine gun, poison gas, armored tanks, and on and on to the grand climax—if it should prove to be—of the experiment on Hiroshima. Nagasaki was bombed too, remember? Or were we already growing accustomed to the idea? And as for Hiroshima, surely it could not have been the notion of sudden death of others that shocked us? How could it be, when in two great wars within one generation we have become familiar with millions of shocking deaths, by sudden violence of most cruel devices, and by agonies prolonged for years in prisons and hospitals and concentration camps. We take with apparent calmness the news of the deaths of millions by flood, famine, plague—no, all the frontiers of danger are down now, no one is safe, no one, and that, alas, really means all of us. It is our own deaths we fear, and so let's out with it and give up our fine debauch of moralistic frenzy over Hiroshima. I fail entirely to see why it is more criminal to kill a few thousand persons in one instant than it is to kill the same number slowly over a given stretch of time. If I have a choice, I'd as lief be killed by an atom bomb as by a hand grenade or a flame thrower. If dropping the atom bomb is an immoral act, then the making of it was too; and writing of the formula was a crime, since those who wrote it must have known what such a contrivance was good for. So, morally speaking, the bomb is only a magnified hand grenade, and the crime, if crime it is, is still murder. It was never anything else. Our protocriminal then was the man who first struck fire from flint, for from that moment we have been coming steadily to this day and this weapon and this use of it. What would you have advised instead? That the human race should have gone on sitting in caves gnawing raw meat and beating each other over the head with the bones?

And yet it may be that what we have is a world not on the verge of flying apart, but an uncreated one—still in shapeless fragments waiting to be put together properly. I imagine that when we want something better, we may have it: at perhaps no greater price than we have already paid for the worse.

1950

MEXICAN

Notes on the Life and Death of a Hero*

❊

The author of *The Itching Parrot* was born November 15, 1776, in Mexico City, baptized the same day, in the parish church of Santa Cruz y Soledad, and christened José Joaquín Fernández de Lizárdi.

His parents were Creoles (Mexican-born Spaniards), vaguely of the upper middle class, claiming relationship with several great families. They were poor, she the daughter of a bookseller in Puebla, he a rather unsuccessful physician, a profession but lately separated from the trade of barber. They made an attempt to give their son the education proper to his birth, hoping to prepare him for the practice of law.

The child, who seems to have been precocious, willful, and somewhat unteachable, spent his childhood and early youth in an immensely Catholic, reactionary, socially timid, tight-minded atmosphere of genteel poverty and desperately contriving middle-class ambitions. Though his parents' heads were among the aristocracy, their feet threatened daily to slip into the dark wallow of the lower classes, and their son witnessed and recorded their gloomy struggle to gain enough wealth to make the worldly show that would prove their claim to good breeding. There was no other way of doing it. In Spain, as in Europe, scholarship might be made to serve as a second choice, but in Mexico there was no place for scholarship. The higher churchly honors were reserved for the rich and nobly born; as for the army, it offered for a young Mexican only the most ignoble end: a father could wield

* Preface to *The Itching Parrot* (*El Periquillo Sarmiento*), by J. J. Fernandez de Lizárdi. Translated from the Spanish by K.A.P. Copyright 1942 by Doubleday & Company, Inc.

as the last resort of authority the threat to send his son to be a soldier.

The outlook was pretty thin for such as our hero. But he was to prove extraordinarily a child of his time, and his subsequent career was not the result of any personal or family plan, but was quite literally created by a movement of history, a true world movement, in which he was caught up and spun about and flung down again. His life story cannot be separated in any particular from the history of the Mexican Revolutionary period. He was born at the peak of the Age of Reason, in the year that the thirteen states of North America declared themselves independent of England. When he was a year old, the United States government decreed religious freedom. In Mexico the Inquisition was still in power, and the Spanish clergy in that country had fallen into a state of corruption perhaps beyond anything known before or since. The viceregal court was composed entirely of Spanish nobles who lived in perpetual luxurious exile; the Indian people were their natural serfs, the mixed Indian and Spanish were slowly forming a new intractable, unpredictable race, and all were ruled extravagantly and unscrupulously by a long succession of viceroys so similar and so unremarkable it is not worth while to recall their names.

The French Revolution occurred when Lizárdi was about fourteen years old. At twenty, he was a student in the University of Mexico, College of San Ildefonso. It is not likely that any new-fangledness in social or political theory had yet managed to creep in there. There was very little thinking of any kind going on in Mexico at that time, but there were small, scattered, rapidly increasing groups of restless, inquiring minds, and whoever thought at all followed eagerly the path of new doctrines that ran straight from France. The air was full of mottoes, phrases, name-words for abstractions: Democracy, the Ideal Republic, the Rights of Man, Human Perfectibility, Liberty, Equality, Fraternity, Progress, Justice, and Humanity; and the new beliefs were based firmly on the premise that the first duty of man was to exercise freedom of conscience and his faculty of reason.

In Mexico as in many other parts of the world, it was dangerous to mention these ideas openly. All over the country there sprang up secret political societies, disguised as clubs for literary discussion; these throve for a good many years before discussion became planning, and planning led to action and so to revolution.

In 1798, his twenty-second year, Lizárdi left the university without taking his bachelor's degree, perhaps because of poverty, for his father died about this time, and there seems to have been nothing much by way of inheritance. Or maybe he was such a wild and careless student as he describes in *El Periquillo*. It is also possible that he was beginning to pick up an education from forbidden sources, such as Diderot, d'Alembert, Voltaire, Rousseau. At any rate, he never ceased to deplore the time he had spent at acquiring ornamental learning, a thing as useless to him, he said, as a gilded coach he could not afford to keep up. The fact seems to be, his failure was a hard blow to his pride and his hopes, and he never ceased either to bewail his ignorance. "To spout Latin is for a Spaniard the surest way to show off his learning," he commented bitterly, and himself spouted Latin all his life by way of example. In later days he professed to regret that his parents had not apprenticed him in an honest trade. However, there was no help for it, he must live by his wits or not at all.

After he left the university without the indispensable academic laurel that would have admitted him to the society of the respectably learned, he disappeared, probably penniless, for seven long years. These years of the locust afterwards were filled in suitably with legends of his personal exploits as a revolutionary. He was supposed to have known Morelos, and to have been in active service with the early insurgents. He says nothing of this in his own account of his life, written a great while afterwards: it is probable that he was a public scrivener in Acapulco. In 1805 he returned to Mexico City and married

Doña Dolores Orendain, who brought him a small dowry. As late as 1811 he appears to have been a Justice of the Peace in Taxco, when Morelos took that town from the Viceroy's troops, and was said to have delivered secretly a store of royalist arms and ammunition to Morelos. For this act he was supposed to have been arrested, taken to Mexico, tried and freed, on the plea that he had acted not of his own will but under threat of death from Morelos' insurgents.

The particularly unlikely part of this story is that the royalist officers would never have taken the trouble to escort Lizárdi, an obscure young traitor to the Spanish throne, all the way from Taxco to Mexico City for trial. It is still a long road, and was then a terrible journey of several days. They would have shot him then and there, without further ceremony. A more unlikely candidate than Lizárdi for gun-toting was never born. He shared with all other humanist reformers from Erasmus onward a hatred of war, above all, civil war, and his words on this subject read like paraphrases from Erasmus' own writings, as indeed many of them were. Lizárdi's services to his country were of quite another kind, and his recompense was meager to the last degree.

Just when those agile wits of his, which he meant to live by, first revealed themselves to him as intransigent and not for sale, it is difficult to discover. As late as 1811 he wrote a poem in praise of the Virgin of Guadalupe, who had protected the capital city and defeated by miracle the insurgent army led by Hidalgo. He wrote another entirely loyal and conventional poem to celebrate the accession of Philip VII to the Spanish throne. He belonged with the Liberal faction, that is, he opposed alike the excesses of the extreme insurgents and the depravities of the viceroys, he began by believing himself to be a citizen of the world, wrote against narrow patriotism, and refused to put himself at the service of any lesser cause than that of absolute morality, in every department of state and church. His literary career began so obscurely that it is difficult to trace its beginnings, but by 1811 he was writing and publishing, on various presses in Mexico City, a copious series of pamphlets, poems, fables, dialogues, all in the nature of moral lectures with rather abstract political overtones, designed to teach broadly social sanity, political purity, and Christian ethics. These were sold in the streets, along with a swarm of broadside, loose-leaf literature by every kind of pamphleteer from the most incendiary Mexican nationalist to the most draggletailed anonymous purveyors of slander and pornography.

A series of rapid events occurred which brought Lizárdi out into the open, decided the course of his beliefs and therefore of his acts, and started him once for all on his uncomfortable career as perpetual dissenter. In 1810 the Council of Cádiz decreed the freedom of the press, for Spain and her colonials. The Viceroy of Mexico, Xavier Vanegas, believed, with his overworked board of censors, that the Mexican press had already taken entirely too much freedom for itself. He suppressed the decree, by the simple means of refraining from publishing it.

By July 1811, the insurgent army under Hidalgo had been defeated, and late in that month the heads of Hidalgo and his fellow heroes, Aldama, Jimínez, and Allende, were hanging as public examples in iron cages at Guanajuato. The Empire was re-established, with Vanegas still Viceroy, and during that year and into the next, the censorship of the press became extremely severe. Every printer in Mexico was required to show a copy of every title he published, and among the items that showed up regularly were quite hundreds of flimsy little folders with such names as "The Truthful Parrot," in which a loquacious bird uttered the most subversive remarks in the popular argot of the lower classes, mixed freely with snatches of rhyme, puns in Mexican slang, and extremely daring double meanings. There were such titles as "The Dead Make No Complaints"; "The Cat's Testimony," a fable imitating La Fontaine; "It Is All Right to Cut the Hair But Don't Take the Hide Too," which

in Spanish contains a sly play on words impossible to translate;
"There Are Many Shepherds Who Shall Dance in Bethlehem,"
another punning title, meaning that many priests shall go to
Belén (Bethlehem), the great prison which exists still in Mexico
City; "Make Things So Clear That Even the Blind May See
Them"; "Even Though Robed in Silk, a Monkey Is Still a
Monkey"; "All Wool Is Hair," which has a most salty double
meaning; "The Nun's Bolero," concerning scandals in convents;
"The Dog in a Strange Neighborhood"; "The Devil's Penitents,"
—these were only a few of the provocations Lizárdi showered
upon the censors, the royalist party, the church, venal politicians
of all parties, social and political abuses of every kind. The
censors could hardly find a line that did not contain willful but
oblique offense, yet nothing concrete enough to pin the author down on a criminal charge, so the Council of Safety con-
tented itself with harrying him about somewhat, suppressing
his pamphlets from time to time, forbidding various presses to
publish for him, and threatening him occasionally with worse
things.

But it is plain that Lizárdi had discovered that he was, in particular, a Mexican, and a patriotic one, though still in general
a citizen of the world. It would seem that those truly heroic
heads of Father Hidalgo and the others in Guanajuato had
brought him down from the airy heights of abstract morality
to a solid and immediate field of battle. For, in June 1812, three
months before the new constitution took effect, Viceroy
Vanegas, who seems to have been a rather weak, shortsighted
man, alarmed by the continued rebelliousness of a people he
had believed he had conquered, took a fateful step. He issued an
edict condemning to death all churchmen of regular or secular
state who might take part in the revolution. This clause dealt
with those many priests who rose to take the place of Father
Hidalgo. All officers from the rank of sublieutenant upwards
were condemned to death. There were all over the country an
immense number of captainless men who went independently

into battle. These were to be decimated on the spot wherever captured. This last clause might seem to have covered the business; but the Viceroy added a final generous provision for wholesale slaughter. After such decimation, those who by chance had escaped death were, if convenient, to be sent to the Viceroy for suitable punishment. If this was not convenient, it was left to the discretion of each commandant to do with them as he saw fit.

So far, the edict was in its nature a fairly routine measure in times of emergency. But there was a further clause condemning to death all authors of incendiary gazettes, pamphlets or other printed matter. This was sensational, considering that unpublished decree granting freedom of the press. The liberal wing of the Constitutionalist (or royalist) party, together with all the forces that aimed for a peaceable settlement and some sort of compromise with the revolutionists, protested against this edict and advised the Viceroy seriously against such drastic means. The Viceroy did not cancel the edict, but as a sop to public opinion, he did publish the Cádiz decree on October 5, 1812, and the Mexican press, theoretically at least, was free.

Lizárdi was ready to take advantage of this freedom. He leaped into print just four days later with the first number of his first periodical, which had for title his own pen name, *The Mexican Thinker*. For two numbers he praised the glories of a free press and the wonders of liberty, but in the third he broke out in high style against the whole Spanish nation, its pride, its despotism; against the corruptions of the viceregal court, the infamies of officials in every station. Seeing that no revenge overtook him, he dared further in a later number: "There is no civilized nation which has a worse government than ours, and the worst in America, nor any other vassal country that has suffered more harshly in its arbitrary enslavement." He turned upon the Spanish governors the very words they had used against Hidalgo. "Cursed monsters," he wrote, and printed, and sold in the streets to be read by all, "you despots and the old evil government are responsible for the present insurrection, not as you say the Cura Hidalgo. It is you together who have stripped our fields, burned our villages, sacrificed our children and made a shambles of this continent."

It is worth noticing here that among his fellow pamphleteers, Lizárdi was famous for his moderate language and his courtesy in debate.

No consequences followed this wrathful page. Lizárdi went on safely enough until the ninth number, published on December 2, 1812. He devoted this number to an appeal to the Viceroy Vanegas to revoke at least that clause of the edict against revolutionaries which called for the trial of insurgent priests before a military court. He also wrote a personal letter to the Viceroy, timed the publication date to coincide with the Viceroy's Saint's Day, and appeared at court with a specially printed copy. With his own hands he delivered this little bombshell into the very hands of Vanegas, and received the viceregal thanks.

It is hardly probable that Vanegas troubled to examine the papers given him, but the Council of Safety, alarmed, informed him of its contents. The following day the Viceroy and his council suspended the freedom of the press, "for reason of the unsettled conditions of the country." They sent for Lizárdi's printer, manager of the Jáurigui press, who admitted that Lizárdi had written the offending article.

On the fifth of December they ordered Lizárdi to appear before the Court. He disappeared into ineffectual hiding in the house of a friend, Gabriel Gil, where, at three o'clock in the morning, December 7, he was seized and taken to prison. He wrote the story ten years later at great length, and he was still as indignant as he was the day it occurred, but he was proud, also, of the number of men who came to help with the arrest. There were more than seventy of the "dirty birds."

It must be remembered that, under the edict, Lizárdi was in danger of death. It would appear his jailors set out methodically to terrorize him, and they succeeded. It does not appear that his judges had any intention of sentencing him to death, but the whole proceedings had the air of making a stern example of troublesome scribblers. They put him in the death cell, where he passed a hideous night, expecting a priest to come to administer the last rites, expecting to be tortured, mistaking the rattle of the jailor's keys for chains. In the morning they took him before a judge he knew, and suspected of having headed the plot to imprison him, where he had to listen patiently to a great deal of foul insult and injury.

Lizárdi, in the speeches of his celebrated hero, El Periquillo, declared repeatedly that he feared physical violence more than anything else. The Periquillo is merry and shameless about it, for cowardice is possibly the most disgraceful trait known to man in Mexico, but his author did not find it amusing in himself. Later in his defense to the Viceroy he admitted quite simply that he had refused to obey the first summons to appear because he feared violence and not because he had a sense of guilt. His fears were reasonable. Worse had happened to other men for less cause, or at any rate for no more.

Still, when he gathered that harsh language was probably going to be the worst of it, and he was not going to be tortured and hanged, or at any rate, not that day, he recovered his spirits somewhat and took a rather bantering tone with his infuriated questioners. He was a tall, slender man of a naturally elegant manner, of the longheaded, well-featured Hidalgo kind; his portrait shows a mouth sensitive almost to weakness, and a fine alert picaresque eye. His judges, being also Spanish, and prone to judge a man's importance by his dress—a reflection of his financial state, which was in turn proof of his caste—were inclined to doubt he was so dangerous as they had thought, since Lizárdi at that moment was "emaciated, pallid, of shabby appearance," with his "black cloak smeared and crumpled from using it as a bed" in his cell; ten years after he remembered with regret that he had no time to clean it properly before having to show

himself. Lizárdi told them that indeed they were right, not he
but two ladies, one respectable, the other plebeian, had written
the articles. They insisted humorlessly that he explain himself.
He sobered down and confessed himself as the author. "The
respectable lady was the constitution of Cádiz, which allowed
him to write on political questions; the plebeian was his own
ignorance which had misled him into believing the Viceroy
would not be angered by a request to revoke an edict distaste-
ful to the people."

Their ferocity rose at this, they demanded an account of his
whole life, and pursued him with questions meant to trap him
until, seeing the affair still threatened to be serious, he grew
frightened again and implicated his friend, Gabriel Gil, as
well as Carlos María Bustamante, an active insurgent, and
writer, who had "warned him his life was in danger and advised him to leave the city."

Probably because of these interesting bits of evidence and
not, as Lizárdi boasted years afterwards, on account of his own
astuteness, for he certainly does not seem to have shown any,
the sentence of solitary confinement was lifted, he was re-
manded to the common jail among a number of his comrade
insurgent prisoners, and Gil was arrested.

Feeling himself betrayed by the man whom he had be-
friended at so much danger to himself, Gil said that Lizárdi
had come to him in distress, and that he, Gil, had done his
best to persuade him to obey the summons. Gil then went on
to make a bad matter worse by saying that Lizárdi had con-
fided that a certain friend had told him he could escape safely
with five hundred insurgents who were about to leave the city.

In panic, Lizárdi denied this and involved another friend,
Juan Olaeta, who had, Lizárdi said, offered to allow him to
escape with the insurgents. Olaeta, brought before the judges,
passed on the responsibility to an unnamed priest from Toluca,
who had overheard a conversation between two persons unknown to him, concerning the plans of five hundred insurgents

who were about to leave the city. Olaeta's part had been merely an offer to Lizárdi to take him to the priest. Lizárdi insisted to Olaeta's face that Olaeta had "told him the Tolucan priest would arrange for his escape with the insurgents. Olaeta insisted that Lizárdi had misunderstood him, and the two, together with Gabriel Gil, were sent back to jail." If they were in the same cell, it must have been a frightfully embarrassing situation for Lizárdi. And he was not done yet.

After nine days in prison, exhausted by repeated questioning and anxieties, he wrote a personal appeal to the Viceroy saying in effect and in short that he had acted innocently in handing him the protest against the edict and that before giving it he had shown it to a priest who approved of it, and by way of justifying himself further, he added with appalling lack of ethical sense that Carlos María Bustamante and a Doctor Peredo had "written with more hostility than he against the same edict." He continued to drag names into the business, adding that of a Señor Torres, and even blaming his error on them.

The first Judge advised the Viceroy to turn Lizárdi's case over to the Captain General and the Military Court. Lizárdi asked for bail which was his constitutional right, but it was refused. He was handed about from court to court, military and civil, for months, gradually modifying his statements, or retracting, or insisting that he had been misunderstood. Gil and Olaeta were freed, Bustamante, Torres and Peredo were never arrested at all, and Bustamante, an admirable and heroic spirit, never held any grudge against him, but wrote well of him afterwards. But Lizárdi lingered on in jail, writing to the Viceroy, asking for an attorney, asking that his case be turned over to the war department, being mysteriously blocked here and there by hostile agencies, and there he might have stayed on to the end if Vanegas had not been succeeded as Viceroy on March 4, 1813, by Calleja.

Lizárdi began a fresh barrage of importunities and explanations to this new, possibly more benign power. He praised him

for the good he hoped for from him, and published this praise
as a proclamation of the Thinker to the People of Mexico. This
got him no new friends anywhere and did not get him his
liberty either. He was allowed now and then to visit his family,
which consisted of his wife, a newly born daughter, and four
unnamed members which, dependent upon him, were almost
starving. He had supported them somewhat while in prison by
getting out number 10 and number 11 of *The Mexican Thinker*,
in December, and number 12 and number 13 in January, but in
a considerably chastened and cautious style.

One of its periodic plagues came upon Mexico City and raged
as usual, and the churches were crowded with people kissing
the statues and handing on the disease to each other. In one
number of *The Thinker*, Lizárdi advised them to clean up the
streets, to burn all refuse, to wash the clothes of the sick not
in the public fountains but in a separate place, not to bury the
dead in the churches, and as a final absurdity, considering the
time and place, he counselled them to use the large country
houses of the rich as hospitals for the poor. None of these things
was done, the plague raged on and raged itself out.

Lizárdi also wrote a statement of his quarrel with the existing state of politics, but a very discreet one, and he could think
of no better remedy, his own situation being still perilous as
it was, than that both sides in the struggle should obey the
counsels of Christ and love one another.

Naturally this sloppy thinking brought upon him the contempt of all sides. The royalists thought no better of him than
before, and the liberals, who favored the new constitution, now
distrusted him, as they had no intention of loving either an
out-and-out royalist or any insurgent, and as for the insurgents
themselves, they damned Lizárdi freely.

All this was going on, remember, while our hero was still in
prison.

In Mexico there was the celebrated "Society of Guadalupe,"
the most effective of such societies which, under cover of more

polite interests, were at the service of Morelos and kept him well informed of events in the capital. The new Viceroy, Calleja, proved to be an even more bitter enemy of the insurgents than Vanegas had been, and Lizárdi's unfortunate eulogy of Calleja had been sent to Morelos with a note by a member of the Society of Guadalupe. "This person," said the note, "is not worth your attention, because when they imprisoned him, he showed his weakness, and has written several pamphlets praising this damnable government, and has most basely harmed several men."

At last the Viceroy, finding no new things against Lizárdi, wearied of the case; the last judge who took it over recommended that Lizárdi be set free, and so he was, on July 1, 1813, after nearly seven months in prison. "Enough to ruin me, as I was ruined, with my family," he wrote.

This is the least handsome episode of Lizárdi's life, and he behaved like a green recruit stampeded under his first fire, who may yet become as good a soldier as any man. Lizárdi became a better soldier than most, and if he had been once afraid to die, he was not afraid to suffer a long, miserable existence for the sake of his beliefs. He was by no means ruined. He had scarcely been scotched. He returned to his dependents, his six-month-old daughter and the wife who had almost died at her birth, to a brazier without coals and a cupboard without food; and sat down at once to write indignantly against all the causes of misery and the effects of injustice in this maddening world.

The Holy Office of the Inquisition had recently been abolished by decree. Lizárdi, with that unbelievable speed of his, wrote a history of that institution, a very bitter history, and he rejoiced over its downfall. He published it on September 30, 1813, as a number of *The Thinker*, and went on with his many projects for local reforms, not attacking the government except by indirection. He wrote against ignorant doctors; against the speculators in food who hoarded for higher prices; he wrote rebuking the Creoles, telling them they had the vices of both the Indians and the Spaniards. If he had poured boiling oil upon them he could not have offended them more bitterly. He wrote against the depravity of the lower classes, and the plague of thieves, beggars, and drunkards in the streets. In November he enjoyed a small popular triumph. A crowd gathered at sight of him and cheered him in the street, shouting that he told them the naked truth. ("La Verdad Pelada" was one of his most lively efforts.) But no royalist or liberal or insurgent or priest or anyone that mattered then was in this cheering rabble; these were the shirtless ones, the born losers no matter which side might win. They shouted his name, and worsened his reputation, but they did not follow his advice and could not if they would. They liked him because he was sharp and angry, full of their own kind of humor, and talked to them in their own language. It was the first time they had ever seen their own kind of talk in print. The flattery was great and they responded to it; for a few centavos they could buy this highly flavored reading matter which expressed all their secret wrongs and grudges and avenged them vicariously; and his words worked afterwards in their thoughts; they trusted him and believed him.

In December 1813, three months after Lizárdi's attack, the Inquisition was re-established. The absolutist monarch Ferdinand VII after his eclipse was back on the throne of Spain, and all grudgingly granted liberties were at an end again for Spain and her colonies.

Lizárdi was by then a man without a party indeed. For in that month someone of the Society of Guadalupe sent Morelos a marked copy of Lizárdi's attack on the native-born Mexicans, commenting: "Merely to show you how this author abuses us. We know his weakness since the time of his imprisonment, and we wish that in the press of Oaxaca you shall give him a good shaking up [literal translation] as a mere sycophant."

And one month later, January 14, 1814, a priest called the

attention of the head Inquisitor, Flores, to *The Mexican Think-er's* denunciation of the Inquisition. More than a year later Flores sent the article to two priests for examination, and in June 1815, they denounced it as "a mass of lies, impostures, in-iquitous comparisons, scandals, seductions, offensive to pious ears, injurious to the sanctity of the sovereign Popes, and the piety of our monarch."

Once more the harassed manager of the Jáuregui press was tracked down, this time by an officer of the Inquisition. The printer said that Lizárdi lived in Arco Street, number 3, tene-ment A, then reconsidered and said Lizárdi had lived there when he wrote the article but was now living in Prieto Nuevo Street. Lizárdi was always moving about from one poverty-stricken tenement in a shabby back street to another. Nothing more came of this affair just then.

The only sign Lizárdi gave that he knew he had been de-nounced to the Inquisition was a softening in the tone of his indignation, a generally lowered quality of resistance, a method-ical search for themes on which he might express himself freely without touching too dangerous topics. That year he wrote some rather sensible plans for relieving the sufferings of lepers; against gambling and gambling houses; and criticisms of the prevailing system of public education. He began a campaign for modern education, based on the ideas of Blanchard, a Jesuit priest who had modified Rousseau's theories as expressed in *Emile* "to suit the needs of Christian education."

Sometime during 1815 Lizárdi tried a new series of pamphlets under a single title, "Alacena de Frioleras," meaning a cupboard of cold food, scraps, leftovers. He fell into disgrace with the censors at the second number, and was refused license to print it. He was bitterly discouraged, but not without some resources still. He decided to try his hand at a novel; what censor would look for political ideas in a paltry fiction?

Lizárdi's friend Dr. Beristain, a man of letters, who was writ-ing and compiling a Library of Northern Spanish Americana, did not agree with the censors, but declared Lizárdi to be "an original genius, native of New Spain." Dr. Beristain also believed that Lizárdi, for his knowledge of the world and of men, and for his taste in literature, merited to be called "if not the American Quevedo, at least the Mexican Torres Villaroel . . . he has now in hand a life of Periquito Sarniento, which judging by what I have seen of it, much resembles Guzman de Alfarache."

The censor's report for February 1816, mentions the appearance of *El Periquillo* from the prologue to chapter 6; in July, another series of chapters; the third series was suppressed on November 29, 1816, because it contained an attack on the system of human slavery.

This is the first mention of that book, undertaken as Lizárdi's last hope of outwitting the censorship, as well as of making a living by its sales as it was being written. He finished it, but it was not published in full until after his death.

There followed a long dreary period of pamphlet writing, against bullfighting, against dandyism—his Don Catrín remains a stock character in that line until today—calendars, almanacs, stainless essays on morals and manners, hymns and little songs for children. In the meantime the insurgents, who had been growing in strength, were weakened and the Liberal-Constitutionalist party got into power. At once they suppressed both the Inquisition and the Board of Press Censorship, and at once Lizárdi was ready for them. He founded a small periodical called *The Lightning Conductor* and began to tell again the naked truth.

There were to be several changes of government yet during Lizárdi's lifetime, but there was never to be one he could get along with, or accept altogether. After twenty-four numbers of *The Lightning Conductor*, he could not find a printer who would risk printing his periodical for him. Lizárdi by no means defended the entire Constitutionalist idea, he only defended those tendencies which led to such reforms as he had just witnessed in regard to the Inquisition and the censorship. But in doing this he offended again the rockbound royalist clergy, who used the whip of spiritual authority to force their parishioners to oppose the constitution, as it curtailed the Spanish power and automatically their own. These and all other die-hard royalists hated Lizárdi; the insurgents distrusted him. He was a gadfly to the Viceroy, always addressing complaints directly to him: he was opposed to war still, civil war above all, and considered the insurgents to be almost as obnoxious to the good of the country as the royalists themselves. He considered himself "as Catholic as the Pope," but the clergy hated and attacked him bitterly. A priest named Soto wrote such a vicious pamphlet against him that the censors suppressed it.

During that period, almost frantic in his hornets' nest of personal and public enemies, Lizárdi found time and a little money to open a reading room, where for a small fee the public might read the current books, newspapers, pamphlets. Almost nobody came to read, he lost his money and closed the place after a few months.

The struggle between Mexico and Spain was approaching the grand climax, and with peculiar timeliness Lizárdi did precisely the thing calculated to get him into trouble. In February 1821, Augustín Iturbide and Canon Monteagudo, at the head of the Anti-constitutionalist party, boldly declared themselves ready to separate Mexico from Spain, without any further compromises. The Liberal party had held out for an independence to be granted by Spain, peacefully. The new constitution granted when Vanegas was Viceroy had been a makeshift affair, with no real concessions in it. Iturbide's party appeared to be only the acting head of the insurgents, for this seizing of independence for Mexico was exactly what the insurgents had been fighting for all along. Iturbide, with an ambition of his own, decided to use the strength of the insurgents and the growing nationalist spirit to his own ends. He and Monteagudo published their program as the Plan of Iguala.

In the meantime, Lizárdi had been writing on this topic, too. Just four days after the Plan of Iguala was published, Lizárdi printed a pamphlet which was described as a serio-comic dialogue between two popular and sharp-tongued characters called Chamorro and Dominiquín. They discussed the possibilities of independence for Mexico, and looked forward to the day of freedom, believed it would be a good thing for both countries, but still hoped it might be granted legally by the Spanish government.

The liberal constitutionalist but still very royalist government, with its free press, saw nothing to laugh at in this work, suppressed it at once, arrested Lizárdi and kept him in jail for several days. On this occasion he flattered no one, implicated no one, and retracted nothing. He was released, and wrote a halfhearted pamphlet on the beauties of reconciliation between factions. And in his next pamphlet he stated boldly a change of mind. "It is true that if we do not take our independence by force of arms, they will never concede us our liberty by force of reason and justice."

When he had been imprisoned, he was accused of being a follower of Iturbide, and a supporter of the Plan of Iguala. Lizárdi replied merely that he had not known about the plan when he wrote his own suggestions; in effect no answer at all, and perhaps true in itself. But immediately after this last pamphlet boldly counselling the violent way to freedom, the next thing we know, Lizárdi is showing a letter from Iturbide to a certain Spaniard, and this Spaniard is supplying him with money and equipment and a horse, and Lizárdi, by urgent request of Iturbide, is riding toward Tepotzotlan to take charge of the insurgent press there. This press was devoted entirely to the doctrine of Mexican independence and the necessity of gaining it by force.

Iturbide's troops fought their way steadily through the country toward Mexico City, and Lizárdi was close on their heels with his press turning out patriotic broadsides. Iturbide entered the capital in triumph on September 21, 1821. The great deed was accomplished, the eleven years of revolutionary war came to a close, and Mexico was declared an independent government. Lizárdi naturally entered the city in triumph also, with his press still going at top speed. Let the censors fume. He had a whole victorious army with him.

There was still no thought in anyone's mind of establishing a Republic. Lizárdi expressed the hopes of the victors clearly: that Iturbide should be made Emperor by acclamation, at the first session of Congress. "Oh," cried our misguided hero, who had waited so long to espouse any faction, and now had taken to heart so utterly the wrong one, "may I have the joy of kissing once the hand of the Emperor of America, and then close my eyes forever in death."

How little becoming to Lizárdi was this new garment of acquiescence. It was never made for him and he could not carry it off. Two months later his eyes, closed in enthusiasm, were opened violently, he gazed clearly upon the object of his infatuation, and rejected it. He saw that Iturbide had done as other ambitious men do. He had used the force of a great popular movement to seize power for himself, and meant to set himself up as head of a government more oppressive if possible than the old.

Lizárdi wrote a pamphlet called "Fifty Questions to Whoever Cares to Answer Them," and the questions were very embarrassing to the new Emperor, to the church authorities leagued with him, and to all who had promised reforms in government. Iturbide had at least gone through the formality of having himself elected Emperor, and Lizárdi accused the priests of controlling the election. They called Lizárdi unpatriotic, hostile to religion, accused him of political ambitions. Iturbide was disconcerted by the sudden defection of a man to whom he had given money and a press and a horse to boot, and finding that Lizárdi was abusing the freedom of the press, urged that a new censorship be established.

Finding himself the chief obstacle to that freedom of the press which had now become his main object in life, Lizárdi proceeded to multiply his offenses. Freemasonry had been creeping in quietly from France by way of Spain. It was the nightmare of the Church everywhere and two Popes had issued bulls against it: Clement XII in 1738, Benedict XIV in 1751. The alarmed clergy in Mexico republished these bulls in 1821, and by way of response Lizárdi wrote a pamphlet called plainly "A Defense of the Freemasons." He used arguments that were in the main those of a good Christian, an informed Catholic and a fairly good student of the Bible. It was also a heated, tactless and illogical performance, and the Church simply came down on him like a hammer. Nine days after the pamphlet was published, Lizárdi was publicly and formally excommunicated by the board of ecclesiastical censorship, and the notice was posted in all the churches.

So it was done at last, and The Thinker passed a little season in hell which made all his former difficulties seem, as he would say, "like fruit and frosted cake." He was kept more or less a prisoner in his own house, where by the rules no member of his own household was supposed to speak to him, or touch him, or help or serve him in any way.

It is improbable that this state of affairs ever existed in that family, but the neighbors would not speak to his wife or daughter, they had great hardships procuring food, and no servant would stay in the house. When he ventured out certain persons drew aside from him; at least once a small mob gathered and threatened to stone him; a group of friars also threatened to come and beat him in his own house, and he advised them defiantly to come well prepared. They did not come, however. He had no defenders for no one would defend an excommunicated man. His wife went to appeal to the Vicar-General, who would not allow her to approach or speak, but waved her away, shouting, "In writing, in writing," since it was forbidden to speak to any member of his family.

Lizárdi, announcing that he was "as Catholic as the Pope," which in fact he does not seem to have been, began to defend himself. It was a sign of the times that he could still find presses to print his pamphlets. He appealed to Congress to have the censure of the Church lifted within the prescribed legal period, and asked that body to appoint a lawyer to defend him in the secular courts, but nothing was done in either case. He continued to harry the government, giving sarcastic advice to Iturbide, and recorded with pride that after he had been cut off from human kind by his excommunication his friends were more faithful than ever. It is true he did enjoy some rather furtive moral support from radical sources, but he was bold as if he had all society on his side. He wrote a second defense of the Freemasons, wrote a bitter defense of his entire career and beliefs in the famous "Letter to a Papist," and dragged on his miserable life somehow until 1823, when Iturbide was overthrown by General Antonio López de Santa Ana, head of a "Federalist" party which pretended to found a Republic based on the best elements of the American and French models. It turned out to be another dictatorship which lasted for about thirty years, with Santa Ana at its head. The Catholic Church was still the only recognized religion, a blow to Lizárdi, but he took hope again. The appearance of the written Constitution deceived him momentarily, and as unofficial uninvited member of the Federalist party he began again agitating for all those reforms so dear to his heart: Freedom of the press, first, last and forever, compulsory free education, religious liberty, liberty of speech and universal franchise, and naturally, almost as a result of these things, justice, sweet justice, for everybody, regardless of race, class, creed or color.

Almost at once he found himself in jail again.

He gives his account of it as follows, tongue in cheek: "In the month of June (1823), I was imprisoned for writing an innocent little paper called 'If Congress Sits Much Longer We Shall Lose Our Shirts.' I described a dream I had in which a set of petty thieves were debating the best way of robbing us . . . they denounced me . . . on the strength of the title alone, arrested me and I was forced to labor again in my own defense." ("Letter to a Papist.")

This must have blown over, for on the 20th of that same June he was again prisoner in St. Andrés' hospital, but this was probably one of those dreary mischances which befall poor people unable to keep up with the rent: at any rate he insulted the landlady and she threw him out of the house, lock, stock, and barrel, accusing him of defamation of her character. He got out of this, too, and in revenge wrote a poem called "Epithalamium" in which he seems to have married off the judge and the landlady with appropriate ribaldry; but they could do nothing as he mentioned no names.

By then no printer would publish for him: he appears to have got hold of a press of his own, but the authorities forbade newsboys to sell his papers in the streets. At last he left the city for a while, but there was no fate for him in such a case except death in exile. He returned and late in December 1823, he wrote a letter to the ecclesiastical board of censorship, saying he would no longer attempt to defend himself by civil law, and asked for absolution. This was granted and the documents were published in a periodical in January, 1824.

"Time will mend all things," he wrote at about this time, "in effect, today this abuse will be remedied, tomorrow, another . . . in eight or ten years everything will go as it should." He lived by, and for, this illusion, but these are the words of a mortally weary man. He had never been strong and he was already suffering from the tuberculosis of which he was to die. He had at this time an intimation of approaching death.

He began a small bi-weekly sheet called *The Yokel and the Sacristan,* and in June 1825, a number of this was pronounced heretical. He was given eight days in which to make a reply, and asked for three months, which was not granted. He allowed himself even a little more time than he had asked for, then made an evasive and unsatisfactory reply. He was not pursued any further about this.

The reason may have been that Lizárdi had quarreled successfully, even triumphantly, just five months before, with the Bishop of Sonora. This Bishop had issued a manifesto pronouncing the new Federalist Constitution of Mexico Anti-Catholic (in spite of that clause legalizing the Church alone which had so nearly broken Lizárdi's spirit). The Bishop argued for the divine right of Kings, and said that God had been deprived of his rights. Lizárdi replied with a defense of the republican form of government, in his usual animated style. The public response to him was so great a governmental commission waited upon the Bishop, escorted him to Acapulco and put him on board a ship which returned him to Spain for good. And Santa Ana's government suddenly gave Lizárdi a pension of sixty-five pesos a month "to reward him for his services to the revolution, until something better could be found." The something better was the editorship of the official organ of the new government, called *The Gazette*, at a salary of 100 pesos a month. For the times, this was not a bad income for a man who had never had one and this short period was the only one of his life in which Lizárdi was free from financial misery. He was at once pestered by his enemies who coveted no doubt the fortune he had fallen into, and though he went on with the job for a year or two, in the end he quarreled with everybody and was out of favor again. . . .

So it went, to the end. The rest of the history has to do with suits for defamation, plays about to be produced and failing, troubles with the censors, suppressions rather monotonously more of the same. "Let the judges answer whether they are fools or bought men," he wrote, when they found for his enemy in a slander trial. He maintained this spirit until the end. He wrote publicly denying that he had ever yielded to the ecclesiastical

censors, or asked for absolution. The fact is clear that if he had
not done so, the sentence of excommunication would never have
been lifted. He boasted of his prudence in the business, and hinted
at secret, important diplomatic strategy. Let it go. In the end,
it was a matter of yielding, or of starving his family and himself
to death.

In 1825, General Guadalupe Victoria, then President, pro-
claimed the end of slavery. One might have thought this would
please Lizárdi, and perhaps it did in a measure. But at once he
discovered that the proclamation referred only to Negro slaves,
and to the outright buying and selling of human flesh. It did not
refer to the slavery of the Indian, which he found as bitter and
hopeless under the Creole Republic as it had been under the
Spanish Viceroys. . . . He pointed out this discrepancy, and insisted that it should be remedied. By that time, he had such a
reputation for this kind of unreasonableness, the new government
decided to ignore him as far as they were able. He was dismissed
from consideration as a crackbrained enthusiast.

By the end of April 1827, Lizárdi knew that death was near.
Someone reported on his state of health: he was "a mere skele-
ton." Lying in bed, he wrote and had printed his "Testament and
Farewell of The Mexican Thinker." At some length, and with
immense bitterness, he repeated for the last time his stubborn
faiths, his unalterable beliefs, his endless opposition to every form
of social, political, and human wrong, to every abuse of power
and to every shade of dishonesty, particularly the dishonesty of
those in power. He still considered himself as Catholic as the
Pope, but he could not admit the infallibility of His Holiness. He
still did not believe in the apparitions of saints, calling them
"mere goblins." He was as good a patriot as ever, but he was
still no party man, and he could not condone in the republican
government those same abuses he had fought in the days of the
Empire. With sad irony he willed to his country "A Republic
whose constitution denies religious freedom; a Cathedral on
which the canons would at the first opportunity replace the

Spanish coat of arms; an ecclesiastical chapter which ignores the
civil law altogether; streets full of stray dogs, beggars, idle police;
thieves and assassins who flourish in criminal collusion with cor-
rupt civil employees," and so on as ever, in minute detail, no evil
too petty or too great for attack, as if they were all of one size
and one importance. I think this does not argue at all a lack of the
sense of proportion, but is proof of his extraordinary perception
of the implicit relationship between all manifestations of evil,
the greater breeding and nourishing the lesser, the lesser swarming to support and confirm the greater.

He advised the President of the Republic to get acquainted
with the common people and the workers, to study his army and
observe the actions of his ministers; and he desired that his wife
and friends should not make any loud mourning over him; they
were not to light candles around him, and they were to bury him
not in the customary friar's robe, but in the uniform of a soldier.
Further, he wished that his wife would pay only the regular
burial fees of seven pesos, and not haggle with the priest, who
would try to charge her more for a select spot in the cemetery.
He wished that his epitaph might be: "Here lies the ashes of The
Mexican Thinker, who did what he could for his country."

For long days and nights he strangled to death slowly in the
wretched little house, number 27, Fuente Quebrado (The Broken
Fountain), with his wife and young daughter watching him die,
unable to relieve his sufferings with even the most rudimentary
comforts, without medical attendance, without money, almost
without food. He called two priests to hear his final confession,
wishing them to be witnesses for each other that he had not died
without the last rites; but he put off receiving Extreme Unction
because he hoped the ritual might be attended by a number of
former friends who believed him to be a heretic. The friends for
some reason failed to arrive for this occasion. Lizárdi lingered on,
hoping, but no one came; and on June 27, still hoping, but refusing the ceremony until his witnesses should arrive, he died.
Almost at once it was rumored abroad that he died possessed of

the devil. The friends came then, to see for themselves, and his pitiable corpse was exposed to public view in the hovel where he died, as proof that the devil had not carried him off.

The next day a few former acquaintances, his family and a small mob of curious busybodies followed the body of Fernández de Lizárdi to the cemetery of San Lázaro, and buried him with the honors of a retired Captain. Neither the epitaph that he composed for himself, nor any other, was inscribed on his gravestone, for no stone was ever raised. His wife died within four months and was buried beside him. His fifteen-year-old daughter was given in charge of a certain Doña Juliana Guevara de Ceballos, probably her godmother, or a female relation, who seems to have handed her over to the care of another family whose name is not known. This family removed to Vera Cruz shortly, and there Lizárdi's daughter died of yellow fever.

So the grave closed over them all, and Mexico almost forgot its stubborn and devoted Thinker. The San Lázaro cemetery disappeared, and with it his unmarked grave. His numberless pamphlets disappeared, a few into private collections and storerooms of bookshops; a great many more into moldering heaps of wastepaper. In effect, Lizárdi was forgotten.

His novel, his one novel that he had never meant to write, which had got itself suppressed in its eleventh chapter, is without dispute The Novel of the past century, not only for Mexico but for all Spanish-speaking countries. It was published in full in 1830, three years after Lizárdi's death, and there were eight editions by 1884. In spite of this, in 1885 there appeared an edition, "corrected, explained with notes, and adorned with thirty fine illustrations," and announced as the second edition, though it was really the ninth.

After that, no one troubled any more to number editions correctly or not. Until the recent disaster in Spain, a big popular press in Barcelona reprinted it endlessly at the rate of more than a million copies a year, on pulp paper, in rotten type, with a gaudy paper cover illustrating some wild scene, usually that of the corpse-robbing in the crypt. In Mexico I used to see it at every smallest sidewalk book stall; in the larger shops there were always a good number of copies on hand, selling steadily. It was given to the young to read as an aid to manners and morals, and for a great while it must have been the one source of a liberal education for the great mass of people, the only ethical and moral instruction they could have, for Lizárdi's ideas of modern education got no foothold in Mexico for nearly a century after him.

It is not to be supposed that anybody ever read a picaresque tale for the sake of the sugar plums of polite instruction concealed in it, but Lizárdi had the knack of scattering little jokes and curious phrases all through his sermons, and he managed to smuggle all his pamphlets into the final version of *El Periquillo*. They were all there, at great length; the dog in the strange neighborhood, the dead who make no noise, the monkey dressed in silk; with all his attacks on slavery, on bullfighting, on dishonest apothecaries and incompetent doctors; his program for enlightened education, his proposals for cleaning the city in time of plague; against the vicious and mercenary clergy, the unscrupulous politicians; against gambling, against—ah well, they are all there, and the trouble for the translator is getting them out again without leaving too many gaps. For try as he might, by no art could the good Thinker make his dreary fanatic world of organized virtue anything but terrifying to the reader, it was so deadly dull. But once these wrappings are stripped from the story, there is exposed a fine, traditional Rogue's Progress, the history of a true pícaro, a younger brother of Guzman de Alfarache, as Dr. Beristain said, or of Gil Blas. He has English relations too—Peregrine Pickle, Roderick Random, Tom Jones, all of that family of lucky sinners who end well. In the best style, more things happen to El Periquillo than might reasonably happen to one man, events move at top speed, disasters pile up; but he comes through one way or another, shedding his last misadventure with a shake of his shoulders, plunging straightway into the next. Like all his kind, he is hard and casual and thickskinned and sentimental, and he shares their expedient, opportunist morality, which always serves to recall to his mind the good maxims of his early upbringing when his luck is bad, but never once when it is good.

The typical pícaro also is always the incomplete hero of his own story, for he is also a buffoon. Periquillo is afflicted with the itch, he loses his trousers during a bullfight in the presence of ladies, he is trapped into the wrong bed by the malice of his best friend, he is led again and again into humiliating situations by wits quicker than his own.

Living by his wits, such as they are, he is a true parasite, attaching himself first to one then another organism to feed upon. He is hardly ever without a "master" or "mentor" or "patron" and this person is always doing something for him, which El Periquillo accepts as his right and gives nothing, or as little as possible, in return.

Only once does he feel real gratitude. After leaving the house of the Chinese Mandarin, improbable visitor from the Island Utopia, whom Periquillo has succeeded in gulling for a while, he has been beaten and called a pimp by three girls. None of his other disgraces could equal this, so he gets drunk and goes out to hang himself. He fails of course, goes to sleep instead, and wakes to find himself robbed and stripped to the shirt by wayside thieves. He is rescued by a poor old Indian woman who clothes and feeds him. In an untypical rush of tenderness, he embraces and kisses the unsightly creature. This is almost the only truly and honestly tender episode in the book, uncorrupted by any attempts to point a moral, for Lizárdi's disillusionment with human nature was real, and based on experience, and most of his attempts to play upon the reader's sentiments ring false.

As El Periquillo's adventures follow the old picaresque pattern, so do those of the other characters, for they are all pretty much fairly familiar wares from the old storehouse. But the real heroes of this novel, by picaresque standards, are some of El Periquillo's comrades, such as Juan Largo, and the Eaglet. One is hanged and one dies leading a bandit raid, neither of them repents or ponders for a moment, but goes to his destined end in good form and style. Juan Largo says, "A good bullfighter dies on the horns of the bull," and El Periquillo answers that he has no wish to die a bullfighter's death. Indeed, he wants no heroics, either in living or dying. He wants to eat his cake and have it too and to die at last respectably in a comfortable bed surrounded by loving mourners. He does it, too. A thoroughly bad lot.

As in all picaresque literature, the reader has uneasy moments of wondering whether it is the hero or the author who is deficient in moral sensibility; or whether the proposed satire has not staggered and collapsed under its weight of moral connotation. When Januario is about to become a common thief, there is a long and solemn dialogue between him and Periquillo, Januario holding out firmly against Periquillo's rather cut-and-dried exhortations to honesty, or at any rate, as a last resort, plain prudence. Januario there repeats word for word the whole Catechism. Having done this, he goes out on his first escapade, and is half successful—that is he escapes from the police, but leaves his swag. On this occasion, Lizárdi, by the demands of the plot, is hard beset to have Periquillo present, a witness, yet innocent. The best he can manage is to have him act as lookout, by distracting the watchman's attention and engaging him in conversation. Periquillo then believes that this act does not involve him in the least, and is most virtuously outraged when he is arrested and accused as confederate.

Again, Periquillo, in prison, and watching for a chance to cheat at cards, reflects at length and piously on the illicit, crafty methods of the trusty for turning a dishonest penny by cheating the prisoners. Thinking these thoughts, Periquillo refrains from cheating only because he realizes that he is in very fast company and will undoubtedly be caught at it. Don Antonio, a jail mate, formerly a dealer in contraband, in telling his story of how he lost his ill-gained fortune, innocently assumes and receives the complete sympathy of his hearers, not all of them mere thugs

either. This Don Antonio, by the way, who is meant to shine as
an example of all that is honorable, upright and unfortunate in
human nature, is certainly one of the most abject and nitwitted
characters in all fiction. He is smug, pious, dishonest, he feels
dreadfully sorry for himself, and his ineptitude and bad manage-
ment of his affairs cause much suffering to innocent persons. In
fact, Lizárdi was singularly uninspired in his attempts to portray
virtue in action. In his hands it becomes a horrid device of boredom, a pall falls over his mind, he retreats to the dryest kind of
moral saws and proverbs. He seemed to realize this, seemed to
know that this kind of goodness, the only kind he dared recom-
mend or advertise, was deadly dull. He tried to make it interesting but could not, and turned again with relief to his tough
thieves and merry catchalls and horners and unrepentant bandits.
Their talk is loose and lively, their behavior natural; he cheers
up at once and so does his reader.

A contemporary critic complained that the book was "an uneven and extravagant work in very bad taste . . . written in an
ugly style, with a badly invented plot . . . made worse by the
author's treatment." He then confessed that what really annoyed
him was the author's choice of characters, who were all from the
lowest walks of life. They talked and behaved exactly like the
vulgar people one saw in the streets, and their language was the
sort heard in taverns. This left-handed praise must have pleased
Lizárdi, who had aimed at precisely this effect. The critic went
on to say that the vices of polite society were perhaps no less
shocking, but they seemed less gross because it was possible to
gloss them over, decorate them, polish them up a bit, and make
them less ridiculous. "When a rich man and a poor man drink
together," answered Lizárdi, in a little jingle, "the poor man gets
drunk, but the rich man only gets merry."

Lizárdi's infrequent flights into a more rarefied social atmosphere are malicious, comic, and a conventional caricature, designed to confirm in his lower-class readers all their worst sus-
picions regarding the rich and titled. Now and again he drags in

by the ears a set speech on the obligations of nobility to be truly noble, and of the poor to be truly virtuous, in the most Lizárdian sense of those words, but he makes it clear that he has no real hopes that this will come to pass.

For him, the very rich and the very poor are the delinquent classes, to use a current sociological phrase. He called aloud for the pure mediocrity of morals and manners, the exact center of the road in all things. The middling well off, he insisted, were always good, because they practiced moderation, they were without exorbitant desires, ambitions, or vices. (That this was what made them middling was what Lizárdi could never see, and that only those born to the middling temperament, rather than middling fortune, could practice the tepid virtues.) Every time El Periquillo falls into poverty, he falls also into the vices of the poor. When by his standards he is rich, he practices at once the classical vices of the rich. His feelings, thoughts, and conduct contract and expand automatically to the measure of his finances. He was always astounded to meet with morality in the poor, though he did meet it now and then, but never once did he find any good among the rich. His favorite virtue was generosity, and particularly that generosity practiced toward himself, though he almost never practiced it toward others. Even during a period of relative respectability, financially speaking, when El Periquillo is planning to marry, he discusses with Roque, one of his fly-by-night friends, the possibility of Periquillo's Uncle Maceta standing as security for the bridegroom's finery at the tailor's and the silversmith's, along with a plot to rid himself of his mistress, a girl whom he had seduced from a former employer. All goes smoothly for a time: the Uncle is complacent, the mistress is thrown out of the house in good time, the marriage takes place, with bad faith on both sides, El Periquillo's transitory small fortune is thrown away on fast living, and the Uncle is rooked out of his money. El Periquillo comments that it served him right for being such a stingy, unnatural relative.

So much for the Parrot as the faulty medium of Lizárdi's social and moral ideas: some of his other characters were hardly less successful in this role . . . for example, his army officer, a colonel, in Manila.

This man is a brilliant example of what a military man is not, never was, could not in the nature of things be, yet Lizárdi introduces him quite naturally as if he believed him to be entirely probable. The Colonel is full of the most broadly socialistic ideas, democratic manners, with agrarian notions on nationalism. He believes that rich deposits of gold and silver are a curse to a country instead of the blessings they are supposed to be, and that the lucky country was one which must depend upon its fruits, wool, meats, grain, in plenty but not enough to tempt invaders. He notes that Mexico and the Americas in general are deplorable examples of that false wealth which caused them to neglect agriculture and industry and fall prey to rapacious foreigners. . . . The Colonel, in his fantasy, is no more strange than the entire Manila episode. El Periquillo is deported there as a convict. It is hardly probable that Lizárdi ever saw Manila, though there was a legend that he had visited there during the vague "lost years." It is more probable that while he lived in Acapulco he listened to stories of storm and shipwreck and life in strange ports. That he loved the sea is quite plain, with a real love, not romantic or sentimental; he expresses in simple phrases a profound feeling for the deep waters and the sweet majesty of ships. But otherwise, the Manila episode has the vague and far-fetched air of second-hand reporting.

It is not his moral disquisitions, then, nor his portrayal of character, nor his manner of telling his story, that keeps El Periquillo alive after more than a hundred years: it is simply and broadly the good show he managed to get up out of the sights and sounds and smells of his native town. His wakes, funerals, weddings, roaring drunken parties, beggars in their flophouses, the village inns where families rumbled up in coaches, bringing servants, beds, food, exactly as they did in medieval Europe: they all exist with extraordinary vividness, and yet there is very little actual description. There are dozens of scenes which stick in the memory: Luisa standing in the door, greeting with cool scorn her former lover; the wake with the watchers playing cards through the night, and as their own candles give out, borrowing one by one the blessed candles from the dead; the robbing of the corpse, with its exaggerated piling of horror upon horror; the hospital scenes, the life in prisons; all this is eye-witness, first-hand narrative, and a worm's-eye view beside. It is a true picture of the sprawling, teeming, swarming people of Mexico, ragged, eternally cheated, crowding about the food stalls which smoke along the market side, sniffing the good smells through the dirt and confusion, insatiably and hopelessly hungry, but indestructible. Lizárdi himself was hungry nearly all his life, and his Periquillo has also an enormous, unfailing preoccupation with food. He remembers every meal, good or bad, he ever ate, he refers punctually three times a day to the fact that he was hungry, or it was now time to eat: "And my anxious stomach," says Periquillo, in one of the more painful moments of his perpetual famine, "was cheeping like a bird to gobble up a couple of plates of chile sauce and a platter of toasted tortillas." Even in exile, in Manila, when he had almost forgotten persons he had known, could hardly remember the lovely face of his native city, he still remembered with longing the savory Mexican food. . . .

Lizárdi was once insulted by a picayune critic, who wrote that his work was worthless and he himself a worthless character who wrote only in order to eat. This was not altogether true, for if it had been, Lizárdi might easily have been much better fed than he was: but he did, having written, do what he could to sell his work to gain his bread, and though he did not choose the easy way, still he was bitterly stung by this taunt, poor man, and to save his pride, mentioned that at least he had lived by what he made, and not squandered his wife's dowry.

The Thinker's style has been admired as a model of clarity in Mexican literature by some of his later friends, but I think that must be the bias of loyalty. By the loosest standard, that style was almost intolerably wordy, cloudy, vague, the sentences of an intricate slovenliness, the paragraphs of inordinate length; indeed it was no style at all, but merely the visible shape of his harassed mind which came of his harassed life. He nearly always began his pamphlets, as he began his novel, with great dignity, deliberation and clearness, with a consciously affected pedantry, with echoes of the grand manner, a pastiche of Cervantes or Góngora, but he knew it could not last; he knew also his readers' tastes; he could do no more than promise a patchwork, and patchwork it was. There are times too when it is apparent he wrote at top speed in order to get the number finished and handed to the printer, needing desperately the few pesos the sale would bring him, padding and repeating, partly because his mind was too tired to remember what he had written, and partly because he must give his readers good weight for the money, or they would not buy.

The censors complained constantly of his obscenity and use of double meanings, and indeed he was a master in this mode. All of his writings I have seen are full of sly hints and some not so sly, curious associations of ideas one would need to be very innocent indeed to miss. The Mexicans love them with a special affection, the language is a honeycomb of them, no doubt Lizárdi enjoyed writing them, and it was a certain device for catching his readers' undivided attention. He did not need to invent anything, he had only to listen to the popular talk, which was and is ripe and odorous. Some of it is very comic and witty, some of it simply nasty, humorless, and out of place in a translation where the meaning could be conveyed only by substituting a similar phrase in English, since they are often untranslatable in the technical sense. And was he—to imitate one of his own rhetorical questions—so simple as to believe that his readers would take the trouble to wade through his moral dissertations if he did not spice them with the little obscenities they loved? He was not, and he did his best by them in the matter of seasoning. At least a hundred million readers have found his novel savory, and perhaps a few of them repaid his hopes by absorbing here and there in it a little taste of manners and morals, with some liberal political theory besides. Certainly the causes for which he fought have been never altogether defeated, but they have won no victory, either: a lukewarm, halfway sort of process, the kind of thing that exasperated him most, that might well end by disheartening the best and bravest of men. Lizárdi was not the best of men, nor the bravest, he was only a very good man and a very faithful one. If he did not have perfect courage or judgment, let him who has require these things of him.

Yaddo, December 10, 1941

Why I Write About Mexico

A LETTER TO THE EDITOR OF
"THE CENTURY"

❋

I write about Mexico because that is my familiar country. I was
born near San Antonio, Texas. My father lived part of his youth
in Mexico, and told me enchanting stories of his life there; therefore the land did not seem strange to me even at my first sight
of it. During the Madero revolution I watched a street battle between Maderistas and Federal troops from the window of a cathedral; a grape-vine heavy with tiny black grapes formed a screen,
and a very old Indian woman stood near me, perfectly silent, holding my sleeve. Later she said to me, when the dead were being
piled for burning in the public square, "It is all a great trouble
now, but it is for the sake of happiness to come." She crossed herself, and I mistook her meaning.

"In heaven?" I asked. Her scorn was splendid.

"No, on earth. Happiness for men, not for angels!"

She seemed to me then to have caught the whole meaning of
revolution, and to have said it in a phrase. From that day I watched
Mexico, and all the apparently unrelated events that grew out of
that first struggle never seemed false or alien or aimless to me. A
straight, undeviating purpose guided the working of the plan.
And it permitted many fine things to grow out of the national
soil, only faintly surmised during the last two or three centuries
even by the Mexicans themselves. It was as if an old field had been
watered, and all the long-buried seeds flourished.

About three years ago I returned to Mexico, after a long absence, to study the renascence of Mexican art—a veritable rebirth, very conscious, very powerful, of a deeply racial and personal art. I was not won to it by any artificial influence; I recognized it at once as something very natural and acceptable, a feeling for art consanguine with my own, unfolding in a revolution which returned to find its freedoms in profound and honorable sources. It would be difficult to explain in a very few words how the Mexicans have enriched their national life through the medium of their native arts. It is in everything they do and are. I cannot say, "I gathered material" for it; there was nothing so mechanical as that, but the process of absorption went on almost unconsciously, and my impressions remain not merely as of places visited and people known, but as of a moving experience in my own life that is now a part of me.

My stories are fragments, each one touching some phase of a versatile national temperament, which is a complication of simplicities: but I like best the quality of aesthetic magnificence, and, above all, the passion for individual expression without hypocrisy, which is the true genius of the race.

I have been accused by Americans of a taste for the exotic, for foreign flavors. Maybe so, for New York is the most foreign place I know, and I like it very much. But in my childhood I knew the French-Spanish people in New Orleans and the strange "Cajans" in small Louisiana towns, with their curious songs and customs and blurred patois; the German colonists in Texas and the Mexicans of the San Antonio country, until it seemed to me that all my life I had lived among people who spoke broken, laboring tongues, who put on with terrible difficulty, yet with such good faith, the ways of the dominant race about them. This is true here in New York also, I know: but I have never thought of these people as any other than American. Literally speaking, I have never been out of America; but my America has been a borderland of strange tongues and commingled races, and if they are not American, I am fearfully mistaken. The artist can do no more than deal with familiar and beloved things, from which he could not, and, above all, would not escape. So I claim that I write of things native to me, that part of America to which I belong by birth and association and temperament, which is as much the province of our native literature as Chicago or New York or San Francisco. All the things I write of I have first known, and they are real to me.

1923

Leaving the Petate

✳

The petate is a woven straw mat, in shape an oblong square, full of variations in color and texture, and very sweet smelling when it is new. In its ordinary form, natural colored, thick and loosely contrived, it is the Mexican Indian bed, an ancient sort of sleeping mat such as all Oriental peoples use. There is a proverb full of vulgar contempt which used to be much quoted here in Mexico: "Whoever was born on a *petate* will always smell of the straw." Since 1910, I shall say simply to fix a date on changes which have been so gradual it is impossible to say when the transition actually was made, this attitude has disappeared officially. The *petate*, an object full of charm for the eye, and immensely useful around any house, is no longer a symbol of racial and economic degradation from which there is no probable hope of rising. On the contrary, many of the best 1920 revolutionists insisted on smelling of the straw whether they were born on the *petate* or not. It was a mark of the true revolutionary to acknowledge Indian blood, the more the better, to profess Indian points of view, to make, in short, an Indian revolution. All the interlocking advances of the *mestizo* (mixed Spanish and Indian) revolution since Benito Juarez have been made for the Indian, and only secondarily by him—much as the recent famous renascence of Indian sculpture and painting was the work of European-trained *mestizos*. No matter: this article is not going to deal with grand generalities. I am interested in a few individual human beings I have met here lately, whose lives make me believe that the Indian, when he gets a chance, is leaving the *petate*.

And no wonder. He wraps himself in his *serape*, a pure-wool blanket woven on a hand loom and colored sometimes with vegetable dyes, and lies down to rest on his *petate*. The blankets are very beautiful, but they are always a little short, and in this table-land of Mexico at least, where the nights are always cold, one blanket is not enough. The *petate*, beautiful as it is, is also a little short, so the man curls down on his side, draws his knees up and tucks his head down in a prenatal posture, and sleeps like that. He can sleep like that anywhere: on street corners, by the roadside, in caves, in doorways, in his own hut, if he has one. Sometimes he sleeps sitting with his knees drawn up to his chin and his hat over his eyes, forming a kind of pyramid with his blanket wound about him. He makes such an attractive design as he sits thus: no wonder people go around painting pictures of him. But I think he sleeps there because he is numbed with tiredness and has no other place to go, and not in the least because he is a public decoration. Toughened as he may be to hardship, you can never convince me he is really comfortable, or likes this way of sleeping. So the first moment he gets a chance, a job, a little piece of land, he leaves his *petate* and takes as naturally as any other human or brute being to the delights of kinder living. At first he makes two wooden stands, and puts boards across them, and lays his *petate* on a platform that lifts him from the chill of the earth. From this there is only a step to thin cotton mattresses, and pillows made of lumps of rags tied up in a square of muslin, and thence. . . .

There were presently three women near me who had lately left the *petate*: Consuelo, Eufemia and Hilaria. Consuelo is the maid of a young American woman here, Eufemia was my maid, and Hilaria is her aunt. Eufemia is young, almost pure Aztec, combative, acquisitive, secretive, very bold and handsome and full of tricks. Hilaria is a born intriguer, a carrier of gossip and maker of mischief. Until recently she worked for a hot-headed

Mexican man who managed his servants in the classical middle-class way: by bullying and heckling. This gentleman would come in for his dinner, and if it was not ready on the instant, he would grab his hat and stamp shouting into the street again. "My señor has an incredibly violent nature," said Hilaria, melting with pride. But she grew into the habit of sitting in my kitchen most of the time, whispering advice to Eufemia about how best to get around me; until one day the señor stamped around his house shouting he would rather live in the streets than put up with such a cook, so Hilaria has gone back to her native village near Toluca—back, for a time at least, to her *petate*. She has never really left it in spirit. She wears her *reboso*, the traditional dark-colored cotton-fringed scarf, in the old style, and her wavy black hair is braided in two short tails tied together in the back. Her niece Eufemia came to me dressed in the same way, but within a week she returned from her first day off with a fashionable haircut, parted on the side, waved and peaked extravagantly at the nape—"In the shape of a heart," she explained—and a pair of high-heeled patent-leather pumps which she confessed hurt her feet shockingly.

Hilaria came over for a look, went away, and brought back Eufemia's godmother, her cousins and a family friend, all old-fashioned women like herself, to exclaim over Eufemia's haircut. They turned her about and uttered little yips of admiration tempered with rebuke. What a girl! but look at that peak in the back! What do you think your mother will say? But see, the curls on top, my God! Look here over the ears—like a boy, Eufemia, aren't you ashamed of yourself! and so on. And then the shoes, and then Eufemia's dark-red crochet scarf which she wore in place of a *reboso*—well, well. . . .

They were really very pleased and proud of her. A few days later a very slick pale young man showed up at the house and with all formality explained that he was engaged to marry Eufemia, and would I object if now and then he stopped by to salute her? Naturally I should never object to such a thing.

He explained that for years upon years he had been looking for a truly virtuous, honorable girl to make his wife, and now he had found her. Would I be so good as to watch her carefully, never allow her to go on the street after dark, nor receive other visitors? I assured him I would have done this anyhow. He offered me a limp hand, bowed, shook hands with Eufemia, who blushed alarmingly, and disappeared gently as a cat. Eufemia dashed after me to explain that her young man was not an Indian—I could see that—that he was a barber who made good money, and it was he who had given her the haircut. He had also given her a black lace veil to wear in church —lace veils were once the prerogative of the rich—and had told her to put aside her *reboso*. It was he who had advised her to buy the high-heeled shoes.

After this announcement of the engagement, Eufemia began saving her money and mine with miserly concentration. She was going to buy a sewing machine. In every department of the household I began to feel the dead weight of Eufemia's sewing machine. Food doubled in price, and there was less of it. Everything, from soap to a packet of needles, soared appallingly until I began to look about for a national economic crisis. She would not spend one penny of her wages, and whenever I left town for a few days, leaving her the ordinary allowance for food, I always returned to find the kitten gaunt and yelling with famine and Eufemia pallid and inert from a diet of tortillas and coffee. If all of us perished in the effort, she was going to have a sewing machine, and if we held out long enough, a brass bed and a victrola.

In the meantime, Consuelo came down with a mysterious and stubborn malady. Her young American woman briskly advised her to go to one of the very up-to-date public clinics for treatment. Consuelo at once "went Indian," as her employer defines that peculiar state of remoteness which is not sullenness nor melancholy, nor even hostility—simply a condition of not-thereness to all approach. So long as it lasts, a mere foreigner might as well save his breath. Consuelo is Totonac, speaks her own tongue with her friends, is puritanically severe, honest and caretaking. Her village is so far away you must travel by train for a day or so, and then by horseback for two days more, and in her sick state she turned with longing to this far-off place where she could get the kind of help she really trusted.

Somehow she was prevented from going, so she called in a *curandera* who came from this same village. A *curandera* is a cross between a witch wife and an herb doctor. She steeped Consuelo in home-made brews and incantations, and what we had feared was a tumor the *curandera* identified as a rib which had been jarred from its moorings. Whatever it was, Consuelo recovered, more or less. Consuelo has two cousins who left the *petate* and are now nurses in a famous American homeopathic sanitarium. They send her long lists of dietary rules and hygienic counsels, which her American employer follows with great effect. Consuelo prefers to stick to her own witch doctors, and lets the foreign ones alone.

Hilaria is a *curandera*, and so is Eufemia in a limited way, and both of them remind me very much of the early American housewife who kept her family medicine chest supplied with her own remedies from tried recipes. They have extensive herb knowledge, and Eufemia was always bringing me a steaming glassful of brew for every smallest discomfort imaginable. I swallowed them down, and so ran a gamut of flavors and aromas, from the staggering bitterness of something she called the "prodigious cup" to the apple-flavored freshness of manzanilla flowers. Hilaria pierces ears when the moon is waning, to prevent swelling, and ritually dabs the ear with boiling fat, which should be an excellent antiseptic. To cure headache, a bottle of hot water at the feet draws the pain from the head. This works better if the sign of the cross is made over the head and the bottle. Every benefit is doubled if given with a blessing, and Eufemia, who knows the virtues of rubbing alcohol, always began my alcohol bath with "In the name of the Father, and of the Son, and of the Holy Ghost, may this make you well," which was so gracious an approach I could hardly refuse to feel better.

She agrees with Hilaria that a small green *chile* rubbed on the outer eyelid will cure inflammation of the eye, but you must toss it over your shoulder from you, and walk hastily away without glancing back. During my illness she moistened a cloth with orange-leaf water and put it on my head as a cure for fever. In the morning I found between the folds a little picture of the Holy Face. Eufemia takes up readily with every new thing, and uses iodoform, lysol, patent toothpaste, epsom salts, bicarbonate of soda, rubbing alcohol and mustard plasters very conveniently. Hilaria sticks firmly to her native herbs, and to cure colds puts a plaster of *zapote*—a soft black fruit—heated red hot, on the chest of her patients. Both remedies are remarkably helpful. But Eufemia is leaving the *petate*, and Hilaria is going back to it.

I sympathized with Eufemia's ambitions, even to her fondness for toilet articles of imported German celluloid, her adoration for Japanese cups and saucers in preference to the Mexican pottery which I so love. But I had not reckoned on providing a dowry for a young woman, and the time came for us to part. I set the day two weeks off, and she agreed amiably. Then I gave her her month's wages and two hours later she had packed up her bed and sent it away. Her young man came in and professed astonishment at the state of affairs. "She is not supposed to go for two weeks," I told him, "and at least she must stay until tomorrow." "I will see to that," said the oily Enrique, "this is very surprising." "Tomorrow she may go and welcome, in peace," I assured him.

"Ah, yes, peace, peace," said Enrique. "Peace," I echoed, and we stood there waving our hands at each other in a peculiar horizontal gesture, palms downward, crossing back and forth at our several wrists, about eye level. Between us we wore Eufemia down, and there was peace of a sort.

But in the meantime, she had no bed, so she slept that night on a large *petate* with two red blankets, and seemed very cheerful about it. After all, it was her last night on a *petate*. I discovered later that it was Enrique who had suggested to her that she leave at once, so they might be married and go to Vera Cruz. Eufemia will never go back to her village. She is going to have a brass bed, and a sewing machine and a victrola, and there is no reason why a good barber should not buy a Ford. Her children will be added to the next generation of good little conservative right-minded dull people, like Enrique, or, with Eufemia's fighting spirit, they may become *mestizo* revolutionaries, and keep up the work of saving the Indian.

My new cook is Teodora. "Think of Eufemia going away with just a barber," she says. "My cousin Nicolasa captured a chauffeur. A chauffeur is somebody. But a barber!"

"Just the same, I am glad she is married," I say.

Teodora says, "Oh, not really married, just behind the church, as we say. We marry with everybody, one here, one there, a little while with each one."

"I hope Eufemia stays married, because I have plans for her family," I tell her.

"Oh, she will have a family, never fear," says Teodora.

1931

The Mexican Trinity

REPORT FROM MEXICO CITY,
JULY 1921

❊

Uneasiness grows here daily. We are having sudden deportations of foreign agitators, street riots and parades of workers carrying red flags. Plots thicken, thin, disintegrate in the space of thirty-six hours. A general was executed today for counter-revolutionary activities. There is fevered discussion in the newspapers as to the best means of stamping out Bolshevism, which is the inclusive term for all forms of radical work. Battles occur almost daily between Catholics and Socialists in many parts of the Republic: Morelia, Yucatán, Campeche, Jalisco. In brief, a clamor of petty dissension almost drowns the complicated debate between Mexico and the United States.

It is fascinating to watch, but singularly difficult to record because events overlap, and the news of today may be stale before it reaches the border. It is impossible to write fully of the situation unless one belongs to that choice company of folk who can learn all about peoples and countries in a couple of weeks. We have had a constant procession of these strange people: they come dashing in, gather endless notes and dash out again and three weeks later their expert, definitive opinions are published. Marvelous! I have been here for seven months, and for quite six of these I have not been sure of what the excitement is all about. Indeed, I am not yet able to say whether my accumulated impression of Mexico is justly proportioned; or that if I write with profound conviction of what is going on I shall not be making a profoundly comical mistake. The true story of a people is not to be had exclusively from official documents, or from guarded talks with diplomats. Nor is it to be gathered entirely from the people themselves. The life of a great nation is too widely scattered and complex and vast; too many opposing forces are at work, each with its own intensity of self-seeking.

Has any other country besides Mexico so many types of enemy within the gates? Here they are both foreign and native, hostile to each other by tradition, but mingling their ambitions in a common cause. The Mexican capitalist joins forces with the American against his revolutionary fellow-countryman. The Catholic Church enlists the help of Protestant strangers in the subjugation of the Indian, clamoring for his land. Reactionary Mexicans work faithfully with reactionary foreigners to achieve their ends by devious means. The Spanish, a scourge of Mexico, have plans of their own and are no better loved than they ever were. The British, Americans and French seek political and financial power, oil and mines; a splendid horde of invaders, they are distrustful of each other, but unable to disentangle their interests. Then there are the native bourgeoisie, much resembling the bourgeoisie elsewhere, who are opposed to all idea of revolution. "We want peace, and more business," they chant uniformly, but how these blessings are to be obtained they do not know. "More business, and no Bolshevism!" is their cry, and they are ready to support any man or group of men who can give them what they want. The professional politicians of Mexico likewise bear a strong family likeness to gentlemen engaged in this line of business in other parts of the world. Some of them have their prejudices; it may be against the Americans, or against the Church, or against the radicals, or against the other local political party, but whatever their prejudices may be they are pathetically unanimous in their belief that big business will save the country.

The extreme radical group includes a number of idealists,

somewhat tragic figures these, for their cause is so hopeless. They are nationalists of a fanatical type, recalling the early Sinn Feiners. They are furious and emotional and reasonless and determined. They want, God pity them, a free Mexico at once. Any conservative newspaper editor will tell you what a hindrance they are to the "best minds" who are now trying to make the going easy for big business. If a reasonable government is to get any work done, such misguided enthusiasts can not be disposed of too quickly. A few cooler revolutionists have been working toward civilized alleviations of present distresses pending the coming of the perfect State. Such harmless institutions as free schools for the workers, including a course in social science, have been set going. Clinics, dispensaries, birth-control information for the appallingly fertile Mexican woman, playgrounds for children—it sounds almost like the routine programme of any East Side social-service worker. But here in Mexico such things have become dangerous, bolshevistic. Among the revolutionists, the communists have been a wildly disturbing element. This cult was composed mostly of discontented foreigners, lacking even the rudiments of the Russian theory, with not a working revolutionist among them. The Mexicans, when they are not good party-revolutionists, are simple syndicalists of an extreme type. By party-revolutionists I mean the followers of some leader who is not an adherent of any particular revolutionary formula, but who is bent on putting down whatever government happens to be in power and establishing his own, based on a purely nationalistic ideal of reform.

The present government of Mexico is made up of certain intensely radical people, combined with a cast-iron reactionary group which was added during the early days of the administration. In the Cabinet at the extreme left wing is Calles, the most radical public official in Mexico today, modified by de la Huerta at his elbow. At the extreme right wing is Alberto Pani, Minister of Foreign Relations, and Capmany, Minister of Labor. The other members are political gradations of these four minds.

The pull-and-haul is intense and never ceases. Such a coalition government for Mexico is a great idea, and the theory is not unfamiliar to American minds: that all classes have the right to equal representation in the government. But it will not work. Quite naturally, all that any group of politicians wants is their own way in everything. They will fight to the last ditch to get it; coalition be hanged!

The revolution has not yet entered into the souls of the Mexican people. There can be no doubt of that. What is going on here is not the resistless upheaval of a great mass leavened by teaching and thinking and suffering. The Russian writers made the Russian Revolution, I verily believe, through a period of seventy-five years' preoccupation with the wrongs of the peasant, and the cruelties of life under the heel of the Tsar. Here in Mexico there is no conscience crying through the literature of the country. A small group of intellectuals still writes about romance and the stars, and roses and the shadowy eyes of ladies, touching no sorrow of the human heart other than the pain of unrequited love.

But then, the Indians cannot read. What good would a literature of revolt do them? Yet they are the very life of the country, this inert and slow-breathing mass, these lost people who move in the oblivion of sleepwalkers under their incredible burdens; these silent and reproachful figures in rags, bowed face to face with the earth; it is these who bind together all the accumulated and hostile elements of Mexican life. Leagued against the Indian are four centuries of servitude, the incoming foreigner who will take the last hectare of his land, and his own church that stands with the foreigners.

It is generally understood in Mexico that one of the conditions of recognition by the United States is that all radicals holding office in the Cabinet and in the lesser departments of government must go. That is what must be done if Mexico desires peace with the United States. This means, certainly, the dismissal of everyone who is doing constructive work in lines

254

MEXICAN

that ought to be far removed from the field of politics, such as education and welfare work among the Indians.

Everybody here theorizes endlessly. Each individual member of the smallest sub-division of the great triumvirate, Land, Oil, and the Church, has his own pet theory, fitting his prophecy to his desire. Everybody is in the confidence of somebody else who knows everything long before it happens. In this way one hears of revolutions to be started tomorrow or the next day or the day after that; but though the surface shifts and changes, one can readily deduce for oneself that one static combination remains, Land, Oil, and the Church. In principle these three are one. They do not take part in these petty national dissensions. Their battleground is the world. If the oil companies are to get oil, they need land. If the Church is to have wealth, it needs land. The partition of land in Mexico, therefore, menaces not only the *haciendados* (individual landholders), but foreign investors and the very foundations of the Church. Already, under the land-reform laws of Juarez, the Church cannot hold land; it evades this decree, however, by holding property in guardianship, but even this title will be destroyed by re-partition.

The recent encounters between Catholics and Socialists in different parts of Mexico have been followed by a spectacular activity on the part of the Catholic clergy. They are pulling their old familiar wires, and all the bedraggled puppets are dancing with a great clatter. The clever ones indulge in skillful moves in the political game, and there are street brawls for the hot-heads. For the peons there is always the moldy, infallible device; a Virgin— this time of Guadalupe—has been seen to move, to shine miraculously in a darkened room! A poor woman in Puebla was favored by Almighty God with the sight of this miracle, just at the moment of the Church's greatest political uncertainty; and now this miraculous image is to be brought here to Mexico City. The priests are insisting on a severe investigation to be carried on by themselves, and the statue is to be placed in an *oratorio*, where it will be living proof to the faithful that the great patroness of Mexico has set her face against reform.

The peons are further assured by the priests that to accept the land given to them by the reform laws is to be guilty of simple stealing, and everyone taking such land will be excluded from holy communion—a very effective threat. The agents who come to survey the land for the purposes of partition are attacked by the very peons they have come to benefit. Priests who warn their congregations against the new land-laws have been arrested and imprisoned, and now and then a stick of dynamite has been hurled at a bishop's palace by a radical hot-head. But these things do not touch the mighty power of the Church, solidly entrenched as it is in its growing strength, and playing the intricate game of international politics with gusto and skill.

So far, I have not talked with a single member of the American colony here who does not eagerly watch for the show to begin. They want American troops in here, and want them quickly— they are apprehensive that the soldiers will not arrive soon enough, and that they will be left to the mercy of the Mexicans for several weeks, maybe. It is strange talk one hears. It is indulged in freely over café tables and on street-corners, at teas and at dances.

Meanwhile international finance goes on its own appointed way. The plans that were drawn up more than a year ago by certain individuals who manage these things in the United States, are going forward nicely, and are being hampered no more than normally by upstarts who have plans of their own. Inevitably certain things will have to be done when the time comes, with only a few necessary deviations due to the workings of the "imponderables." The whole program has been carefully worked out by Oil, Land, and the Church, the powers that hold this country securely in their grip.

La Conquistadora

Rosalie Caden Evans was an American woman, born in Galveston, Texas. She married a British subject, Harry Evans, who became owner of several haciendas in Mexico during the Diaz regime. They lost their property in the Madero revolution, and for several years lived in the United States and in Europe. In 1917 Mr. Evans died while in Mexico, after an unsuccessful attempt to regain his property under the Carranza administration. Mrs. Evans returned to Mexico, and for more than six years she proved a tough enemy to the successive revolutionary governments, holding her hacienda under almost continuous fire. This contest required a great deal of attention from three governments, Mexico, Great Britain, and the United States, and furnished a ready bone of contention in the long-drawn argument between Mexico and foreign powers respecting the famous Article 27 of the new Mexican Constitution, which provides among other things that the large landholdings of Mexico shall be repartitioned among the Indians, subject to proper indemnification to the former owner.

H. A. C. Cummins, of the British Legation, was expelled from Mexico for his championship of Mrs. Evans, and a fair amount of trouble ensued between Mexico and Great Britain about it. The case of Mrs. Evans was cited in the United States as an argument against our recognition of the Obregon government. An impressive volume of diplomatic correspondence was exchanged between the three governments concerning the inflexible lady, who held her ground, nevertheless, saying that she could be removed from her holdings only as a prisoner or dead.

In August 1924, the news came that Mrs. Evans had been shot from ambush by a number of men while driving in a buckboard from the village of San Martin to her hacienda, San Pedro Coxtocan.

Reading the letters Rosalie Evans wrote her sister, Mrs. Daisy Caden Pettus, from Mexico, this adventure takes on all the colors of a lively temperament; the story is lighted for us like a torch. The aim in publishing the letters was to present Mrs. Evans to a presumably outraged Anglo-Saxon world as a martyr to the sacred principles of private ownership of property: to fix her as a symbol of devotion to a holy cause. "Some Americans," says Mrs. Pettus in a foreword to the volume, "in ignorance of Mexican conditions, have said the fight carried on by Mrs. Evans was unwise, if not unworthy, in that it is charged that she was resisting the duly established laws and principles of the Mexican people. This is very far from true."

It is true, however, that she opposed, and to her death, the attempts of the Mexican people to establish those laws and principles which were the foundation of their revolution, and on which their national future depends. She cast her individual weight against the march of an enormous social movement, and though her fight was gallant, brilliant and wholehearted, admirable as a mere exhibition of daring, energy and spirit, still I cannot see how she merits the title of martyr. She was out for blood, and she had a glorious time while the fight lasted.

Her letters are a swift-moving account of a life as full of thrills and action as any novel of adventure you may find. They are written at odd moments, dashed off in the midst of a dozen things all going at once: the episodes are struck off white-hot. The result is a collection of letters that could scarcely be equaled for speed, for clarity, for self-revelation, for wit and charm. We are shown the most fantastic blend of a woman: fanaticism, physical courage, avarice, mystical exaltation and witch-wife superstition; social poise and financial shrewdness, a timeless feminine coquetry tempered by that curious innocence which

is the special gift of the American woman: all driven mercilessly by a tautness of the nerves, a deep-lying hysteria that
urges her to self-hypnosis. Toward the last she had almost lost
her natural reactions. Anger, fear, delight, hope—no more of
these. She was a Will.

Mrs. Evans returned to Mexico to take up her husband's fight
when he had wearied to death of it. Belief in private property
had not yet become a religion. She was animated by sentiment
for her dead husband. All feminine, she insisted that his shade
still guarded and directed her. The demon that possessed her
was by no means of so spiritual a nature as she fancied: she
was ruled by a single-minded love of money and power. She
came into Mexico at harvest time, and after a short, sharp battle
she got hold of the ripened wheat on her main hacienda. This
victory fired her, and was the beginning of the end. Shortly
afterward the shade of her husband left her. "I stand alone."

No single glimmer of understanding of the causes of revolution or the rights of the people involved ever touched her
mind. She loved Spaniards, the British, the Americans of the
foreign colony. She thought the Indians made good servants,
though occasionally they betrayed her. She writes with an-
noyance of Obregon's taking Mexico City and creating a dis-
turbance when she was on the point of wresting from the
Indians her second crop of wheat—"gold in color, gold in reality!" She is most lyrical, most poetic when she contemplates
this gold which shall be hers, though all Mexico go to waste
around her. Carranza's flight interested her merely because it
menaced her chances of getting the only threshing machine in
the Puebla Valley.

Of all the machinations, the crooked politics, the broken faiths,
the orders and counter orders, the plots and counter-plots that
went on between literally thousands of people over this single
holding, I have not time to tell. Mrs. Evans was passed from
hand to hand, nobody wanted to be responsible for what must
eventually happen to her. She pressed everybody into her serv-

ice, from her maids to the high diplomats. Every man of any official note in Mexico, connected with the three governments, finally got into the business, and she shows them all up in turn.

The story of the double dealing here revealed is not pretty, showing as it does some of our eminent diplomats engaged in passing the buck and gossiping behind each other's backs. But sooner or later they all advised her to listen to reason, accept 100,000 pesos for her land and give way. At least they perceived what she could not; that here was a national movement that must be reckoned with.

At first she would not. And later, she could not. She loved the romantic danger of her situation, she admired herself in the role of heroine. Her appetite for excitement increased; she confessed herself jaded, and sought greater danger.

Speaking of a safe conduct she obtained in order to go over her hacienda and inspect the crops, she says: "You see it means a chance of gaining 80,000 pesos besides the adventure." After each hairbreadth encounter with sullen Indians armed with rope and scythe, with troops bearing bared arms, she was flushed with a tense joy. Later, when she came to open war, she would ride into armed groups with her pistol drawn, singing *"Nous sommes les enfants de Gasconne!"* She cracked an Indian agrarian over the head with her riding whip during an altercation over the watercourse and patroled the fields during harvest with a small army.

Her love of the drama was getting the upper hand of principle. If at first her cry was all for law and justice, later she refers to herself merrily as an outlaw. "You have no idea how naturally one takes to the greenwood!" She became a female conquistador—victory was her aim, and she was as unscrupulous in her methods as any other invader.

There is not a line in her letters to show that she had any grasp of the true inward situation, but her keen eye and ready wit missed no surface play of event. She maintained peaceable relations first with one, then another of the many groups of rebels. Inexplicably the situation would shift and change, her allies would vanish, leaving her mystified. She had all Mexico divided into two classes: the Good, who were helping her hold her property, and the Bad, who were trying to take it from her.

She could be self-possessed in the grand manner, and seemed to have second-sight in everything immediately concerning herself. She sat for three days and fed her pigeons while serious persons advised her to pay the 300 pesos ransom demanded for her majordomo, kidnaped to the hills. She refused. It was too much to pay for a majordomo, and she felt they would not shoot him anyhow. They did not. When he returned she sent him back with a present of $80 to the kidnapers.

At another crisis she played chess. After a brilliant encounter with some hint of gunfire, she came in and washed her hair. At times she studied astronomy, other times she read Marcus Aurelius or poetry. At all times she played the great lady. Her love for her horses, her dogs, her servants, her workers and allies was all of a piece, grounded in her sense of possession. They were hers; almost by virtue of that added grace she loved them, and she looked after them in the feudal manner.

There was something wild and strange in her, a hint of madness that touches genius; she lived in a half-burned ranch house with her dogs, near a haunted chapel, hourly expecting attack, and longed to join the coyotes in their weird dances outside her door. She foretold the manner of her own death, and related for sober fact the most hair-raising ghost story I have ever read:

The last night I was there I had been in bed an hour perhaps and was growing drowsy when I heard some one crying at my window. The most gentle attenuated sobbing; the most pitiful sounds you ever heard. I never for a minute thought of the spirits, but called the girl to light the candle. She heard it too—but the strange part is, *I* said it was at the back window and *she* heard it at the front, and neither did *she* think of spirits. As she opened to see who was there, IT came in sobbing—and we looked at each other and closed the windows.

Perhaps you think we were frightened or horrified? I can only answer for myself—it filled me with an intense pity. I only wanted to comfort it and I said to the girl: "If it would *only* be quiet." I then promised to have the mass said and invite the people, and it left, sobbing. And we, of course, both went to our beds to sleep dreamlessly till morning.

Revolution is not gentle, either for those who make it or those who oppose it. This story has its own value as a record of one life lived very fully and consciously. I think the life and death of Mrs. Evans were her own private adventures, most gladly sought and enviably carried through. As a personality, she is worth attention, being beautiful, daring and attractive. As a human being she was avaricious, with an extraordinary hardness of heart and ruthlessness of will; and she died in a grotesque cause.

1926

Quetzalcoatl

❊

The Plumed Serpent is a confession of faith, a summing up of the mystical philosophy of D. H. Lawrence. Mexico, the Indians, the cult of the Aztec god Quetzalcoatl—the Plumed Serpent—all these are pretexts, symbols made to the measure of his preoccupations. It seems only incidentally a novel, in spite of the perfection of its form; it is a record of a pilgrimage that was, that must have been, a devastating experience. Lawrence went to Mexico in the hope of finding there, among alien people and their mysterious cult, what he had failed to find in his own race or within himself: a center and a meaning to life. He went to the Indians with the hope of clinching once for all his argument that blood-nodality is the source of communion between man and man, and between man and the implacable gods. He desired to share this nodality, to wring from it the secret of the "second strength" which gives magic powers to a man. But blood itself stood between him and his desire.

"She had noticed that usually, when an Indian looked at a white man, both stood back from actual contact, from actual meeting of each other's eyes. They left a wide space of neutral territory between them. . . ." This acute flash of insight he gives to Kate Leslie, the Irish woman, the only white person among his chief characters. She carries all the burden of doubt and fear for the author, and is the most valid human being in the book. With all his will, his psychoanalytic equipment, and his curiosity, which is like a steel probe, Lawrence could not cross this neutral territory. These, and his poetic imagination touched to wonder drive him resistlessly within touching distance. His mind sniffs out delicately, the filaments of his thought are like living nerve-ends, they shudder and are repelled at the nearness of a secret steeped, for him, in cosmic possibilities. He remains a stranger gazing at a mystery he cannot share, but still hopes to ravish, and his fancy dilates it to monstrous proportions.

He has confessed somewhere that he was in a raging temper from the moment he passed over the line from the United States to Mexico. He blames this on the vibrations of cruelty and bloodshed in the country, the dark hopelessness that rises from the Indians and the very soil in an almost palpable vapor. He felt that the Mexican motive of existence is hatred. Lawrence is a good hater; he should know hate when he sees it. But it was not altogether an occult effluvium from the earth. His terror came halfway to meet it. A serpent lies coiled in the Indian vitals; their eyes are centerless. He cannot acknowledge blood-kin with them. He gives them a soul and takes it away again; they are dragon worshipers, only half-created; he surmises reptilian ichor in their veins. Yet he loves their beauty, and with all his soul he adores their phallic god; and so he remains a stranger, but makes his obeisance.

The genius of Lawrence lies in his power to create out of his own inner experience, his own sensitized fibers, a personal world which is also our world, peopled with human beings recognizably of our own time and place. His world is a place of complex despair, his tragedies are of the individual temperament in double conflict, against the inner nightmare and the outer unendurable fact. Terror of death and nausea of life, sexual egotism and fear, a bitter will-to-power and an aspiration after mystical apartness, an impotent desire for the act of faith, combine into a senseless widdershins; they spin dizzily on their own centers of sensation, with a sick void at the core.

Lawrence has turned away from this world, these persons, exhausted by their futility, unable to admit that their despairs and futilities are also his own. "Give me the mystery and let the world live again for me," Kate cried in her own soul. "And deliver me from man's automatism!" This woman is a perfect study of that last upsurge of romantic sex-hunger, disguised as a quest of the spirit, that comes with the grand climacteric. Lawrence identifies her purpose with his own, she represents his effort to touch the darkly burning Indian mystery. It could not happen: he is too involved in preconceptions and simple human prejudice. His artificial Western mysticism came in collision with the truly occult mind of the Indian, and he suffered an extraordinary shock. He turned soothsayer, and began to interpret by a formula: the result is a fresh myth of the Indian, a deeply emotional conception, but a myth none the less, and a debased one.

For sheer magnificence of writing, Lawrence has surpassed himself. His style has ripened, softened, there is a melancholy hint of the over-richness of autumn. Who looks for mere phrases from him? He writes by the passage, by the chapter, a prose flexible as a whiplash, uneven and harmonious as breakers rolling upon a beach, and the sound is music. His language rises from the page not in words but in a series of images before the eye: human beings move in vivid landscapes, wrapped in a physical remoteness, yet speaking with a ghostly intimacy, as if you were listening to the secret pulse of their veins.

All of Mexico that can be *seen* is here, evoked clearly with the fervor of things remembered out of impressions that filled the mind to bursting. There is no laborious building up of local color, but an immense and prodigal feeling for the background, for every minute detail seen with the eyes of a poet. He makes you a radiant gift of the place. It is no Rousseau-like jungle of patterned leaves and fruits half concealing impersonally savage beasts. The skies change, the lights and colors, the smells and feel of the air change with the time of day; the masses of the Indians move with purpose against this shifting landscape; the five chief characters live out a romantic drama of emotions, accompanied by all the commonplaces of every day, of dress, of food, of weather. A nation-wide political and religious movement provides the framework for a picture that does not omit a leaf, a hanging fruit, an animal, a cloud, a mood, of the visible Mexico. Lawrence puts in besides all his own accumulated protests against the things he hates: his grudge against women as opposed to his concept of woman, his loathing of the machine. His contempt for revolution and the poor is arrogant, not aristocratic: but he is plainly proud of his attitude. It is a part of his curiously squeamish disgust of human contact.

The triumph of this book as a work of art lies in this: that out of his confusions, the divisions of his mind, he has gained by sheer poetic power to a fine order, a mystical truth above his obsessions and debased occult dogma.

Mexico pulls you down, the people pull you down like a great weight! But it may be they pull you down as the earth pull of gravitation does, that you can balance on your feet. Maybe they draw you down as the earth draws down the roots of the tree so that it may be clenched deep in the soil . . . Loose leaves and aeroplanes blow away on the wind, in what they call freedom . . . All that matters to me are the roots that reach down beyond all destruction.

Thus Ramon, the Spanish-Indian scholar who has taken upon himself the role of the living Quetzalcoatl. "God must come to the Mexicans in a blanket and huaraches, else he is no god of the Mexican. . . . We live by manifestations." A full-blooded Indian joins him in the role of Huitzilopochtli, the god of war. Kate Leslie goes with them as Malintzi, wife of the war-god. They set about to restore the old phallic cult, based on an ancient religious tenet of the human race: that the male element is godhead, that man carries the unique secret of creation in his loins, that divinity originates in the potent germ. "I look . . . for my own manhood," says the living Quetzalcoatl. "It comes from the middle—from God. . . . I have nothing but my manhood. The God gives it to me, and leaves me to do further."

And again: "The universe is a nest of dragons, with a perfectly unfathomable life mystery at the center of it. . . . If I call the mystery the Morning Star, what does it matter? . . . And man is a creature who wins his own creation inch by inch from the nest of cosmic dragons." "Man is a column of blood, woman is a valley of blood." And man must be saved again by blood. Blood touches blood in the Morning Star, and thus the otherwise incommunicable secret will be shared.

And what, in fact, is the conclusion after all this grandiose preparation? The Indians must still be saved by a superior expert tribal Messiah and by means of the same worn-out devices. The living Quetzalcoatl works through the cumbrous machinery of drums, erotic-mystic ritual, ceremonial bloodshed. He is a marvelous study of the priestly pedagogue fired with a fanatic vision of a world saved and standing at his right hand praising his name forever. This is the answer we are given to a great quest for the meaning of life: man is not a god, and he must die. But he may hypnotize himself into momentary forgetfulness by means of ceremonial robes and a chorus of mystic mumblings, accompanied by synthesized gesture in praise of his own virility, that most variable and treacherous of all his powers.

The hymns of Quetzalcoatl form a broken cycle through the story, curious interruptions to the muscular power of the prose. There are many beautiful lines: "And say to thy sorrow, 'Ax, thou art cutting me down. Yet did a spark fly out of thy edge and my wound.'" Mostly they are booming, hollow phrases, involved as the high-sounding nonsense of a sixteenth-century Spanish mystic; their ecstasy follows the pattern of artificial raptures, self-conscious as a group of Gurdjieff's American disciples revolving in a dervish dance.

Altogether Lawrence cannot be freed from the charge of pretentiousness in having invaded a mystery that remained a mystery to him, and in having set down his own personal reactions to a whole race as if they were the inspired truth. His Indians are merely what the Indians might be if they were all

D. H. Lawrences. The three characters who act as his mouth-pieces are simply good Europeans at bottom—further variations of Lawrence's arch-type, the flayed and suffering human being in full flight from the horrors of a realistic mechanical society, and from the frustrations of sex.

When you have read this book read *Sons and Lovers* again. You will realize the catastrophe that has overtaken Lawrence.

1926

The Charmed Life

In 1921, he was nearly eighty years old, and he had lived in Mexico for about forty years. Every day of those years he had devoted exclusively to his one interest in life: discovering and digging up buried Indian cities all over the country. He had come there, an American, a stranger, with this one idea. I had heard of him as a fabulous, ancient eccentric completely wrapped up in his theory of the origins of the Mexican Indian. "He will talk your arm off," I was told.

His shop was on the top floor of a ramshackle old building on a side street in Mexico City, reached by an outside flight of steps, and it had the weathered, open look of a shed rather than a room. The rain came in, and the dust, and the sunlight. A few battered show-cases and long rough tables were piled up carelessly with "artifacts," as the Old Man was careful to call them. There were skulls and whole skeletons, bushels of jade beads and obsidian knives and bronze bells and black clay whistles in the shape of birds.

I was immensely attracted by the air of authenticity, hard to define, but easy to breathe. He was tough and lean, and his face was burned to a good wrinkled leather. He greeted me with an air of imperfect recollection as if he must have known me somewhere. We struck up an easy acquaintance at once, and he talked with the fluency of true conviction.

Sure enough, within a quarter of an hour I had his whole theory of the origin of the ancient Mexicans. It was not new or original; it was one of the early theories since rejected by later scientists, but plainly the Old Man believed he had discovered it by himself, and perhaps he had. It was a religion with him, a poetic, mystical, romantic concept. About the lost continent, and how the original Mexican tribes all came from China or Mongolia in little skiffs, dodging between hundreds of islands now sunk in the sea. He loved believing it and would listen to nothing that threatened to shake his faith.

At once he invited me to go with him on a Sunday to dig in his latest buried city, outside the capital. He explained his system to me. He had unearthed nearly a half-hundred ancient cities in all parts of Mexico. One by one, in his vague phrase, he "turned them over to the government." The government thanked him kindly and sent in a staff of expert scientists to take over, and the Old Man moved on, looking for something new.

Finally by way of reward, they had given him this small and not very important city for his own, to settle down with. He sold in his shop the objects he found in the city, and with the profits he supported the digging operations on Sunday.

He showed me photographs of himself in the early days, always surrounded by Indian guides and pack-mules against landscapes of cactus or jungle, a fine figure of a man with virile black whiskers and a level, fanatic eye. There were rifles strapped to the bales on the pack-mules, and the guards bristled with firearms. "I never carried a gun," he told me. "I never needed to. I trusted my guides, and they trusted me."

I enjoyed the company of the Old Man, his impassioned single-ness of purpose, his fervid opinions on his one topic of conversation, and the curiously appealing unhumanness of his existence. He was the only person I ever saw who really seemed as independent and carefree as a bird on a bough.

He ate carelessly at odd hours, fried beans and tortillas from a basket left for him by the wife of his head digger, or he would broil a scrawny chicken on a stick, offer me half, and walk about directing his men, waving the other half. He had an outdoors sort of cleanliness and freshness; his clothes were clean, but very old and mended. Who washed and mended them I never knew. My own life was full of foolish and unnecessary complications, and I envied him his wholeness. I enjoyed my own sentimental notion of him as a dear, harmless, sweet old man of an appealing sociability, riding his hobby-horse in triumph to the grave, houseless but at home, completely free of family ties and not missing them, a happy, devoted man who had known his own mind, had got what he wanted in life, and was satisfied with it. Besides he was in perfect health and never bored.

Crowds of visitors came and bought things, and he dropped the money in a cigar-box behind a showcase. He invited almost everybody to come out and watch him dig on Sundays, and a great many came, week after week, always a new set. He received a good many letters, most of them with foreign postmarks, and after a few rapid glances he dropped them into the drawer of a long table. "I know a lot of people," he said, shuffling among the heap one day. "I ought to answer these. Big bugs, too, some of them."

One day, among a pile of slant-eyed clay faces, I found a dusty, dog-eared photograph of a young girl, which appeared to have been taken about fifty years before. She was elegant, fashionable, and so astonishingly beautiful I thought such perfection could belong only to a world-famous beauty. The Old Man noticed it in my hand. "My wife," he said in his impersonal, brisk tone. "Just before we were married. She was about eighteen then."

"She is unbelievably beautiful," I said.

"She was the most beautiful woman I ever saw," he said, matter-of-factly. "She is beautiful still." He dropped the photograph in the drawer with the letters and came back talking about something else.

After that, at odd moments, while he was polishing jade beads or brushing the dust off a clay bird, he dropped little phrases about his wife and children. "She was remarkable," he said. "She had five boys in eight years. She was just too proud to have anything but boys, I used to tell her."

Again, later: "She was a perfect wife, perfect. But she wouldn't come to Mexico with me. She said it was no place to bring up children."

One day, counting his money and laying it out in small heaps, one for each workman, he remarked absently: "She's well off, you know—she has means." He poured the heaps into a small sack and left the rest in the cigar-box. "I never wanted more money than I needed from one week to the next," he said. "I don't fool with banks. People say I'll be knocked in the head and robbed some night, but I haven't been, and I won't."

One day we were talking about a plot to overthrow the Government which had just been frustrated with a good deal of uproar. "I knew about that months ago," said the Old Man. "One of my politician friends wrote me . . ." He motioned toward the table drawer containing the letters. "You're interested in those things," he said. "Would you like to read some of those letters? They aren't private."

Would I? I spent a long summer afternoon reading the Old Man's letters from his international big bugs, and I learned then and there that hair *can* rise and blood *can* run cold. There was enough political dynamite in those casually written letters to have blown sky-high any number of important diplomatic and financial negotiations then pending between several powerful governments. The writers were of all sorts, from the high-minded and religious to the hearty, horse-trading type to the worldly, the shrewd, the professional adventurer, down to the natural moral imbecile, but they were all written in simple language with almost boyish candor and an indiscretion so complete it seemed a kind of madness.

I asked him if he had ever shown them to anyone else. "Why, no," he said, surprised at my excitement.

I tried to tell him that if these letters fell into certain hands, his life would be in danger. "Nonsense," he said vigorously.

"Everybody knows what I think of that stuff. I've seen 'em come and go, making history. Bah!"

"Burn these letters," I told him. "Get rid of them. Don't even be caught dead with them."

"I need them," he said. "There's a lot about ancient Mexican culture in them you didn't notice." I gave up. Perhaps the brink of destruction was his natural habitat.

A few days later, I went up the dusty stairs and, there, in a broad square of sunlight, the Old Man was sitting in a cow-hide chair with a towel around his neck, and a woman was trimming his mustache with a pair of nail scissors. She was as tall as he, attenuated, with white hair, and the beauty of an aged goddess. There was an extraordinary pinched, starved kind of sweetness in her face, and she had perfect simplicity of manner. She removed the towel, and the Old Man leaped up as if she had loosed a spring. Their son, a man in middle age, a masculine reincarnation of his mother, came in from the next room, and we talked a little, and the wife asked me with gentle pride if I did not find the shop improved.

It was indeed in order, clean, bare, with the show-windows and cases set out properly, and tall vases of flowers set about. They were all as polite and agreeable to one another as if they were well-disposed strangers, but I thought the Old Man looked a little hunched and wary, and his wife and son gazed at him almost constantly as if they were absorbed in some fixed thought. They were all very beautiful people, and I liked them, but they filled the room and were not thinking about what they were saying, and I went away very soon.

The Old Man told me later they had stayed only a few days; they dropped in every four or five years to see how he was getting on. He never mentioned them again.

Afterward when I remembered him it was always most clearly in that moment when the tall woman and her tall son searched the face of their mysterious Wild Man with baffled, resigned eyes, trying still to understand him years after words wouldn't work any more, years after everything had been said and done, years after love had worn itself thin with anxieties, without in the least explaining what he was, why he had done what he did. But they had forgiven him, that was clear, and they loved him.

I understood then why the Old Man never carried a gun, never locked up his money, sat on political dynamite and human volcanoes, and never bothered to answer his slanderers. He bore a charmed life. Nothing would ever happen to him.

1942